THE FAMILY NOBODY WANTED

The Family
Nobody Wanted

HELEN DOSS

with a new introduction by MARY BATTENFELD
and a new epilogue by the author

Northeastern University Press
BOSTON

Northeastern University Press

Copyright 1954 by Helen Doss

Originally published in 1954 by Little, Brown & Company. Reprinted 2001
by arrangement with Helen Doss.

Library of Congress Cataloging-in-Publication Data

Doss, Helen Grigsby.
The family nobody wanted / Helen Doss ; with a new introduction by Mary
Battenfeld, and a new epilogue by the author.
p. cm.
Originally published: Boston: Little, Brown, 1954.
Includes bibliographical references.
ISBN 1-55553-503-8 (alk. paper)—ISBN 1-55553-502-x (pbk. : alk. paper)
1. Doss, Helen Grigsby—Family. 2. Doss, Carl—Family. 3. Interracial
adoption—California. 4. California—Biography. I. Title.

CT275.D8653 D6 2001
306.85—dc21   2001037018

Printed and bound by Edwards Brothers, Inc., Lillington, North Carolina.
The paper is EB Natural, an acid-free stock.

MANUFACTURED IN THE UNITED STATES OF AMERICA
05 04 03 02 01   5 4 3 2 1

TO CARL
*Without Whose Help
This Book Could Never Have Been Written,
and Without Whom
It Never Would Have Happened*

Contents

Introduction

In my prayers, I give thanks that we never had children of our own, after all. Of our own blood, I mean, because children couldn't be any more my own than these. Somehow I feel that our family was meant to be just this way.

Helen Doss, *The Family Nobody Wanted*

THE NIGHT BEFORE they are to finalize the adoption of the last of their twelve children, Helen Doss turns to her husband, Carl, and affirms the central message of *The Family Nobody Wanted*. "Our family was meant to be just this way," Doss declares, claiming her children, adopted at different ages and from a variety of racial and cultural backgrounds, as "my own." For the original baby boom audience of *The Family Nobody Wanted*, and even for many twenty-first-century readers of this new edition, that declaration is likely to sound perplexing, if not absurd. The cultural belief that adoptive families are "less than" biological ones is so entrenched that Doss must sidestep the biological connotations of the phrase "children of our own" with the qualification "Of our own blood, I mean, because children couldn't be any more my own than these." Despite that powerful declaration, others doubt Helen Doss's claim.

Even in the last chapter of *The Family Nobody Wanted*, a neighbor known as "Mrs. Pickles" tells the Dosses as they leave for the county courthouse to adopt three more children, "I'll admit I don't understand what you're doing" (266).

Nearly fifty years have passed since the original publication of *The Family Nobody Wanted*, but it is clear that a majority of Americans still "don't understand" adoption. The Evan B. Donaldson Institute's 1997 *Benchmark Adoption Survey* found that half the Americans polled felt that adoption "is not quite as good as having one's own child."[1] The survey confirms conclusions of scholars such as David Schneider, who contends that Americans ascribe to the biological family an "almost mystical commonality and identity."[2] Such views have helped to create a contemporary America that, according to Elizabeth Bartholet, a law professor and adoptive mother, "glorifies reproduction, drives the infertile to pursue treatment at all costs, socializes them to think of adoption as a second-class form of parenting to be pursued only as a last resort, and regulates adoption in a way that makes it difficult, degrading, and expensive."[3] Bartholet's comments were borne out by two cover stories in popular magazines that appeared during the week this essay went to the publisher.[4] Although both articles included positive points, these cover stories also encouraged readers to regard adoption as an arduous and questionable way to form a family. Thus, *U.S. News and World Report*'s "The Adoption Maze" reminded readers of the "difficult, expensive and potentially heartbreaking" side of adoption, while *People*'s cover tag line, "How Stars Find Their Babies," commodified and objectified those babies, and linked the lives of both birth parents and adoptive parents to the far-from-normal lives of celebrities. These articles, like most reviewed for a 1988 survey of film and print stories about adoption in the mass media, ultimately depict adoption "as a troubling and troublesome issue."[5]

Transracial adoptive families such as the Dosses are met with even more suspicion, in part because they continue to constitute a small minority of adoptive families.[6] Research on transracial adoption is limited, and the most recent statistics available suggest that only about 8 percent of adoptions occur across racial lines. The continued rarity of transracial adoption can be traced to concerns about appropriate support of a child's racial identity, as well as to more general fears about interracial relationships. Even the 1994 Multiethnic Placement Act, which removed legal barriers to transracial adoption, has not resulted in demonstrably greater numbers of transracial placements. For example, in 1998 only 15 percent of adoptions from U.S. foster care were transracial.[7]

Discomfort with transracial adoption also has roots in the widespread cultural belief that "real" children look like their parents. The author of a recent *Salon.com* "Mothers Who Think" column describes what is to her the self-evident value of birth over adoptive children. "Like everybody else, I just want a child who looks like me and talks like me and fits into my family—just as if he or she was born into it. Is that a crime?"[8] While not a crime, the views of this "mother who thinks" do suggest the extent to which she and our culture still see adoption as acceptable only in cases where a family can "pass" for one linked through the double helix chain of DNA. Indeed, a recent survey showed that social workers continue to believe that it is valuable to match physical and mental characteristics of adoptive parents and children.[9] The beliefs of these contemporary social workers mirror those of adoption practitioners encountered fifty years ago by Carl and Helen Doss. One social worker dismissed the couple's request for a mixed-race child because, she said, "I would rather see a child raised in an orphanage, than by parents who look so *different*"(30). Given these widespread and enduring attitudes, it is no wonder that adoptive families today continue to face intrusive questions from strangers, neighbors, friends, and family who doubt that parents and children "who look so *different*" constitute a "real" family.

The Family Nobody Wanted offers emphatic, vivid, humorous, and loving evidence that adoptive families *are* as valid as those with "blood ties." Readers who, like me, are members of the adoption triad (birth parents, adoptive parents, and adopted persons), will find in Helen Doss's story a much-needed affirmation of ourselves and our lives. Doss's 1954 memoir also continues to bring an important message to those many Americans whose views of adoption have been shaped by decades of secrecy and silence, broken intermittently by sensational news stories featuring degenerate birth mothers, desperate adoptive parents, corrupt adoption agencies, and victimized children. As 2001 began, the public face of adoption was represented by a bizarre and tragic transatlantic custody battle involving a birth mother, two sets of adoptive parents, a dubious adoption facilitator, and the six-month-old twins at the center of the dispute.[10]

Such distorted media images have tended to go unexamined, since scholarship on adoption has traditionally been the province of social workers and psychologists, whose interests are clinical rather than cultural. The research that has been done, as Katarina Wegar argues, has "served to perpetuate rather than correct dominant stigmatizing biases against adoptive families."[11] Scholarship has been particularly limited on transracial adoption, which, as Susan Ito, a transracial adopted person, notes, "has existed far too long with neither academic attention nor practical support."[12] Only recently have scholars begun to analyze the historical and cultural meanings of this important method of family formation.[13] Given this context, it is hardly surprising that many continue to see adoption as a strange, unnatural, and inferior way to create and live in a family. In showing readers that the Doss family is normal and "meant to be just this way," *The Family Nobody Wanted*, both in 1954 and today, thus performs the vital cultural work of legitimizing and normalizing adoptive kinship relationships.

Helen Doss begins with the poignant utterance "All in the world I wanted was a happy, normal little family" (3). At this point, as the Dosses struggle with infertility, a "happy, normal" family means to Helen Doss, and to her readers, a blood family. Yet by the end of *The Family Nobody Wanted*, the meaning of family has changed. Helen Doss's intelligent and eloquent personal account convinces us that a family formed by adoption can be, as another book by Doss says, a "really real family."[14] Against all odds, Doss creates the happy, normal, although far from little, family she wants. Against even greater odds, readers come to accept that this international family, made up of white parents and twelve children whose heritages span much of the globe—from Korea, Japan, the Philippines, Malaysia, and Burma to France, Spain, Mexico, Hawaii, and the Native American Chippewa, Blackfoot, and Cheyenne nations—is in fact a normal and happy American family.

As Doss wrote, "It is the outsiders who imagine that our family is made up of incompatible opposites" (165). Helen Doss recognized that "outsiders" would find her family alien and unwanted, a view alluded to in the title. In fact Doss's first choice for a title, *All God's Children*, was demonstrably more positive than *The Family Nobody Wanted*. Yet the irony in the title is clear. The stories of how Donny, Laura, Susan, Teddy, Rita, Timmy, Alex, Diane, Elaine, Gregory, Richard, and Dorothy became Dosses demonstrate emphatically that each child was a wanted child. Indeed, almost every page of *The Family Nobody Wanted* offers proof of the title's fallacy. By the time nine-year-old Richard says, "I wouldn't want to live anywhere else" (265), we as readers have to agree. Helen Doss's insider's view of her diverse, happy, and successful household has transformed the Dosses into a family that anybody would want.

America first met "the family nobody wanted" in Helen Doss's August 1949 *Reader's Digest* article.[15] The appeal of the Doss family was evident in initial responses to that article. Helen Doss reported that "we were flooded by letters from all over the United States, and clear around the world, asking for the rest of the story in a book."[16] By the end of

1951, *Life* magazine had featured the Doss family, and a nationwide NBC radio show had named them the "Christmas Family of the Year." Intense interest in the family's story led publishers to ask Helen Doss for a book. Initially reluctant to publish a story that would put her children in the spotlight and keep her from writing a novel, Helen Doss was finally convinced that a book about her family would have value. That book, composed in spare moments between dishwashing and diaper changing, was *The Family Nobody Wanted*.[17]

Helen Doss may have questioned the appropriateness of making "our own family . . . the *subject* of my first book," but her readers have never had such doubts.[18] Since its original publication in January 1954, *The Family Nobody Wanted* has inspired, instructed, and engaged the hearts of two generations of American readers. Although the book never achieved "blockbuster" status, its publishing history, like the Doss story itself, is one of persistence, loyalty, and love over the long haul. Other books can boast of more immediate sales than *The Family Nobody Wanted*, but few have achieved such longevity. The book went through more than two dozen printings and was translated into seven languages before going out of print in North America in 1984. *McCall's* serialized the book, while a number of book clubs, including the Sears Peoples Choice Book Club and Scholastic Books, sold *The Family Nobody Wanted*. These inexpensive editions made the book available to a large and diverse audience. Two film versions, one made soon after the original publication and the other in 1975, provide further evidence of the book's enduring and widespread popular appeal.[19]

Even after going out of print, *The Family Nobody Wanted*
has continued to inspire a passionately loyal readership.
Comments of readers who have posted reviews on Amazon.
com suggest this, as do the high prices and limited availabil-
ity of out-of-print editions of the book. A reader from Idaho
echoed the sentiments of many Internet reviewers when she
described the book as "one that I will always treasure. I
would like to scream to every person, 'Please read this
book!' " [20] If these loyal readers wanted to buy *The Family
Nobody Wanted*, they could expect to pay more than one
hundred dollars for a copy in good condition.[21]

The enduring appeal of *The Family Nobody Wanted* can be
traced in part to the composition of its original audience.
Recommended by libraries and educational associations,
and sold through Scholastic Books, *The Family Nobody
Wanted* was soon required reading at many elementary,
middle, and high schools. The *Horn Book Magazine* placed
its review of *The Family Nobody Wanted* in a section that
highlighted "books of interest to high school students."[22] In
giving its endorsement to the 1975 ABC television version
of *The Family Nobody Wanted*, a National Education Association press release noted that although "prime time TV
specials have been given the NEA Seal, this marks the first
time it has been awarded to a prime time television
movie."[23] Helen Doss even today continues to receive letters from teachers who use tattered copies of *The Family Nobody Wanted* in their elementary or secondary school
classrooms.[24] Thus, a large group of readers first encountered the Doss family as preteens or teenagers. Moreover,
much of that younger audience read the book along with

teachers in the institutional context of American public schools. For example, a classroom teacher described how "I would read it to my class as literature. Every now and then, I had to stop reading to fight back the tears. One of my students must have fallen in love with it too because it disappeared one day."[25]

Helen Doss envisioned *The Family Nobody Wanted* as a book for adults. Yet I, along with almost everyone I have asked, can date a first reading of the book to the late elementary- or middle-school years. Three-quarters of the Amazon.com reviewers of *The Family Nobody Wanted* mention that they first read the book as a child or young adult. Many note that they have read and reread the book numerous times, both as children and as adults. These readers recall that the initial appeal of *The Family Nobody Wanted* lay in its charming descriptions of family life. A Maine reader described it as "wonderful, full of love and triumph, through some very trying times, as well as a lot of fun!" Another reader feared that the book would be filled "with big words that nobody understood." Instead, *The Family Nobody Wanted* captured her interest so completely that "I couldn't wait to finish this book." A Massachusetts reader who claims to have read "this book about 100 times as a child" remembers it as "great to read—full of details of life with a houseful of kids and not much money!"[26]

This original baby boom audience of *The Family Nobody Wanted* could find in Helen Doss's story of a woman raising twelve children a reflection of the traditional nuclear family enshrined in popular situation comedies of the era. Yet while the size of the Doss family links it to dominant images of the family in the postwar years, in most ways the family is far from typical. Recognizing this, readers have particularly stressed the importance of the book to shaping their views of adoption. As one reader said, "I'm sure this book was an inspiration to many people to adopt children that 'nobody wanted.'" Another Amazon.com reviewer credited *The Family Nobody Wanted* with influencing her decision to adopt several Asian children.[27]

The family's adoptive status is not the only thing that sets it apart from dominant images of the postwar American family. Unlike the affluent Cleaver and Brady families of television fame, the Dosses, as the Massachusetts reader quoted earlier realized, had "a houseful of kids and not much money." The Dosses are so far from the consumerism urged by the affluent fifties that one of the children responds to the overabundance of goods given the family for being "the Christmas Family of the Year" by observing, "Santa Claus brought you too many things" (219). And while television rarely if ever showed its housewives hard at work, Helen Doss gives us scenes in which she wallpapers a room with children underfoot, copes with a broken furnace in her husband's absence, and does backbreaking, financially needed labor in a family garden. Perhaps most important, unlike the same-race families that even today set the standard for popular images of the American family, the Doss family was visibly multiracial. In such ways *The Family Nobody Wanted* opened important cultural fault lines, providing its original readers a glimpse at difference during a period in which dominant images of the American family stressed and promoted its homogeneity.

Like other books that have made a mark on both children and adults, *The Family Nobody Wanted* walks a narrow line between cultural mainstream and margin. Thus one reader of the original edition described it as "a good, clean, and Christian book to have in any home,"[28] words applicable to another book that has appealed to both children and adult readers, Alcott's *Little Women*. Yet *The Family Nobody Wanted* advocates for the radical, democratic tradition of Christianity that shaped both the antislavery activism of the Alcotts and the antisegregation work of the Dosses. As Carl Doss tells a neighbor, "We Americans can't keep one tenth of our population in an inferior position. . . . It isn't Christian and it isn't democratic, and most of us claim to be both" (187–188). Similarly, like Mark Twain's *The Prince and the Pauper*, which moves quickly from humorous boyish pranks to horrifying images of women being burned at the stake, *The Family Nobody Wanted* contains episodes both charming and frightening.

For example, the chapter "Taro" describes in humorous detail the "wild and woolly times" (88) of four boys at play. Yet we also learn that Taro came to the Dosses as a foster child after his entire family, with the exception of his father, died in the internment camps in which Japanese Americans were imprisoned. The chapter concludes with a bitter Thanksgiving message when Taro's father arrives for dinner, his face "battered, swollen, with a large bandage over one ear, his lip split in an ugly cut, and one eye almost closed" (90). Taro's father, the victim of "patriotic" neighbors who punch and kick him nearly to death because "the only good Jap's a dead one," is saved by a white U.S. ser-

viceman married to a Japanese American woman. The story
takes another dramatic turn when the soldier describes how
in Italy "a Nisei boy saved my life—my life, at the cost of
his" (91). In a fashion typical of *The Family Nobody Wanted*,
the episode shows us both the ugly face of American racism
and the redeeming hope of a multiracial American democracy.

  The Family Nobody Wanted was published four months before the landmark *Brown v. Board of Education* ruling, and
the book's appeal can be traced in part to the way in which
it presents and views race relations. Published reviews and
unpublished letters to Helen Doss from readers stress the
impact of the book's message of racial tolerance. One reader
from the Sears, Roebuck Company's "Peoples Jury" described *The Family Nobody Wanted* as "wonderful for the
whole family to read—and for anyone who wants to have
a better feeling toward the different races of people in our
country."[29] A *Library Journal* review praised "the true spirit
of brotherly love and tolerance which pervades the book."[30]
A woman from Tennessee who read the book as a teenager
credited it with "giving me the open mind and loving heart
that I now have."[31] The book's numerous examples of both
racism and racial tolerance reinforce this message, as do the
many overt statements contained in chapters such as
"Taro," "All God's Children," and "Little Beaver and the
War Orphan."

  Like Lillian Smith's *Killers of the Dream*, *The Family Nobody Wanted* gave readers a white woman's personal view of
race and family in America.[32] Unlike Smith's work, however, *The Family Nobody Wanted* was marketed to and read

avidly by young people. Vivid scenes of family life and a writing style described by the *New York Times* as "the friendly simplicity of a woman talking over a back fence"[33] made the book both compelling and accessible. For *The Family Nobody Wanted* does not make a merely theoretical argument for racial tolerance. Throughout the book, we see Helen Doss "walking the talk" in a particularly personal way. Helen and Carl Doss learn from and advocate for their children, even as they outspokenly preach for integration and tolerance from inside a multiracial family.

Life magazine featured the Doss family for reasons also related to racial tolerance, but with an important difference. To *Life*, the Doss family was good propaganda. When the Dosses balked at exposing their family to public scrutiny, *Life*'s reporter Dick Pollard exclaimed, "I wish you could realize how a general knowledge of your 'United Nations' family could help our country! Anti-American propaganda abroad emphasizes our intolerant side. If people in other countries could open a copy of *Life* and learn about your interracial family, they would see our better side, a glimpse of democracy in action." Carl Doss himself suggests this view when he tells a neighbor who has accused him of being a radical, "Every time one of us steps on someone because of his color, we do as much harm to our country as if we were Communist saboteurs" (188). Pictures of this happy interracial family would show the Soviet Union and other cold war "anti-American" forces that Americans of different races do get along. A *San Francisco Chronicle* reviewer described "the Dosses' experiment" as "more important than the work of the Atomic Energy Commission," while the syndicated columnist Dolly Reitz contended, "I can't think of a better book to be translated into foreign languages."[34]

The *Life* article and reviews that link *The Family Nobody Wanted* to the United States' image abroad offer provocative evidence of how mainstream American culture attempted to fit this transracial adoptive family into a world bordered internationally by World War II, the cold war, and Third World nationalism, and domestically by the internment of Japanese Americans, a nascent civil rights movement, and the elevation of the nuclear family. Even as *Life* labeled the Doss family "a one-family United Nations," the magazine's photographs and captions located this far-from-typical family within mainstream ideals of 1950s America. One photograph, for example, shows the children at school, reciting the pledge of allegiance. Another captures the five Doss girls, whose ethnic backgrounds include Chinese, Japanese, Mexican, and Native American Indian, dressed in identical "best white dresses" for a walk to church. Carl Doss is identified in the article's subtitle as a Methodist minister, and photographs of the family attending church are prominently featured. The photograph that heads the article, which appears on this edition's cover, offers the telling image of Helen and Carl Doss seated with the two youngest children on their laps while the other children climb a rope ladder.[35]

Life thus led readers to see the Doss family as a clear example of an American success story. To *Life* magazine and the dominant culture that labeled them a "one-family U.N.," the Dosses were a symbol of racial tolerance and integration. Their assimilated, mixed-race children would be given opportunities to climb any ladder to social acceptance and economic mobility. And in many ways, *Life*'s view was correct. The family, and the children, did succeed within the American mainstream, offering proof of the potential of a color-blind society. This message, which Helen Doss recently rearticulated to me as "I hope my readers will realize that there is just one race; the human race," is profoundly important, and it had special significance to its original audience. *The Family Nobody Wanted* helped readers of the fifties, sixties, and seventies have faith in what one reviewer called "the universal brotherhood of man." As that reviewer went on to say, "I shall always feel better for having read this book. And so will you."[36] For readers confronted with racial violence, from a church in Birmingham exploding with its youngest worshipers inside, to white mothers in Boston throwing rocks at buses holding black children, Doss's example and message were invaluable. As a Sears book club reader put it, the story of the Doss family "truly offers an example of what we could be."[37] *The Family Nobody Wanted* thus lent hope to a civil rights–era generation struggling to comprehend and overcome the failures of American democracy.

The Family Nobody Wanted tells us that we are capable of overcoming those failures, but it does not gloss over them. Helen Doss's pointed comments on the effects of internment on Japanese Americans, on misguided race-matching adoption policies, and on the racial name-calling that hurt her children, graphically illustrate racism's presence and dangers. As Doss tells her readers, "Carl and I must prepare our children to stand up in the face of prejudice. We know they will someday share the fate of many Americans who, like Taro's father, are sometimes forced to live on the edge of danger because their skins are dark or their eyes 'slant' " (170). At the same time, Helen and Carl Doss recognize and reject the privilege conferred by their white skin. To a social worker who warns them that adopting a child of another race will "drag" them "down to the level of the subjugated minority," the Dosses respond that "skin color . . . should not give us the right to lord it over those who are born with darker skin"(31).

Helen Doss also critiques the racial matching in adoption practice. When they attempt to adopt a biracial German child, the Dosses are greeted with suspicion by neighbors and relatives and with red tape from adoption agencies. As Carl says to Helen, "Some of the intermediaries probably object to placing a Negro child in a so-called 'white' home, and just haven't the courage to come out and say so" (190). Earlier, a social worker angrily rejects the Dosses' request for a mixed-race child: "Crossing racial lines is against all our *principles* of good social-work practice" (30). Figures on transracial adoption indicate that these principles of good social work practice were seldom violated. In 1953 statistics gathered by the U.S. Children's Bureau and the Child Welfare League of America showed only 32,872 nonrelated adoptions, and during this period only 7 percent of all adoptions were transracial.[38] Even though they were in 1951 celebrated as the "Christmas Family of the Year," as an international and multiracial family the Dosses were still a cultural rarity and very much "the family nobody wanted."

As a member of a transracial family, Doss also raises questions relevant to the 1950s liberal racial ideology of "color-blindness." For example, the story of biracial Gretchen ends when the Dosses find an African American couple to adopt the little girl. Helen Doss concludes the chapter with an acknowledgment of the difficult identity issues facing black children with white parents. Doss reminds us that Gretchen has found a home with "a father and a mother and a brother, all the same warm toast shade that she was, and she would know that her own color was just right for *her*" (191). Gretchen finds her permanent family in an African American family, and Taro is reunited with his Japanese American birth father. When Teddy comes home in tears after a playground episode of racial name-calling, his mother reminds him that "God made more dark-skinned people than any other kind! . . . So I think God must especially love little brown children" (173). Shortly after this, Donny tells Teddy a Filipino legend about the creation of human beings. In the legend, which Donny learned from Taro's father, God finally gets human beings right when he creates "a beautiful, warm-toned brown" person, "just exactly the way a man should be" (87).

Thus, *The Family Nobody Wanted* suggests the ways in which people of different races and cultures are both the same and different. Even as Doss reminds us that we are all part of the human race, she also celebrates her children's individual cultures and differences. A similar pattern is found in two of many children's books Doss published after *The Family Nobody Wanted*. One, *All the Children of the World*, highlights cultural differences in children's lives. Another, *Friends around the World*, shows how children around the world share similar tastes and interests.[39] Doss neither denies the importance of race and culture in a person's life nor reduces those aspects of identity to an essentialist foundation. Her eye as a mother, writer, and social observer is too sharp for color-blindness and too sensitive to individual differences to see nothing but race or color.

This balance, important for readers of the 1950s, is equally crucial today. As Cornell West wrote in *Race Matters*, "To establish a new framework, we need to begin with a frank acknowledgment of the basic humanness and Americanness of each of us."[40] Whether poking fun at a teacher who believes that Rita's Mexican heritage makes her genetically disposed to like chili peppers (166), or reminding us of the institutionalized racism that brought "discrimination in jobs and housing, an Orientals Exclusion Act, and the 'relocation centers' of World War II" (170), Helen Doss helps us to see how the "Americanness of each of us" is undercut in both small and large ways by racial intolerance and racial essentialism. In writing the story of our multiracial society through one multiracial family, Helen Doss makes race matter in an intimate, familial, and believable context.

Indeed, the enduring appeal of *The Family Nobody Wanted* lies in part in its ability to take on such large social issues while never losing sight of the particular. Every chapter of *The Family Nobody Wanted* contains moments of trenchant social commentary, but Doss's insights are delivered in the very specific context of her family and their vividly rendered lives. As one reader said, "I liked the details about their everyday life and I felt as if I could have been right there in their home."[41] This balanced attention to both household and world affairs is a unique and important quality of *The Family Nobody Wanted*. A scene in which Helen Doss pulls out a map to show six-year-old Teddy the Philippines is emblematic of the family's relationship to the world. Doss tells Teddy, who is of Filipino and Malay heritage, about "where some of your ancestors came from" (173). She promises her son that if possible, the whole family will visit the Philippines some day. The geography lesson is followed with practical advice about how to cope with the cruel and racist taunts of some of his schoolmates. Clearly, the Doss home is no protected, isolationist haven. The world is part of this household, from the rich culture of the Philippines to the distressing realities of young children's prejudice.

Reviews of the book all praised the warm stories of family life, and the *New York Times* entitled its review of *The Family Nobody Wanted* "A World Inside One Household."[42] However, as the mother of Asian, Native American, Hispanic, and mixed-race children, and a member of a socially rather than biologically constructed family, Doss necessarily confronts and writes about public attitudes and institutions. Family, considered by American culture as a separate and private sphere, is visibly public for a transracial family such as the Dosses, who cannot pretend a biological link to their Asian, Hispanic, and Native American children. The family's celebrity, generated by the *Life* article, the national radio program, and the book itself, further breaks down the idea of family as a privileged private space.

For while *The Family Nobody Wanted* happily celebrates family life, it also offers a radical revision of the American family of the postwar era. The first two sentences, "I didn't yearn for a career, or maids and a fur coat, or a trip to Europe. All in the world I wanted was a happy, normal little family," place Helen Doss's story and longings for children within dominant cultural ideals for women and families in the 1950s. Postwar America, as Elaine Tyler May has argued, needed and wanted large families, and encouraged women to find their identity in motherhood. Through these large families, America could demonstrate "optimism and abundance, a sign of faith in a better future."[43] Helen Doss, however, struggles with infertility and with adoption bureaucracies before finally attaining her large baby boom family. She reminds us after another unsuccessful attempt to adopt a second child that "I felt tired and discouraged, but so did the whole world" (32).

Moreover, Doss's discouragement does not end until she takes on the whole world, in the form of public attitudes and regulations about adoption and race. We first see the public nature of Doss's path to motherhood as she types letters to hundreds of adoption agencies in search of "unwanted" mixed-race children. Whether knocking on adoption agency doors, writing letters to social workers across the country, traveling to bring her children to their new home, or standing in a judge's chambers to finalize an adoption, Helen Doss becomes a mother in a visible and public way. The public sphere intrudes into her home once she becomes a mother as well. For example, Doss describes an encounter with a state social worker in terms that make readers aware of the public links to her family life. " 'I don't like the reports on this latest one you've taken,' she [the social worker] said, as she sat in our living room"(60). Thus, while much of the action of *The Family Nobody Wanted* takes places in the Doss home, that home is far from a private world. In addition, Helen Doss's desire to have children and, later, to support her children leads her to make many forays into the world outside the home.

Such facts enable readers to understand that while the mother/narrator of *The Family Nobody Wanted* is fulfilled by marriage and children, she is not "only" a wife and mother. In addition to being a persistent and outspoken advocate for adoption, Helen Doss is a writer throughout her marriage. She also contributes greatly to the family "kitty" through such work as planting a garden and painting houses. Halfway through the book, Doss leaves her family to go to college, and she graduates shortly before the publication of *The Family Nobody Wanted*. In an article written for the Sears Peoples Book Club, Doss defines herself as above all an author. "As far back as I can remember, I wanted to be a writer," Doss begins.[44] As the biographer and mother of the very public "family nobody wanted," Doss implicitly challenges the postwar relegation of women to a protected and privatized home.

Moreover, in writing as a mother, Doss challenged the cultural authority of educated, often male professionals to speak for and about American women. Touted in publicity as a "true story," *The Family Nobody Wanted* gained credibility and popular acclaim in part because Helen Doss used her status as an adoptive mother to reply to the social workers, doctors, scientists, psychiatrists, psychologists, and other professionals whose "expert" advice in the 1950s focused largely on the problems, rather than the promise, of adop-

tion.[45] In offering American culture the clear, warm, and
unapologetic voice of a parent who loves her children and
is a proud advocate for adoption, Doss countered psychoan-
alysts such as Barbara Kohlsaat and Adelaide M. Johnson,
who in a March 1954 article warned of "neurotic character
traits" in adoptive parents, as well as child psychologists
such as Marshall Schecter, who asserted, with little evidence, that adopted children were highly likely to exhibit
"neurotic and psychotic states."[46] Against the "science" of
social workers and psychologists, Doss placed her own experience.

For their part, social workers, as Julie Berebitsky has
shown, worried that such popular writings on adoption
"were seen by many Americans as a trustworthy and author-
itative voice on the subject."[47] Articles in popular magazines
from *Reader's Digest* to *Ladies Home Journal* to *Ebony* presented alternative views of adoption, and in many of these
stories adoption professionals did not fare well. Notable was
a 1948 *Reader's Digest* story that disparagingly quoted the
head of a large adoption agency who answered, "We don't
handle dented cans," when asked to explain the agency's rejection of mixed-race, older, and special-needs children.[48] In
The Family Nobody Wanted, social work experts also tend to
be the villains of the story, first telling Doss that she and
her husband have too little money to adopt, and later react-
ing with horror to the family's inquiry about adopting a
mixed-race child. The reliance of social workers on statistics
unsupported by experience particularly comes under attack
in *The Family Nobody Wanted*. In one humorous but pointed
episode, we see a social worker, "tapping her pencil on her

notes," tell Doss, " 'the facts are here before you' " (61). By the end of the chapter, however, even the social worker recognizes that the Doss children are not abstract "facts," but specific and unique individuals.

Doss was not alone in challenging professional opinions through personal experience. The same year *The Family Nobody Wanted* hit bookstores, Jean Paton's seminal collection, *The Adopted Break Silence*, was also published.[49] The combination of Doss's voice as an adoptive parent and Paton's as an adopted person marked an interesting and rare moment of positive cultural attention to adoption. During the same period, Pearl Buck, who corresponded with Helen Doss and wrote the introduction to the Japanese edition of *The Family Nobody Wanted*, founded Welcome House, whose mission was to find families for children who, like the Doss children, were considered "unadoptable" because of race or physical or mental disability. Buck also used her status as a well-known author to promote transracial adoption, arguing in a 1958 *Ebony* magazine article that "The crucial necessity in adoption is not similarity of religion or race, but love."[50]

The rise of such popular writings on adoption coincided with, and contributed to, the growth in adoption in America. As Julie Berebitsky has noted, the postwar years of 1946–1970 marked a moment in which "adoption won widespread cultural legitimacy and there were more unrelated adoptions each year than ever before or ever since."[51] At the time of *The Family Nobody Wanted*'s original publication, approximately 33,000 nonrelated adoptions took place in the United States yearly. During the period in which Americans eagerly read the Doss family saga, adoption in

America continued to rise, peaking in 1970, when 89,200 nonrelated adoptions were recorded.[52] Helen Doss's memoir was thus part of a growing and intense cultural interest in adoption.

In addition to this actual increase in the number of adoptions, the reasons for adopting and the kinds of children typically adopted changed. In earlier years, children available for adoption tended to be older, either orphaned or the offspring of married couples who could not afford to raise them. Parents typically adopted for reasons other than infertility. Indeed, as Elaine Tyler May says, "The term [infertility] itself was not even used before 1940."[53] By the forties and fifties, however, adoption in its modern form emerged. Regulated by agencies, adoption became an often expensive option for infertile couples seeking healthy white infants. The children they adopted were typically born to young, unwed women.[54] A variety of factors, including an increase in infertility and cultural messages about the importance of marriage and motherhood to women's identities, led more married couples to adoption. While out-of-wedlock births increased in this period, cultural attitudes toward illegitimacy were also changing.[55] This is evident in *The Family Nobody Wanted* when Carl Doss reassures a sympathetically portrayed unwed birth mother: "If you've decided to keep your baby, I'm sure you're doing the best thing. Who has a better right to raise that child?" (27). These factors meant that, as the Dosses discovered, "each [adoption] agency had a waiting list as long as from here to the moon, and a dozen eager couples clamored for every baby needing a home" (5).

Simultaneously, and not coincidentally, the era of *The Family Nobody Wanted* also marked the period in which secrecy and closed records became the norm in American adoption. As Wayne Carp has noted, between 1937 and 1939 states began to reevaluate or revise their adoption laws. By the time Helen Doss had published *The Family Nobody Wanted*, all states kept original birth records sealed, a departure from procedures that had been followed since the founding of the United States.[56] In this context of increased secrecy around adoption, the Doss family's story and their culture's response are illuminating. During the fifties, adoptive parents were advised to keep the fact of their children's adoption secret, and laws supported such secrecy. The idea was to create an illusion of a biologically created family. Thus, after an adoption, original birth records were sealed and a new birth certificate generated.

Yet as a transracial adoptive family, the Dosses could not be part of this illusion, nor did they wish to be. To a neighbor who suggested that they "pass off" a child as "a dark Spanish child," Carl Doss responded: "But secrets have a way of leaking out. If we lied about that one thing, could our daughter trust us about anything else?" (190). Carl Doss's response demonstrates that the Dosses' understanding of adoption was far more complex and advanced than their culture's. In contrast, comments of the Dosses' neighbors suggest the extent to which average Americans, even during the period in which adoptions reached an apex, continued to doubt, distrust, and hide this alternative method of family formation. That distrust was evident in the popular media as well. Adoption was listed under "Special Problems" in Dr. Spock's _Baby and Child Care_. A _Saturday Evening Post_ article on adoption had the title "Babies for the Brave." And the popular 1956 film _The Bad Seed_ (based on the 1954 novel of the same title) depicted an adopted child with a pathological genetic disposition to evil.[57]

Against a background of such negative images Helen Doss placed her family's story. That story still resonates in part because the issues the Doss family faced in 1954 remain relevant to adoptive families today. Estimates place the number of adoptees in America at between five and six million, and a 1997 survey found that 58 percent of Americans claim a "personal experience" with adoption, in the sense that they, or a close friend or family member, have adopted, been adopted, or relinquished a child for adoption.[58] In recent decades, nonrelated adoptions have hovered near 50,000 a year, with a growing number of international adoptions. During the last decade international adoption grew dramatically, from 7,093 children adopted from abroad by U.S. citizens in 1990 to 18,539 in 2000.[59] Yet it is still clear that most Americans define a "real family" as one with a blood tie or, failing that, at least the appearance of one. As Wayne Carp has said, "When it comes to family matters, most Americans view blood ties as naturally superior to artificially constructed ones."[60]

Nonetheless, if we are becoming, as Adam Pertman writes, an "adoption nation," it is in part because of the example set by Helen Doss and her family. Our culture contains many images of adoption's problems, but few if any works have ever spoken so directly and so lovingly about the joys and wonders of adoption. Particularly for members of transracial adoptive families, *The Family Nobody Wanted* offers a convincing and moving counterexample to the views of those who, as Helen Doss says, "have never ventured beyond the white bars of their self-imposed social cages" (165). This is especially important given what Beth Waggenspack has called "the symbolic crisis of adoption." Waggenspack notes the need for positive adoption symbols to counteract the powerful negative images that permeate popular culture and the mass media.[61] *The Family Nobody Wanted* has been in the past and now can be again a much-needed validating symbol of adoptive family life.

Yet *The Family Nobody Wanted* is relevant not only to what my daughter calls "families like ours." In asserting and showing that her family "was meant to be this way," Helen Doss's still-compelling story forces us to reconsider fundamentally held beliefs about the American family. Just as it did in 1954, the family today occupies a peculiarly immutable space in the American cultural landscape. Protected by literal and metaphoric fences, the family is the haven to which we retreat to escape the economic pressures, political disputes, and diverse populations of the public arena. Moreover, that public sphere is notable for its dynamic, autonomous, and socially constructed spaces. We build our skyscrapers, schools, and institutions, choose our presidents and our soft drinks, and are told that we can accomplish anything if we "just do it."

But at the same time, an older slogan reminds us that "you can choose your friends but not your family." The only way to fit adoption into that slogan is to see members of the adoption triad as driven not by positive choice but by the negative necessities of infertility, poverty, and loss. While those elements are part of the Doss family story, they are far from its sum total. As Helen Doss breaks down "the walls of Jericho" to bring first one, then two, and eventually twelve children into her family, we come to understand that families may be chosen. We also see the variety of ways in which economic, social, and political factors shape a family's journey to and through adoption. Above all, we come to believe and understand Helen Doss when she tells us that her heterogeneous adoptive family is exactly the family that she wanted. After reading *The Family Nobody Wanted*, we are ready to exclaim along with Dorothy Doss, "*gosh, I wished I lived in that family.*"

May 2001   MARY BATTENFELD

Notes

This introduction could not have been written without the support and example of Helen Doss Reed. Barbara Melosh's comments on my paper at the October 2000 American Studies Association conference in Detroit, Michigan, also were invaluable. Finally, I would never have reread *The Family Nobody Wanted* without the presence in my life of my daughters, Priya and Varsha.

1. Evan B. Donaldson Institute, *Benchmark Adoption Survey: Report on Findings* (Washington, D.C.: Princeton Survey Research Associates, October 1997).

2. David Schneider, *American Kinship: A Cultural Account* (Chicago: University of Chicago Press, 1988), 25.

3. Elizabeth Bartholet, *Nobody's Children: Abuse and Neglect, Foster Drift, and the Adoption Alternative* (Boston: Beacon Press, 1999), 181.

4. "The Baby Chase," *People*, March 5, 2001, 60–70, and "The Adoption Maze," *U.S. News and World Report*, March 12, 2001, 62–69.

5. George Gerbner, *Adoption in the Mass Media: A Preliminary Survey of Sources of Information and a Pilot Study* (Philadelphia: Annenberg School of Communication, 1988); cited in Katarina Wegar, *Adoption, Identity, and Kinship* (New Haven: Yale University Press, 1997), 110.

6. The term "transracial adoption" is sometimes used to refer to the adoption of African American children by white parents. However, the term more properly refers to any adoption across racial lines. See, for example, Christine Adamec and William Pierce, *The Encyclopedia of Adoption*, 2d ed. (New York: Facts on File, 2000), 272–275.

7. See, for example, K. S. Stolley, "Statistics on Adoption in the United States," *The Future of Children* 3, no. 1 (Spring 1993): 26–42; and Karen Spar, *Foster Care and Adoption Statistics* (Washington, D.C.: Congressional Research Service, 1997).

8. Barb Reinhold, "What's Wrong with Foreign Adoption?" *Salon.com*, September 28, 2000 (http://www.salon.com/mwt/feature/2000/09/28/Russian_adoption/index.html).

9. See Katarina Wegar, "Adoption, Family Ideology, and Social Stigma: Bias in Community Attitudes, Adoption Research, and Practice," *Family Relations* 49, no. 4 (October 2000): 363–370.

10. For thoughtful discussions of this case, see Ellen Goodman, "Who Will Own these Lovely Twins?" *Boston Sunday Globe*, January 28, 2001, F7, and Madelyn Freundlich, "The Internet Twins Case," *Adoptive Families* 34, no. 2 (March/April 2001): 10.

11. Wegar, "Adoption, Family Ideology, and Social Stigma," 369.

12. Susan Ito, "An Intimate Rapport," review of Sandra Lee Patton, *BirthMarks: Transracial Adoption in Contemporary America*, *Adoptive Families* 34, no. 2 (March/April 2001): 54.

13. For recent work see, for example, Wayne Carp, *Family Matters: Secrecy and Disclosure in the History of Adoption* (Cambridge, Mass.: Harvard University Press, 1998), Julie Berebitsky, *Like Our Very Own: Adoption and the Changing Culture of Motherhood, 1851–1950* (Lawrence: University Press of Kansas, 2000), and Adam Pertman, *Adoption Nation: How the Adoption Revolution is Transforming America* (New York: Basic Books, 2000).

14. Helen Doss, *The Really Real Family* (Boston: Little, Brown, 1959).

15. Helen Doss, "Our International Family," *Reader's Digest* 55 (August 1949): 55–59.

16. Helen Doss, "The Case of the Deferred Novelist," *Sears Peoples Book Club* 11, no. 11 [1954].

17. Ibid.

18. Ibid.

19. Helen Doss estimates that *The Family Nobody Wanted* sold more than 500,000 copies. Little, Brown did not keep sales figures, so I have been unable to confirm how many books were sold. Letter from Andrew Sheltry, Little, Brown and Company, August 11, 2000 (in my possession), and personal interview with Helen Doss, July 24, 2000.

20. Amazon.com, "Customer Reviews of *The Family Nobody Wanted*," December 18, 1999 (http://www.amazon.com/exec/obidos/ts/book [April 11, 2000]).

21. At the time this went to press, the range of prices for used booksellers advertising through Barnes and Noble and Amazon.com was $65.00 to $185.00.

22. Margaret C. Scoggin, "The Outlook Tower," *Horn Book Magazine* 31, no. 1 (February 1955): 25.

23. From an ABC press release on "The Family Nobody Wanted," January 27, 1975, in Helen Doss's personal papers.

24. Conversation with Helen Doss, January 18, 2001.

25. Amazon.com, "Customer Reviews of *The Family Nobody Wanted*," June 25, 1999 (accessed February 7, 2001).

26. Ibid., March 11, 2000, June 21, 2000, and April 25, 2000.

27. Ibid., April 25, 2000, and May 2, 1999.

28. Mrs. Ray Severance, "Your Peoples Jury Says," *Sears Peoples Book Club* 11, no. 11 [1954].

29. Mrs. Glen Powell, "Your Peoples Jury Says," *Sears Peoples Book Club* 11, no. 11 [1954].

30. Elizabeth Nichols, *Library Journal* 79 (September 15, 1954), 1583.

31. Amazon.com, "Customer Reviews of *The Family Nobody Wanted*," July 30, 1999 (accessed February 7, 2001).

32. Lillian Smith, *Killers of the Dream* (New York: W. W. Norton, 1949).

33. Ben Bradford, "A World Inside One Household," *New York Times Book Review*, November 21, 1954, 34.

34. Jane Voiles, *San Francisco Chronicle*, October 3, 1954, 18. Dolly Reitz, quoted in *The Washington Farmer* (undated), in Helen Doss's personal papers.

35. Wayne Miller, "Life Visits a One-Family U.N.," *Life* (November 21, 1951), 157–162.

36. Godfrey Winn, *Women's Illustrated* (England). Quoted in *The Washington Farmer* (undated), in Helen Doss's personal papers.

37. Doris E. Wellman, "Your Peoples Jury Says," *Sears Peoples Book Club* 11, no. 11 [1954].

38. Adamec and Pierce, *Encyclopedia of Adoption*, xxvii, and Michael Schapiro, *Study of Adoption Practice* (New York: Child Welfare League of America, 1957), 9.

39. Helen Doss, *All the Children of the World* (New York: Abingdon Press, 1958), and Doss, *Friends around the World* (New York: Abingdon Press, 1959).

40. Cornell West, *Race Matters* (New York: Random House, 1994), 8.

41. Verna Kozak, "Your Peoples Jury Says," *Sears Peoples Book Club* 11, no. 11 [1954].

42. Bradford, "A World Inside One Household," 34.

43. Elaine Tyler May, *Barren in the Promised Land: Childless Americans and the Pursuit of Happiness* (New York: Basic Books, 1995), 137.

44. Helen Doss, "The Case of the Deferred Novelist," and Carl Doss, "We're All Proud of Mama," *Sears Peoples Book Club* 11, no. 11 [1954].

45. See, for example, Carp, *Family Matters*, and Judith Modell, *Kinship with Strangers: Adoption and Interpretations of Kinship in American Culture* (Berkeley: University of California Press, 1994).

46. Barbara Kohlsaat and Adelaide M. Johnson, "Some Suggestions for Practice in Infant Adoptions," *Social Casework* 35 (March 1954): 92. Marshall Schecter is quoted in Carp, *Family Matters*, 127.

47. Berebitsky, *Like Our Very Own*, 15.

48. Frederick G. Brownwell, "Why You Can't Adopt a Baby," *Reader's Digest* 53 (September 1948): 58. See also M. W. Jackson, "Always Room for One More," *Ladies Home Journal* 67 (January 1950): 111–114, and Pearl S. Buck, "Should White Parents Adopt Brown Babies?" *Ebony* (June 1958): 31.

49. Jean Paton, *The Adopted Break Silence* (Philadelphia: Life History Study Center, 1954).

50. Buck, "Should White Parents Adopt Brown Babies?" 31. For Welcome House, see Peter Conn, *Pearl S. Buck: A Cultural Biography* (New York: Cambridge University Press, 1996), 313.

51. Berebitsky, *Like Our Very Own*, 16. Barbara Melosh made the same point in her comments following the session "Race and Adoption in National and Transnational Contexts" at the American Studies Association Convention in Detroit, October 2000.

52. Cited in Berebitsky, *Like Our Very Own*, 189.

53. May, *Barren in the Promised Land*, 142.

54. See May, *Barren in the Promised Land*, Modell, *Kinship with Strangers*, and Carp, *Family Matters*.

55. See, for example, May, *Barren in the Promised Land*, 140–143, and Berebitsky, *Like Our Very Own*, 16.

56. Carp, *Family Matters*, 25.

57. "Babies for the Brave," *Saturday Evening Post* 227, no. 5 (July 31, 1954): 26–27.

58. Adam Pertman, "U.S. Adoptees May Approach 6 Million," *Boston Globe*, March 8, 1998, A35.

59. V. E. Flango and C. R. Flango, "How Many Children Were Adopted in 1992?" *Child Welfare* 74, no. 5 (September/October 1995): 1018–1032. Also "Intercountry Adoptions Reach All-Time High in 2000," *Adoptive Families* 34, no. 2 (March/April 2001): 12. Unfortunately, this essay was completed before the 2000 U.S. Census figures on adoption became available.

60. Carp, *Family Matters*, 1.

61. Beth M. Waggenspack, "The Symbolic Crisis of Adoption: Popular Media's Agenda Setting," *Adoption Quarterly* 1, no. 4 (1998): 57–82.

THE FAMILY NOBODY WANTED

CHAPTER 1

In the Beginning

I DIDN'T yearn for a career, or maids and a fur coat, or a trip to Europe. All in the world I wanted was a happy, normal little family. Perhaps, if God could arrange it, Carl and I could have a boy first, and after that, a little girl.

God didn't arrange it.

In fact, as our doctor regretfully informed us, Carl and I couldn't have *any* children of our own. No children, no sticky fingerprints on the woodwork, no childish tears and laughter, no small beds in the other bedroom. Just barren, empty years, stretching aimlessly into a lonely future.

I felt quite provoked with God about this, at first. Most of my friends were having their first babies, and some were starting on their second round. The interminable stork showers, where I had to watch complacent Madonnas in maternity clothes preside over their tissue-wrapped gifts, always sent me home for equally interminable weeping spells in my pillow. I couldn't pass a layette display in a store window without getting a lump the size of a baby rattle in my throat. Every time I walked down the street and saw a fulfilled mother strutting along the sidewalk behind a baby buggy, I was possessed with violent jealousy, envy, and acute self-pity.

Carl, who is a patient man, finally had enough.

"For heaven's sake stop mooning, or you'll have us both neurotic," he said. "If having a baby is that important, why don't we adopt one?"

The more I mulled the idea over, the better I liked it. Wasn't motherhood compounded more of love than biology? Once I made up my mind, I was eager to cradle our adopted baby in my arms, to bathe him and give him his bottle, to dress him in fuzzy kimonas and little sweater sets. Warmed with a breathless, motherly inner glow, I planned what must be done.

First, the nursery. I cleared out the extra bedroom and began work on the drab, stucco-finish walls. All the old calcimine had to be scrubbed off, and the walls scraped clean. Carl, who had recently quit his job as a journeyman painter and gone into business as a painting contractor on his own, was obviously too busy to help; so I borrowed brushes and some pale-pink paint, and did the nursery walls and woodwork myself. Then I sailed around downtown Santa Ana, the southern California town where we lived, on a buying spree. A secondhand store yielded a crib and chest of drawers, which I painted blue. Mother Goose decals came from the dime store, to march around the dado and intrigue the future owner of the room. The best crib mattress money could buy, some pink and blue blankets, small white sheets — everything must be ready.

"All right," I told Carl, the morning after the pink and blue rag rug had been laid, the room aired, the crib made, and the sheets turned down, waiting. "Let's go adopt our baby today."

I thought it would be easy. All we would have to do was to walk into the nearest orphanage, specify size, shape, sex, and color, and carry our new infant home.

I was bitterly disappointed.

The so-called "orphanages," we discovered, weren't full of homeless waifs, just waiting to be adopted. Most of the children were living there on a temporary basis, because their homes were broken by divorce, prolonged illness, or other incapacities of parents. Even bona fide orphans usually weren't free for adoption; somewhere for each child there was a relative or guardian, unable or unwilling to provide a home at that particular time.

"If you're looking for a baby," the orphanage superintendent told us kindly, "most couples find one through a licensed adoption agency."

He gave us the addresses of the two which had offices in Los Angeles. I visited them with high hopes; again my hopes were flattened. Each agency had a waiting list as long as from here to the moon, and a dozen eager couples clamored for every baby needing a home.

"We'll send a social worker to make a preliminary study of your home," one agency director said. "We must warn you, however, that it may be two or three years, possibly more, before a baby is placed with you. We must find a child whose background is perfectly matched to yours, and it must also be a child who is not a better match for anyone ahead of you on our waiting list."

It was a dim and distant hope to cling to, but I clung. That is, until the social worker finally made her visit.

"I'm afraid we can't even put you on the waiting list at

this time," she told us. "From the information you have given me — no money in the bank, no insurance, a huge mortgage on your house, in debt for your painting truck and equipment — " She raised her eyebrows. "I am sure you can plainly see that, at this point, you are financially unstable."

"But Carl is doing so well," I protested, "considering that the depression is still on! Anyway, he has all the jobs coming in he can handle, and already he's one of the top painting contractors in Santa Ana."

"Yet his business still is a new one," she said. "Let it get out of the red and on its feet. Wait until your debts are cleared up and you have money in the bank. Then come back and apply again."

That looked far enough away to be forever. My last flicker of hope went out like a snuffed candle, and I started weeping into my pillow again.

"Pull yourself together and find something else to think about," Carl said. "Why don't you get some friends and start a junior women's club in Santa Ana? Or take some postgraduate work at the junior college?"

Although he was gentle with my grief, he was not particularly disappointed that we couldn't adopt a child. He liked children well enough, but he wasn't in any hurry to have one; he had problems enough at that time, without taking on any new ones. It would have been simple if only it were debts worrying him, or the high cost of pig-bristle brushes, or trying to keep good painters on his crew. No, his problems were bigger than that. He was having a tussle with God, too.

Back in his high-school days, Carl had felt a call to the ministry. Either the call was too faint or the pressure of environment too strong; after several frustrated tries, he had given up the idea of working his way through college, and had gone to work as an apprentice painter. He was president of the Epworth League at Santa Ana's First Methodist Church when I joined the group and first met him. I never suspected then, in fact not until several years later, when we married, that Carl was taunted by urges to be something more than a house painter.

"It was just a wild dream," he laughed, when he told me. "Just an idealistic kid's daydream."

As the first months of our marriage passed, and then the first years, I knew it was more than that. I might be troubled because we had no children; but Carl was troubled over the one thing that could be deeper, a man's searching of his soul to find its purpose and meaning. He came home from work every night tired, looking older than his twenty-eight years, his face and hands flecked with paint, and dropped with great weariness into his chair.

"Painting doesn't satisfy the whole *you*, any more than the Junior Women's Club or my classes at the college satisfy the whole *me*," I said, one summer evening. Carl was active in the Junior Chamber of Commerce and was heading up Santa Ana's official *Clean-Up, Paint-Up* drive, but I knew that these things were not enough for him, either. "If we get the business out of the red and the mortgage paid on the house, if our application for adoption is finally accepted . . . After a few years, if we finally get a child — "

Carl took my hand. "That would make you pretty happy, wouldn't it?"

"That's what I'm trying to tell you," I said. "Even if we eventually *do* have one or two children — what I want most in the world — I couldn't be happy. Not unless *you* were satisfied with life, too."

"Distressing, isn't it?" Carl said wryly. "A man just two years short of being thirty, who still hasn't found himself! At least I know what's wrong."

"What?"

"It's hard to explain, exactly, in words. But I feel there's a voice down inside of me, inside all of us. Call it God speaking to us, call it the soul, call it conscience or whatever you like. If we turn to it, we can find help in knowing how to make the most of our lives. But that voice doesn't speak very loud. If we aren't still, if we don't provide solitude for listening — if we don't *try* to listen, then we can't hear it. It's easy to drown out that voice. Just the bustle and noise of everyday living can drown it out."

"Yes," I said. "I know."

"A man can be so busy making a living, he puts off making his life. And then one day he wakes up and finds he's too old, and it's too late."

"You're not too old," I said.

"Maybe not," Carl said. "Maybe not."

The next day I bicycled out to the apartment house which Carl and his crew were painting. I leaned on the handlebars, watching Carl hoist huge ladders and planks as if they were toys, adjusting a swing stage. I liked to come watch him when he was painting; he handled his brush with the quick, sure strokes of an artist. While I was watching, the noon whistle blew. As Carl climbed down the ladder and went for his lunch pail in the truck, he saw me.

"Hi," I said.

He brought his lunch over, pushed the standard down on my bicycle, and dusted off an upturned bucket for me to sit on. He sat on the grass beside me and took off his paint-spattered white cap; the tight band had pressed a mark on his prematurely thin blond hair. He smelled of turpentine and paint thinner.

"I didn't sleep much last night," he said. "Here, have a sandwich."

"I'll eat one when I get back to the house," I said. "I know you didn't. Every time I woke up, I knew you were awake, too."

"And this morning I've been trying to let my soul talk to me, instead of telling it to shut up and quit bothering me. If you're with me, Helen, I'm going to give up my business. I want to go back to college and study for the ministry."

"I'm with you," I said.

"It's asking a lot. I'll need four years of college, then three years postgraduate work at seminary. I don't know *when* you'd get the baby you want."

I shrugged. I had let my maternal feelings become numb, because it didn't hurt so much that way. "That's all right. It would be a long time anyway."

"We're just on the verge of making the business a financial success," Carl said. "If I sell out now, I'll sell at a terrific loss. We'll be lucky to break even."

"We've started from scratch before."

"Our friends will laugh at us," he warned. "Our relatives will think we've lost our minds."

"What was it somebody said? *'If God be for us, who can be against us. . . .'*"

"That's Paul, I think." He laid down his sandwich and took my hands in his. "It won't be easy."

"I know," I said. "I've found that out. The things you want most out of life are never easy."

Carl and I enrolled at the University of Redlands for the fall semester. After selling our house, truck, equipment, paint supplies, and all, and with the remaining payments on everything settled, we had barely enough money to get started. We paid one semester's tuition apiece, one month's rent on a little cottage in an orange grove, and bought enough groceries to stock the shelves. Our remaining few dollars purchased about half the books we needed, and then we were flat broke.

"Everybody says we'll never make it," Carl said. "We'll show them."

There were many times during that first year at Redlands when I thought that maybe we *wouldn't* make it. We tackled any kind of odd job we could find, so that we could keep eating. Carl cleaned chicken houses, and painted for the university on Saturdays; I had a part-time desk job in one of the women's dormitories, and wrote free-lance articles for the *American Girl* magazine. For weeks on end we lived on boiled dry beans, and it was a gay day when we splurged by adding a dime's worth of hamburger. I gleaned dandelion leaves and other edible wild greens, to cook or eat raw, as a vitamin balance to our restricted diet.

We were closest to going without food the time we ate the rattlesnake meat. I had a small can of it, acquired many years ago as a souvenir, and I kept it on my kitchen-window shelf because it was so pretty. I never intended to eat it.

The minister of the University Methodist Church teased us about my souvenir. Carl was helping him out as youth director, and the minister was often at our house for either business or pleasure. The first time he saw the can, he picked it up and admired it.

"When are you and Carl going to open this?" he asked.

I laughed. "As far as I'm concerned, that's purely for decoration. You've *no* idea how hungry we'd have to be to eat *that!*"

Then came the day when our cupboards were as bare as old Mother Hubbard's. We had nothing for breakfast and nothing for lunch. That evening, when classes were over, we stood in our kitchen and looked around, and when our eyes met we knew what we had to do. Carl reached for my gaily colored little can, with the gold lettering that said: *Rattlesnake à la king — canned in Florida.* I took two cards and scraped enough flour from the corners of the flour drawer to make a couple of biscuits. They were a little hard, since I had no shortening or milk, but they weren't too bad. That was more than I could say for the *à la king.*

Rattlesnake is supposed to taste like a cross between chicken and tuna fish. Any resemblance ours might once have had to either certainly had been lost in the long passage of years since it had been canned. It turned out to be something closer to cotton strings in a curdled cream sauce. We ate it because, after all, it had calories.

The minister dropped by that night for a visit. When he went to the kitchen for a drink of water, he reached for the can, which was back in its usual place on the window shelf.

"When are you two going to eat this rattle——" he began, and then broke off in surprise when the can came up light in his hand. He turned it over and stared. Carl had reamed it open from the bottom, washed it out, and replaced it on the shelf for me; a few drops of water still clung to the inside. The minister shook his head, then took out his wallet and laid ten dollars on the kitchen sink.

"Don't argue with me," he said. "I know what your cupboards are like, without looking. Go buy some groceries."

At the end of that school year, Carl attended his first Methodist Annual Conference, the statewide meeting where church business is taken care of and appointments of pastors to churches of the area are made for the coming year. When Carl came back from the conference he announced, "Our money worries are over, honey! Start packing, we're going to Cucamonga!"

"Cuckoo — what?" I said. This was several years before Jack Benny and other comedians began using Cucamonga as a gag name on the radio, and I had never heard of the place.

"It's a little village between here and Los Angeles, on Foothill Boulevard," Carl told me. "They raise grapes in the valley, oranges and lemons toward the mountains. I'll have the student church there, preach on week ends, go to school on week days." He hugged me. "Just think, a salary of nine hundred dollars a year! And that's not all, because there's a house to live in, too!"

We moved into the parsonage, a sagging one-story house across the drive from the square-towered stone church on Archibald Street. The first month was busy, with fixing up the house, trying to marshal my weak memory into remembering the right names to go with the right faces in our little congregation, and, above all, getting used to the idea of being a minister's wife. When I began to feel at home in my new role, with a little time on my hands, I found that my old dreams of having a family just wouldn't stay suppressed any longer.

"This little sleeping porch, right next to our bedroom," I told Carl — "wouldn't it make a wonderful nursery?"

"Stop looking so wistful," Carl said. "No agency in its right mind would give us a baby, now."

"No harm in asking, is there?"

"Now just wait a minute," he protested. "I'm making nine hundred a *year*, not a month. I've got three more years at Redlands. After that, three more doing graduate study at seminary. It's going to be all I can do, just to get through school. How do you think we could support a baby?"

"Would you let me have one, if they offered us one?"

"You're being silly," Carl sputtered. "Of course, after the way you've stood behind me, and all I couldn't — But anyway they wouldn't, and even if they did, we'd never — "

"You know what you kept quoting from Matthew, whenever we hit the low spots last year," I reminded him.

"You said that if we had the faith of a mustard seed, we could move obstacles as big as mountains. I think we need a child, and somewhere a child needs us. And I've got the faith."

My letters to the adoption agencies were filled with the poignancy of my longing. When the summer was over, a social worker came to call. She visited pleasantly in our small, tan-papered parlor, the worn rug on the floor between us, rain drumming wet fingers on the tall, skinny Victorian windows. She took our case history from her brief case and checked over the details with us.

HUSBAND'S NAME: Carl M. Doss
BORN: Long Beach, California
AGE: 29
EDUCATION: Graduated from Santa Ana High School; one year at the University of Redlands
WIFE'S MAIDEN NAME: Helen Louise Grigsby
BORN: Sanderstead, Surrey, England, of American parents
AGE: 27
EDUCATION: Graduated from Maine Township High School at Park Ridge–Des Plaines, Illinois; one year each at Eureka College in Illinois, Santa Ana Junior College, and the University of Redlands.
PROPERTY OWNED: None
OTHER SECURITIES: None
BANK ACCOUNT: None
INSURANCE: None

The social worker droned on, going down the two pages of the questionnaire we had filled in. *Here it comes,* I thought, ready for a last-ditch argument about the things that are more important than money, such as families and love. I waited for her to suggest that we apply again in seven or eight years, when Carl was through college and seminary and settled in the full-time ministry.

She didn't.

God bless her, she shut her portfolio, smiled like an angel, and said, "I have a baby for you."

Just like that. "*I have a baby for you.*"

I couldn't believe my ears. Then I shut my gaping mouth and tried to look reasonably bright. I knew I couldn't have heard right.

The angel smiled indulgently. "He's a chubby little fellow with blue eyes, and a perfect match for you two."

"Where — where is he?" I stammered. "When can we have him?"

"He's in the city," she said. "I'll give you a note for the hospital, and you may pick him up any time in the next few weeks."

"*Weeks!*" I shouted, running to the coat closet. "We'll go right now!"

Carl studied the storm outside. "We'd better wait until tomorrow. The car — " He smiled an apology at the social worker — "the roof on our Model A leaks."

I flung my arms into my coat and grabbed an umbrella, waving it. "No matter," I shouted. "I'll hold this over the baby. Carl, you can wear my rain hat!"

An hour later we were sitting on the edges of our chairs in the hospital and a nurse was laying our Donald in my arms. I had to blink a few times before I could see him clearly. He was six weeks old, and his blue eyes looked at me with a charming, blank stare. Even to the nearly bald blond head, he was a chip off his adopted daddy.

I pulled back the blanket and touched his narrow head with tenderness. "Is he a forceps baby?" The nurse gave me a curious look, so I added lamely, "I just thought his head seemed sort of pinched in."

This brought a big laugh from the nurse. "He has a most normal and beautiful head. You don't know much about tiny babies, do you?"

"I never even *held* a tiny baby before," I confessed.

"You'll learn," she smiled.

"Yes," I said, laughing and crying at the same time in my great happiness. "Yes, I'll learn."

That night Carl helped me fix a makeshift crib beside our bed. For his first few weeks, little Donald slept in a big drawer laid across two facing straight chairs. A quilt folded in the bottom was the mattress, a piece of oilcloth cut from my kitchen tablecloth provided a waterproof cover, and pillowcases were just the right size for sheets.

Donny slept like a doll that first night; the next morning, when I took him up and dressed him for the first time, he seemed unbearably fragile, with arms and legs like matchsticks. I was afraid his limbs might break if I weren't careful, and I picked him up and laid him down as if he were made of glass. The first time I took Donny for his medical check-up, I gasped when the doctor grabbed our baby by one elbow and the opposite leg and swung the poor infant up on the scales. The good doctor was amused at my wide eyes, my hand over my mouth.

"His arms and legs won't come off," he soothed. "Babies are more durable than you think."

Nevertheless, I couldn't bring myself to take chances. It was a month before I could trust myself to lower a soapy baby into a tub of water, and I was nearly as nervous about those first daily sponge baths. Not only did I need space on the round oak dining table for towels, the dishpan filled with warm water, clean diapers, pins, soap, talcum, swab sticks, baby oil, and all the rest of the requirements for the ritual of the bath, but I also needed space to prop my indispensable baby book. Unless I followed the book one step at a time, I was afraid I might leave something out or do something wrong. I was as serious as a small child at a circus, but Carl thought I was uproariously funny.

"Don't just stand there and laugh," I told him the first day. "You could at least hold this book and read off the directions to me as I go." I was testing the water with my elbow and worrying because I didn't have a bath thermometer. The book said you ought to have a bath thermometer.

"You don't need one," Carl said. "Put Donny in, and if he turns red it's too hot, and if he turns blue it's too cold."

"That's an old joke, and not even funny," I said. "Read what comes next, after the part where I remove his clothes and let him kick for five minutes."

"Wring the washcloth in warm, clear water," Carl read, after finding the place, "and gently wipe the baby's face. Take a fresh cotton swab for each ear and nostril, being careful to — "

"Stop!" I cried. "You're going too fast."

"By the time you get to the end of the chapter, the poor little fellow *will* turn blue," Carl said, laying down the book. "Here, let me do it."

As the oldest in a spread-out family of six children, Carl had observed enough about babies to add to the natural self-confidence he had about any new venture. Without hesitation he soaped, rinsed, and dried Donny, slipped him into a shirt, neatly pinned the diaper, then tied on a white kimona.

"Nothing to it," Carl grinned, as he kissed his shining son.

That week the women's society in our church gave a surprise baby shower, with enough blankets and baby clothes to make Donny a well-dressed young man for the rest of his babyhood. The church people took Donny into their hearts, and Donny loved them right back. He was a most sociable baby, perhaps because he went everywhere with us, in his basket or in our arms, to church services, board meetings, house calls, and potluck suppers.

By the time he took his first steps, he was a confirmed explorer, and his exploring nearly always got him into trouble. He was the original little Dennis the Menace.

Since he was no longer able to sit reasonably still during the worship service, his roaming was confined to our fenced back yard during church time. One broiling summer Sunday, the high-school girl who was watching him in the back yard became engrossed in her Sunday school paper, and Donny climbed over the gate. Leaving his sunsuit where it had caught on the fence post, he toddled across the driveway and up the tall front steps to the open door of the church. Completely and unselfconsciously naked, he made a beeline for the pulpit, calling out cheerily, "Hi, Daddy!" as he eluded my frantic clutch from the front pew.

His insatiable curiosity continually drove him to try out new things for taste. He'd put anything into his mouth that would fit and wouldn't bite him first. I knew enough to keep such obvious dangers as iodine, laundry bleach, and kerosene out of his reach, but his imagination was more inventive than mine. To my knowledge he sampled everything from laundry soap to grasshoppers and shoe polish; and it was probably a good thing that many of the undoubtable other things weren't in my knowledge. I worried enough as it was.

One day I found him on the floor with a torn-open package of winter woolens, playing marbles with the moth balls. Suspicious, I looked closer. There were sugary crumbs around his mouth. My heart started to panic in my throat as I snatched him up and smelled his breath. It reeked.

"Donny," I cried, "quick, tell Mama! You didn't *eat* any of those white balls?"

"Naughty, naughty, not eat nassy stuff," he said solemnly. "Don't taste good, nope." He pointed to a chewed-up moth ball, spit out under the bed.

I dashed to the phone and frantically dialed the doctor. Our doctor was used to this.

"He couldn't have eaten enough to harm him," he reassured me. "Give him lots of bread and milk to wash it down. He'll be all right."

Donny's special weakness was for bottles. They fascinated him; if he had been Alice in Wonderland, he would have drunk himself tall, short, and clear out of sight in no time. He tried hair tonic, ink, concentrated vitamins, vanilla, vinegar, liquid shampoo, and anything else he could lay his chubby little fingers on when no one was looking.

"I keep things put away," I sighed, as I dressed Donny in his little white suit to go see the judge. "About the only thing else I can do is to keep my fingers crossed. It's a wonder we've raised him this far."

After Donny had first been placed in our home, a preliminary petition for adoption had been filed at our county superior court. For a year our home had been supervised by regular visits from the social worker. Now her report on Donny's adjustment, and the agency's approval of the adoption, had also been filed at the court; after several delays because of a crowded court docket, we had an appointment with the judge for the granting of the final adoption decree.

As is customary in most adoption cases, the hearings were held in private session in the judge's chambers, instead of in open court. We arrived early and waited in the corridor, restraining Donny from dashes to investigate the elevator buttons, dropped cigarette butts, and a spittoon.

"I feel as tense as I did when I was waiting in the minister's study before our wedding," Carl said. "Of course the social worker said that there would be no trouble, that the adoption would go right through. But I'll still be glad when this is over, and Donny is actually all ours."

When the judge received us in his chambers, it *was* something like a wedding, except that it was more in the mood of a civil one, rather than a church ceremony. The clerk of the court came in and asked us to raise our right hands and solemnly swear to tell the truth, the whole truth, and nothing but the truth, which we did. Then the judge talked to us, pointing out what we already knew, that this was a lasting and permanent obligation, that adoption would grant us the same legal relationship to our son as if he had been born to us, with all the mutual rights, privileges, and responsibilities of natural parents and children.

This should be a ceremony in a church, I thought, *with organ music and candles lighted, and flowers.* These vows, which Carl and I were taking, were just as sacred and enduring and meaningful as the marriage vows we had taken six years before. Would it not be more fitting if we were all standing before an altar, the minister saying, "Do you take this child to be your lawfully adopted son, for better for worse, for richer for poorer, in sickness and in health, to love and to cherish, till death do thee part?" *And Carl and I could answer, with deep feeling, "We do."*

The adoption completed, we each took one of Donny's hands and went back along the corridor, down in the elevator. As we walked down the outside courthouse steps, Donny hopping between us and singing a tuneless song, Carl said, "Well, Helen, have you everything you need to make you happy, now?"

"Almost," I said.

"What else?"

"A little girl," I said. "Donny's such a sociable little boy. He ought to have a little sister."

"Oh, no," Carl groaned. "Give my wife an inch, and she wants a mile."

"I don't want a mile. I just want one more little baby."

"In the first place," Carl said, "I'm much too busy going to school to be bothered by such a family load. In the second place, you know we absolutely couldn't afford another one. And in the third place, lucky for me, I'm positive that no agency would let us have a second child in the first place.

"I'm remembering that mustard seed," I said. "I've still got faith."

CHAPTER 2

Blind Alleys

WE would never have had an interracial family if I had not been blocked by countless blind alleys in my search for a younger brother or sister for Donny. Asking to adopt another child was as futile as asking for the moon.

"You should be thankful you even have a first child," one social worker reproved me. "If you knew how many financially *capable* homes are on our waiting list, with no child at all, you wouldn't even *ask* for a second."

I wasn't discouraged, at first. Month after month we made the futile rounds to different adoption agencies. Endless hours dragged by in agency waiting rooms, with Carl muttering under his breath about the foolishness of the whole quest and trying to read snatches from his schoolbooks, while I jounced Donny on my lap. I was almost ready to give up, when friends began to suggest, "Try this doctor — he sometimes finds homes for babies of unwed mothers." Or, "I know a lawyer . . ."

This was not a black market; babies were not sold, like so much merchandise. It was rather a gray market, because nonlicensed parties who arranged adoptions, no matter how kind the intentions, were working outside the meaning of our California state law. A licensed agency is legally allowed to be a blank wall between natural and adoptive parents; although pertinent information may be exchanged through the agency, this does not include names or addresses. Natural and adoptive parents never meet, and it is best for the child that this is so. The agency also has a large number of babies to place, and an even larger number of homes on the waiting list, so there is room for choice in deciding on the best home for each child. Licensed agencies provide the safe and sane road to adoption; but for us, now, that road was apparently closed.

Why not take the chance? I thought. *If I wait until an agency will approve our home, Donny will be almost old enough to have a child of his own.* I began to contact doctors and lawyers who might have babies to place. With mixed hope and fear, I jumped into the gray market.

One night a doctor in a small maternity hospital in the city called me on the phone.

"Do you remember the unwed mother I told you about when you were here?" he asked. "She's anxious to leave the hospital in the morning, and wants to see her baby girl placed with a reliable couple first. She expressed a preference for a minister's family, so I recommended you."

"We'll come immediately, right now, tonight," I babbled excitedly.

Carl clapped his head, muttered under his breath, and went out to start the car. I was putting together a going-home layette from the nicest things I had saved of Donny's baby clothes, when Carl came back, shrugging.

"Take your coat off, Helen. The car won't start."

He looked like a condemned man who had just had a

reprieve. I shook him. "Honey, if you're stalling – if you're just trying to get out of this, be honest and tell me."

"Call back your doctor," Carl sighed, "and tell him we'll be there before noon. First thing in the morning, we can coast the car down the hill to the garage, and get it fixed."

As I dialed the long-distance operator with a shaky finger, I mumbled, heartsick, "I just know we're going to lose that baby, unless we get there tonight."

"Now don't you worry," the doctor reassured me, when I got him on the phone. "There will be plenty of time to work everything out when you get here tomorrow. I haven't told any others about the baby. The mother has said positively that she won't change her mind. So don't worry."

The next morning Carl put Donny and me into the old Ford and pushed us down the hill to the garage. When the car was fixed, we rattled into the city. I sat on the edge of my seat gripping the box with the baby clothes, while Donny bounced up and down on the seat between us. At the hospital, the doctor took us in for a brief introduction to the mother. She was sitting up in bed, putting on a liberal application of lipstick and looking quite pleased with the prospect of leaving the hospital.

"If I ain't glad it's all over with," she confided. "Now I can live again." She looked us over critically, and nodded. "Yep, I'm glad my kid's going into a preacher's home. Maybe she'll get a good raising, like I never got."

The doctor took us back to the nursery and put into my arms a baby girl with long-lashed blue eyes and soft curls of brown hair. Even Carl began to look interested.

"I've delivered a lot of babies," the doctor said, "but this one's the prettiest yet, for one so young. Bright-eyed, too."

I fell in love with her immediately. So soon, so quick, she seemed like our very own. I hated to give her up to the nurse, although in an hour I would have her back in my arms to keep.

"Now if you'll step down the hall to my office," the doctor said, "I'll tell you what I know of the background. Then we'll go over the papers which you and the mother must sign."

The unmarried mother, he told us, had only a fourth-grade education, and worked as a waitress in a cheap hotel. The baby's father, a bus boy, disappeared before the baby was born. The mother could make legal arrangements to give her child to anyone, subject to later court approval; but if she just walked off and left her baby, she would be liable to arrest for criminal abandonment. If she wished to be dismissed from the hospital without her child, the legal relinquishment papers must be signed first.

I found it hard to sit and listen to the doctor. I yearned to return to the nursery, dress our new baby in the clothes we had brought, and hurry home with her, safe in my arms.

"Ever since the mother entered our hospital," the doctor went on, "she has insisted she has no desire to keep her child. We have suggested several agencies here which could help her. There is one which would board her child for her while she gets on her feet. She just hasn't been interested. She has refused to nurse the infant, even to see it."

With the papers in hand, we returned to the mother's room. My premonition of the night before turned out to be true. She was sitting up against her pillows, her face tear-streaked, and in her arms was the blue-eyed baby. I knew, even then, that we would never take that baby home.

The doctor looked surprised. "I thought you refused to see your child."

She nodded, sniffling. "Everything would of been much better, if I never did see her, too." She looked down at the baby, and fresh tears streaked her heavy make-up. "That little red-haired nurse just busted in here a minute ago and dropped her in my lap. She — she told me to look real good at what I was giving away."

Carl gave the mother one of his understanding smiles. "Don't you worry about us. If you've decided to keep your baby, I'm sure you're doing the best thing. Who has a better right to raise that child?"

"But that's not true!" she sobbed. "That's why I'm all broke up like this, because I knew that getting her adopted was the best thing I could do for her. *I* can't give the kid anything. Besides, all my friends know what — how she — " She blew her nose. "With you, my kid would of had a chance. But now that I seen her, I'm too selfish to give her up. She's too darn cute, like a little doll. Like all the dolls I never had when I was a kid. . . ."

We tiptoed out and left her with her baby. To his eternal credit, Carl didn't once say, "I told you so!"

On the way home, Donny asked, "Daddy, what's the matter with Mama?"

In a gentle voice, Carl said, "Climb up in her lap and give her a great big hug, son. Mama doesn't feel happy inside, today."

.   .   .

Later, I could see that I was luckier than some who dabbled in the gray market. In any placement made outside of a licensed agency, the mother may demand her baby back any time during the minimum of six months to a year, the time it takes to make an adoption final. What if we had brought the little girl home, and the mother had changed her mind several months later, before the child could be legally ours? It would have been like the swooping down of death, to have her pulled up by the roots from our lives and our hearts.

Later I knew I was lucky, but at that time I thought the bottom had dropped out of my world. I wasn't ready to give up, but it was the end of hunting babies from independent sources. I dragged Carl back along the weary rounds of the licensed agencies, back to the old, familiar offices.

The international aspect of our family started quite unexpectedly.

"Too bad you aren't Turkish or Portuguese," the receptionist in one agency said. "We have a little Turkish-Portuguese boy we can't find a home for. The Portuguese don't want him because they say he looks like a Turk. If a Turkish family could be found, I suppose they wouldn't want him because he looked too Portuguese." She shrugged. "That's what happens with those mixed-blood children. *Nobody* wants them."

"Nobody?" I said.

"That's right," she said. "Nobody wants them. They are classed as unadoptable, same as any child with a defect."

The idea shocked me. Children weren't like oranges in

a packing house, to be sorted over, those with defects thrown in the discard heap. They were individuals, equally loved in the sight of God.

"In the first place, I wouldn't call mixed ancestry a defect," I said. "Would you, Carl?"

Carl shook his head. "That's not fair to the child, to label him like that." I knew he was hit in his soft, idealistic heart.

Again the receptionist shrugged. "Don't blame me. Society puts the labels on, I don't. That's just the way it is."

"If I get a child," I said, "it's like getting a Christmas package. It's what's inside that counts. The color of the wrapping doesn't matter."

"There's your second child," Carl said. "If nobody else wants him, let's take him home and be done with it."

"I'm sure the agency wouldn't let *you* have him," the receptionist said. "The rule here is to perfectly match each child to the prospective parents."

I didn't believe her. "Oh, I don't think they'd hesitate to let us have him, if they can't find a matching home." I was that naïve.

When we were admitted to the inner sanctum of the head social worker, the lady quickly quashed the eager light on my face. "I wouldn't even consider such a placement," she said. "The child you speak about is *very* dark-skinned, and you are both fair."

"Color is a superficial thing," Carl said. "It wouldn't make any difference to us if he were black, if he needed a home."

"He could be brown or pink," I added, "red or yellow. We don't care."

The social worker slammed her pencil on her desk and rose to show us to the door. "Either you people haven't given this wild idea the proper thought," she snapped, frost on her words, "or else — " She didn't finish, but I could see that in her mind she was committing us to a mental institution. "I would rather see a child raised in an orphanage, than by parents who look so *different*. Crossing racial lines is against all our *principles* of good social-work practice."

At home, I asked Carl, "Are all social workers that intolerant? Do you suppose that somewhere else we could — "

"All right," Carl said. "All right. You find us a little boy or girl of mixed race. But only *one*, and then we quit adopting, understand? I don't know how I'm going to work my way through college with two children as it is."

I wrote to every agency, in California and out of it, that I had ever heard of. I wrote to the state welfare departments at each state capital, asking for lists of licensed adoption agencies in that state. Night after night, when Donny had been tucked into bed, I typed letters to these hundreds of agencies across the United States. Many were close enough for us to make trips for personal interviews; others sent application forms, asked questions.

"*Why* do you want to take a child of another race?" each agency asked pointedly.

I said we wanted another child because we loved children and didn't want Donny to grow up an only child. A surplus of homes existed for the fair and perfect child, while nobody wanted those of mixed or minority race. So we preferred the child who needed our home the most.

"Won't it be hard not to show prejudice toward a dark-skinned child?" they all wanted to know.

How could we show something we didn't feel? We be-
lieved that all races were basically alike underneath, the
same in range of intellect, the same in capacity for moral
and spiritual growth. Variation in skin color between one
race and another was little greater than the wide variation
already existing within any one race. Differences were
there, and certainly made humans more interesting than if
all were stamped from the same cookie cutter, like so many
gingerbread men; but we didn't feel that such differences
were important.

"Do you really think you can bring a dark-skinned child
up to your social standing?" the agencies asked. "Don't
you realize that it is more likely such a child would drag his
adopted parents down to the level of the subjugated minority groups?"

We were not concerned with social standing. Skin color
was an accident of birth. Such an accident should not give
us the right to lord it over those who are born with darker
skin.

"How about Donny?" we were warned. "Won't he grow
up to be ashamed of a brother or sister of mixed blood?"

Growing up in a tolerant home, Donny doubtless would
not understand or appreciate the prejudices of those who
felt themselves too good to associate as equals with the majority of their fellow men. Always we would be welcoming friends of other races in our home, and anyone small
enough to make snide remarks about Donny's friends — or
brother — might find that he had lost Donny's respect.

"But what about the darker-skinned child in your family?" the agencies asked. "Won't he feel unhappy and inferior, growing up among white people?"

Any American child of dark skin must learn to adjust to a "white" society. We knew we couldn't lighten the skin of any minority-race child we adopted, but we could help lighten the load which society indifferently allowed him to carry. We could teach our child to understand and pity those who were saddled with prejudice.

They kept asking questions, but none gave us a child. One social worker even admitted that her agency had placed no children of mixed race in the past; "unadoptables" had simply been refused agency help, since the chance of placement was so slim.

"I'm so discouraged," I told Carl. "All I want is to give a home to one lone child that nobody wants, and I can't even do that."

I felt tired and discouraged, but so did the whole world. The second World War had exploded the uneasy peace of the past two decades. American boys were dying in Salerno and Guam and on the Normandy beachhead. On top of my own small troubles, I grew depressed with the additional burden of the world's tragic sorrows. We were packing up our books and clothes and cooking utensils, preparing to move back to Illinois, where Carl would continue his graduate work; but I had no heart for the trip.

"How can you be so enthusiastic about going East?" I asked. "We're not getting what we want — "

"*You're* not getting what *you* want," Carl corrected.

"All right, I'm not getting what I want. Even worse, the whole world isn't getting what it wants. Where is there general happiness in the world? What place even has the basic Four Freedoms for *everybody?*"

"We can't make the world better by just giving up," Carl said.

I looked at my husband, packing dishes in a barrel, his face calm.

"I still don't understand," I said. "These last four years have been so long and hard, the world is such a hopeless mess — I don't see how you can still look forward to three more grinding years of school. What's the use?"

Carl wrapped another cup in newspaper and fitted it firmly into the barrel. He stood there looking at me. I could hear our old alarm clock ticking on top of the high-oven stove, and I could smell the fragrance of orange groves on the June breeze which ruffled the curtains at the open kitchen window.

"What's the use of my schooling?" Carl said. "Religion is the only force big enough to save man from his own destruction. Science can produce *things* — and tremendous power. The world desperately needs emotional and spiritual maturity to know how to use these things, this power, for its own good."

"All right, preacher," I said. "I guess I'd have a little more hope for the world, if I had a little more hope for myself."

"If you want to see good things come to pass, you have to work for them, and have faith," Carl said. "Faith for yourself and faith for the world. Remember the mustard seed?"

"I just didn't know there were going to be so many mountains," I said.

CHAPTER 3

And the Walls Came Tumbling Down

FOR three years I had marched around the Jericho citadels of adoption agencies, tooting our family horn, and at last the stubborn walls came tumbling down. Donny was presented with not one little sister, but two.

Carl had begun his last stretch of graduate work at Garrett Biblical Institute, on Northwestern's magnificent campus overlooking Lake Michigan. The Methodist Rock River Conference assigned him to two student churches in northern Illinois: one at Hebron, a small town proud of its cows, its corn, and its championship basketball team; the other a country church at Alden, five miles west. Our parsonage, on Highway 47 in Hebron, was a two-story frame house on a corner lot, with several box elders and a pie-cherry tree around the front yard. On weekdays I lived there alone with Donny, because Hebron was too far for Carl to commute daily. He had a room at the Garrett dormitory and drove home only over Saturdays and Sundays.

As soon as we were settled in our new parsonage, I charged upon all the adoption agencies in the area. Then, showing that often when it rains it pours, two babies turned up almost at the same time.

Laura came first.

I still remember that bright fall day, with the sky lark-spur-blue, the maple leaves and the cornfields rustling yellow, when an adoption agency called long distance from Chicago.

"We have a baby girl for you," the social worker said. "Two months old, a darling little butterball with brown hair and eyes. She's Eurasian. Her mother was Filipino-Chinese, her father English and French."

It was hard to stay by the phone, when I wanted to turn cartwheels around the room. "When can we come for her?"

"She may be seen any day next week. If you think you'd like her, you may take her home."

If, I laughed to myself! No matter what she looked like, I was ready to take her into my heart and love her like my own. I was even mentally naming her already. I would call her Laura, after Carl's mother, to please my husband.

Carl cut classes Monday morning so we could drive down for our new baby. At the hospital, a white-masked nurse pushed through the glass doors from the nursery, carrying a blanketed cocoon which cooed and waved two pink fists.

"She's beautiful!" I burst out. The baby had almond-shaped eyes the color of milk chocolate, and apple cheeks. Carl reached for her first, then handed her to me to hold. "Can we take her home, now?" I asked the nurse.

She nodded. "If you'll give me the clothes you brought, I'll have her ready by the time you've signed the papers in the office."

In the car, with Carl driving and Laura cradled in my arms, I was so happy that I sang "Rock-a-bye Baby" and hummed Brahms's "Lullaby" all the way home.

"Gee, she's little," Donny said, when he greeted us at the

front door. He took Laura's tiny fist in his hand. "Can I show her around the house, now?"

Two weeks later we brought Susan home.

Although blond and blue-eyed like Donny, this wee infant was considered unadoptable. Not only was she frail and sickly, but there was also a disfiguring, tumerous red birthmark on her forehead. With her sallow pinched face, her lifeless straw hair, and her swollen red eyes, she looked more like a miniature, shriveled-up grandma than a baby. She was a blighted bud, with no indication that she would ever flower.

Carl objected violently, at first. "I've got nearly three more years of school ahead of me yet," he exploded. "If I don't know how I can support *two* children, how can I take a third? And a sickly one at that?"

"But nobody else wants her," I said. "Maybe we can pull her through. We couldn't leave her at the hospital all unwanted, could we?"

"I guess we couldn't," Carl said, and then he shook his finger in front of my nose. "But *no* more, understand?"

Two new babies in the house, in addition to three-year-old Donny, kept me so busy I began to wonder how I could stagger through another day. In Cucamonga, when Donny was a baby, Carl had been home nights to take turns on the night feedings. Here at Hebron, I had to manage alone.

Laura called for a bottle every four hours around the clock, and Susie needed one every three hours around the clock. All day long, all night long, too, I was getting one baby up, changing her, holding her bottle, rocking her awhile, and then putting her to bed just as it was nearly time to be getting the other baby up again. In between the round of feedings, there were batches of formula to be made up and kept cold without a refrigerator. Dishes piled up, the house always needed cleaning, and I never seemed to catch up with the laundry. The parsonage had no laundry tubs or automatic hot water. On our old kerosene cookstove I heated buckets of water, lugged them upstairs, and did the family wash in the bathtub.

Long after midnight, down on my knees by the bathtub, wringing out heavy sheets by hand until blisters rubbed raw, dragging down two weary flights to the basement to hang up the dripping wash, I would sometimes wonder, *Is it worth all this to have the little family I wanted so badly?* With bleary eyes I would turn the pages of the calendar, counting the days until the girls would be off their night feedings and I could really go to bed at night, instead of just flopping on the couch between early-morning bottles.

Donny, always into mischief, didn't help matters. Around the house he usually was into whatever he wasn't supposed to be into. When he wandered off, looking for a playmate, he could be exasperating, too. Sometimes he wandered beyond bounds, and I had to comb our little village for him. Sometimes he did unpredictable things, like the time he copied older boys jumping from a chicken-house roof, and cracked a bone in his foot, so that he had to return for a spell to crawling on all fours until the cast came off.

And he was forever losing his shoes.

One day he came in from play in his stocking feet, and I said, "Where are your shoes?"

"My shoes?" he repeated, automatically lifting one foot. He stared, and surprise illumined his small face. He seemed as incredulous as if pixies had just that moment snatched him barefoot.

"Think, Donny," I said. On our budget, a pair of lost shoes was a major disaster. "Where do you remember them last?"

Donny scratched his blond head. " I guess they fell off in the grass."

I took his hand. "Come show Mama which grass."

Soon we were standing on the sidewalk around the corner, in front of an empty lot covered with a summer crop of grassy weeds, solid packed and over waist high.

"Out there, I think," Donny said. "Someplace."

I groaned.

"Shall I go in and get them?" he volunteered.

"Please do," I said.

He dived in and was swallowed in the green jungle. I could see by the waving path above his trail that he was cutting a shallow circle. He emerged with grass seeds in his hair and sticking out of his ears.

"Too bad," he announced. "I can't find any shoes."

"Too bad for you," I said. "You're not through looking. Why did you ever throw them in there, anyway?"

"Didn't throw 'em in," Donny said. "I was a cowboy riding, and the bad men were chasing me, and I couldn't stop." I sent him in again, and after two or three more desultory forays into the green world, he came out and plopped on the sidewalk. "Nothing but grasshoppers in there," he announced. "Let's go home. I'm hungry."

I posted him down at the corner, where he could see our back yard and the baby girls taking sun baths in the play pen.

"You sit there," I ordered, "and keep an eye on your sisters while Mama hunts. You call me if they cry."

Head down, I plunged into the grass, parting the green spears ahead of me and swimming along with a hard-pulling breast stroke, peering through the undersea dimness. After an hour my back felt as if it had been hammered into a sickle. My face was flushed and I had weed seeds in my hair and eyes and nose. I pulled more seeds out of my ears and gasped for breath. I had found one shoe, but I could hear the thin and unmistakable wail of babies crying and I was ready to quit. As I plowed my way out of the grass, I stumbled on the second shoe.

At the corner, Donny was nowhere to be seen, but the two little girls were kicking their feet in the play pen and screaming like fire engines. I tucked a howling baby under each arm and climbed the back steps to the kitchen. Donny was already there, peanut butter everywhere except on the sandwich he was trying to make.

"Time for lunch," he said.

"I know it," I answered grimly, blowing the hair out of my eyes. "And both your sisters are starved for their bottles. See this?" I dropped two small oxfords on the floor and shifted my grip on the babies. "Mama finally found your shoes."

"Oh," Donny said, his mind as full of peanut butter as his mouth. "Was they lost?"

.   .   .

Still, when I made the rounds as I tucked them in at night, when I looked at their sleeping, angelic faces, I knew that everything was worth what it cost. When I wasn't too tired, I really enjoyed the children. Donny was a responsive little fellow, with a curiosity and eager zest for life that were contagious. Susie was too frail yet for much handling, but chubby little Laura loved to be cuddled as much as I loved doing it. When she smiled at me out of her intriguing almond-shaped brown eyes, as if to say, *Hello, Mother. I'm your daughter*, I found my own eyes a little misty in my happiness.

Visitors were attracted to healthy, happy little Laura. "What a little beauty!" they would exclaim, as they came out of her bedroom. Her exquisite ivory skin, her pink-cheeked, china-doll features, entranced everyone.

They were strangely silent after peeking into Susie's crib. After an embarrassed pause, the polite ones would suddenly change the subject. Others were more blunt, and shook their heads. "Doesn't really look as if she would live to grow up, does it?"

One night Susan had convulsions. She moaned, chomping her toothless gums, waving her thin arms and jerking oddly, with her head thrown back and her eyes rolled up. While I waited the frightening half hour it took the doctor to arrive, my shaking hands wrapped her in warm, wet towels. When the doctor came, he gave her some injections. The convulsions eased off and she fell into a deep coma, sleeping for two days without waking for meals, not stirring when I changed her.

If I had thought she was dying when she suffered the

convulsions, I was even more fearful of it during those long hours when she lay nearly lifeless, scarcely breathing. Every night I went in to kneel by her crib, a dozen times in the night; every hour in the day, when I passed her door, I bowed my head in desperate petition.

When Susie finally fought back to life from her coma, she began to gain strength. By the time she was six months old, rosy cheeks had displaced the sallow complexion and she was almost as chubby as Laura. Her eyes had lost their sunken, red rims.

The ugly birthmark, however, had continued to grow until it dominated her face like an oversized strawberry plastered upon her forehead.

"Some birthmarks eventually absorb and disappear," our doctor told us. "The treatment for each type is different." Since Susan's type might continue to grow, he recommended that it be removed with radium treatments.

We took Susan to a clinic in Chicago, a hundred-and-twenty-mile round trip, every two weeks for six long months. Laura had a tiny birthmark on her arm which was treated at the same time. Our family became a familiar sight at the hospital, Carl and I each lugging a baby girl in a basket, Donny clutching a paper sack of lunch. The baby baskets were piled high with extra diapers, blankets, bottles of formula, orange juice, Kleenex, and baby toys. These fortnightly trips were like moving day.

Going up in the hospital elevator, a white-haired lady plucked at my sleeve and whispered, "I've seen you here before. Are these all your children?"

I nodded.

"Both these sweet babies, too?"

"Yes," I smiled. "Two little girls."

"Twins, I suppose?"

"Not exactly." I nodded at Susie, who lay wide-eyed among the bundles in the basket I carried. "This one is two months younger than the other."

Her face puzzled, she peeked toward Carl's basket, where Laura lay asleep on her tummy, her face hidden. "Dear me, yes," she said, her face clearing. "I can see that the other one's considerable bigger than this little mite. The one you've got is blue-eyed and little, like you. I suppose the other one takes after your husband?"

I thought that the dear old soul was merely hard-of-hearing, until Carl and I were leaving the elevator at our floor. She plucked at my sleeve.

"But my dear," she whispered, "wasn't it hard on you, having two babies so close together?"

Carl and I and our three children waited in a small examining room until one of the clinic doctors made the routine general health check-ups on the girls. During the noon hour we held the babies for their bottles, then put them in their baskets for naps; Donny, Carl and I ate sandwiches and apples, and shared a quart of milk. At two o'clock the radiologist and several nurses came in to strap the capsules of radium over the babies' birthmarks.

Our main problem at these bi-weekly sessions was to keep track of Donny, now nearly four years old. Completely unafraid of strange people and surroundings, he would slip away and disappear like a pebble dropped into a lake. One day he wandered out to the main corridor, down in the elevator, to the first-floor pharmacy, where he was having an animated conversation with the druggist. On the next hospital visit we finally discovered him several floors up, cheering an old grandmother in the chronic ward. Again we located him in the surgical ward on another floor; he was helping a doctor and nurses chip the cast from a broken leg, and the doctor insisted he was about ready to take Donny on as an intern.

After our girls had finished two hours of treatment, the doctor and nurses returned to remove the radium, which was encased in wooden blocks and strapped into place with adhesive tape. The invisible radium rays could not be felt, and the adhesive tape, on her smooth arm, did not bother placid little Laura. For Susan, the removal of the radium blocks was more painful. No matter how gently the tape was pulled from the sparse hair, Susie screeched with all her lung power; just having her head held tightly was equally resented. She soon came to the point where she started screaming as soon as she saw doctor or nurse coming.

With the completion of the half year's treatment, Susie's birthmark, like Laura's, had melted completely away. Yet there was an emotional aftermath. Susie had become hysterically afraid of strangers. From her earliest memory, almost all the strangers who came close to her would hurt her, and she couldn't trust outsiders. When we took Susie to church, and a strange woman swooped upon her with coos of delight, Susie retaliated by screaming for five minutes without stopping.

Carl and I decided she must be ignored by strangers, until she felt so safe in their midst that she was ready to make the first overtures of friendship herself. When we went to church for services, social doings, or potluck suppers, I hung signs around Susie's neck, front and back, like a small sandwich board. They read:

DO NOT TOUCH ME!
I AM SHY.
JUST PRETEND I'M NOT HERE,
PLEASE!

As long as nobody made a direct move toward her, Susie felt safe enough to accompany me anywhere. I often took Donny and the two little girls with me to the afternoon meetings of our church women's societies, held in the homes of the members. Laura loved these meetings; completely feminine, even then, she toddled around the hostess's living room, watching the women, studying their make-up, their gestures, the way they crossed their legs. Donny usually managed to wander away and get lost. I didn't worry. He always found his way back in time for refreshments.

At first Susie would crawl under my chair, or behind it, for the whole meeting. She even felt it was too risky to venture out when refreshments were served. Later, she became brave enough to dart out and slip a cookie from my plate, but she ate it in her sanctuary behind my chair. Once in a while a lady would find Susie irresistible, would forget and give her a motherly pat. This would be a setback, for Susie would dive into her hiding place, howling as if she had been stuck with pins.

As the months went by, Susie became even more irresistible. She was not only robust and healthy, but also pert and pretty, with long-lashed blue eyes and softly curling blonde hair. Yet she was too shy to talk, and showed no signs of wanting to be sociable.

Were Carl and I wrong in thinking she could work her own way out of the fears that shackled her? Always Susie seemed surprised that nobody hurt her, that people outside her family usually ignored her; but she was content to cling, speechless, to my side. With no apparent envy she watched Donny and Laura mingling with the ladies, petted and made over. There seemed to be no desire on her own face, as she watched her brother and sister helping themselves to cookies and punch at refreshment time.

At last came the day when her need for recognition became so strong it snapped the fetters of her shyness. She toddled over between Laura and Don, and pulled at the skirt of the lady who was passing out cookies.

"Me, too," she demanded, pointing to the cookie plate. "*Su-sie* tookie, too."

CHAPTER 4

Like Topsy, We Grow

CARL and I might have been satisfied with three children, but our son was not. When Donny was four, he watched his two baby sisters scoot about the floor on their hands and knees.

"You and Daddy got each other," he said wistfully. "And Laura and Susie got each other to play with. But Mama, there isn't *nobody* in this house the right size of me!"

I took him onto my lap. "That's true, isn't it? Mama has the little family she always wanted. Daddy's going to school to get what he wants. I don't see why we can't help you get what *you* want."

I started saving money for stamps, and every time I could get three cents together, I sent a letter to another adoption agency on my list. My letters, to all the states in the union, asked, "Do you have a boy about four years old, of any mixed or minority ancestry, who needs a home?"

Two agencies answered. One, in a nearby state, offered a Mexican-Indian baby girl named Rita. The other, on the West Coast, had a Filipino-Malayan-Spanish boy named Teddy. Nobody wanted to adopt these little youngsters, with their dark hair and dark skins.

"Not that baby girl," Donny said. "We got enough baby girls around here already. "Let's get that Teddy for me."

"That Teddy's not the size of you," I explained. "According to this letter, he's only a couple of months older than the girls."

"Yeah, but we two boys could stick together," Donny said.

"Don't I have anything to say about this?" Carl said. "I told you before, 'No,' and I say again, 'NO.' How can I work my way through seminary with *four* children?"

"It's only one more than three," I said.

"I can count!" Carl thundered. "Wait until I get through school, and then you can adopt a dozen, if you must."

"Who's asking for a dozen? I'm not crazy."

"No?" Carl said. "I'm beginning to wonder."

"Just one more," I pleaded. "That will give us two girls and two boys — a nice, well-rounded family."

"I don't want to be well-rounded," Carl grumbled, as he retired behind a schoolbook. "I'd rather try to get square for a change. Financially square."

I sat in his lap, put his book down, and mussed the top of his head where his hair used to be. "Look, honey, how can you bear it, knowing that nobody wants this little fellow, and when we could, if we wanted to put our minds to it — "

"All *right*," Carl said. "So we could take him, if we put our minds to it. Well, you've put so much mind to it, there isn't any space left for mine."

"Darling!" I said. "You will?"

Carl took out his date book, riffling the pages. "Let's

see. My spring vacation comes up in three weeks. I'll stay
home and study and take care of the girls. You and Donny
can take the train west, and bring home this Teddy."

"Whoopee!" Donny yelled.

"But this is the last one," Carl hollered, waving his date
book in my face. "The very last one, do you understand?"

I squeezed our budget until it whimpered. We ate beans
instead of hamburger. We appropriated the little sum that
was supposed to grow into a washing machine. Three weeks
later, when Carl's spring vacation came up, we had enough
saved for my round-trip ticket by chair car. There was no
money for eating in the dining car, so I took along a shopping bag full of food — perishables for the first day, plus
enough staples, such as canned milk, graham crackers, and
tins of fruit and vegetable juices, to last for the balance of
the trip.

"You look as if you had everything along except the dog
and the kitchen sink," Carl said, as he hoisted Donny and
me, and our lumpy bundles, onto the train at Woodstock.

"A dog wouldn't complicate this trip a bit more than
Donny will," I predicted darkly, as I watched our small
son whizz around the corner and down the aisle, kicking
up his heels like a spring lamb. "I'll bet Donny keeps me in
hot water for the whole trip."

Donny did.

First, I made the mistake of leaving him alone in our seat
with a color book, while I went to the women's washroom.
As I came back down the aisle, I heard people chuckling,
and I just stopped in time when I started to drop into my

seat. Donny had a picnic spread all over the place. With his fingers he was eating cottage cheese from my seat, where it had spilled.

I cleaned up the mess the best I could and marched Donny down to the women's room. After I had him washed and dressed in clean clothes, I made another mistake. I turned my back to comb my frazzled hair. Donny lost no time. He crawled under the washbowl and unscrewed the bottle attached to the liquid-soap dispenser. The bottle crashed down, spilling a slippery mess of soap jelly over the floor. Just then two plump dowagers opened the door, and the train lurched around a curve. The poor ladies lost their balance and skidded across the cubicle, screeching and clutching at everything in sight, to the wide-eyed amazement of Donny.

I tried to keep him out of trouble by amusing him with the bag of color books, crayons, and toys I had assembled especially for the trip; but such inanimate things, inedible in the bargain, could not hold his attention for long. Every time I was lulled into a doze by the clicketty-clicketty-click of the wheels, Donny disappeared. I would find him three cars back, sharing a box of homemade cookies with some soldiers, or up ahead in the dining car with a sweet old lady, being treated to a bottle of soda pop. He would be chattering like a squirrel, as much at home as if he had run into delightful old friends.

At the start of the trip he had been eager to tell everyone where we were going, and why. While we waited to change trains at the Chicago and Northwestern station, he galloped between the benches like a junior Paul Revere.

"We're going to get a brand new little *brother* for me!" he proclaimed to all who were interested, and a good many who were not.

"It isn't polite to bother strangers with our private affairs," I told him, when I coralled him. "Shall we make it our very own secret?"

The secret evidently was too important to be kept. All during the trip to the coast I wondered why the soldiers across the aisle were so solicitous. They leaped across the aisle to help every time I reached for a suitcase or lumpy parcel in the rack overhead.

"Your Donny told us about the addition you expect soon," one confided at the end of the trip, as he helped me off the train with my luggage. "Hope it's another boy! Donny seems so sure it's going to be a *brother*."

For once Donny had been a help. The assistance had been welcome, because we had no money to tip a porter.

At the adoption agency, Donny immediately made friends with the secretary in the outer office. He climbed in her lap to watch her typewriter work, while the social worker took me into her office to explain about Teddy's background.

"This little boy has been in undesirable boarding homes since birth," she said. "The last woman who has been paid to care for him has several older children of her own, but Teddy, with his bright eyes and quick mind, has become her favorite. She even applied to adopt him. As much as we at the agency want Teddy to have a home of his own, we just couldn't see him permanently in this home."

"Was the home so bad?"

She shook her head. "It was a hopeless home for any child, slovenly, broken by drink, a contempt for education. It would be especially bad for a bright little youngster like Teddy, who needs understanding and college opportunities."

"Was the boarding mother resigned to giving him up, then?"

"Hardly. She has tried to fight our agency in the most underhanded way she could — through little Teddy. She has tried to bind him to her emotionally, to make him so fearful of *all* strange women, that he wouldn't adjust to another home. When one of us from the office makes a required supervisory visit, this woman snatches Teddy into her arms and whispers, '*Don't cry. I won't let that bad lady hurt you. I won't let that bad lady take you away!*' Teddy was such a friendly, outgoing little fellow before, and now she has him almost hysterical."

The agency had been fully aware of the situation, but what could be done? Nobody wanted even to board a little brown-skinned boy of mixed race, much less adopt him. No wonder they had been so happy to receive our letter and references, especially because Teddy would have another Eurasian child for a sister.

The social worker left to fetch our new son. An hour later, when she brought him into the office, I wasn't surprised to see the little tyke sobbing in her arms. When I held him, he shrieked through his torrent of tears, his large brown eyes round with fear.

I had planned to stop for a visit with Carl's family at Chico, nearby in California, but I never guessed what an

ordeal that extra short ride would be. Even after we
boarded the bus to go to my father-in-law's ranch, Teddy
was determined to have nothing to do with me. Although
he was worn out with crying and it was past his nap time,
I couldn't soothe him to sleep. To make things worse, the
bus went around one too many nauseating curves, and
Donny lost his dinner all over the place. Donny started to
wail, Teddy was sobbing, and I was tempted to join them.
We were ignored by everyone except a large man with a
serene black face and grizzled white hair who sat across
the aisle. He gathered the white cloths from the back of his
seat, and from several empty seats, and came over.

"You've got more than you can handle, little lady," he
said, handing me the cloths. "Let me rock the baby to
sleep, while you take care of the other little boy."

Teddy looked into the understanding dark face, settled
himself into the gentle arms, and fell asleep. When we
reached Chico, the Negro gentleman was still holding
Teddy. After he was handed back to me, Teddy again began to scream hysterically. Luckily, Carl's family was waiting outside the bus.

"Here," my father-in-law said. "Let me carry that little
fellow for you."

Teddy's arms went quickly around his grandfather's
neck. "Daddy!" he cried, and his tears stopped. The boarding woman had forgotten to make Teddy fearful of men.

Donny continued to feel upset that night. "I ate too
much candy and pop on the train," he groaned. "My
tummy isn't *used* to it."

In the morning his temperature shot up and his breathing

became labored. A hastily summoned doctor gave him a shot of penicillin.

"Pneumonia," the doctor said. "Rig up a steam tent over his bed. That will help his breathing."

For two days, for two fearful, dragging nights, I sat by Donny's bed, listening to his hoarse and raspy breathing inside the sheet which was draped, umbrella-fashion, over his bed. I didn't dare doze off when he needed the kettle boiling for steam. The sheet or bedclothes might drag across the electric hot plate, and set us all on fire.

All this time I was too busy to see much of Teddy, but Teddy didn't care. Carl's younger brothers were home at the time, and Teddy followed his new uncles and his grandfather around the ranch, happily calling them all "Daddy."

The crisis past, Donny's abundant good health stood him in good stead. He convalesced quickly. By the end of the week, the doctor said he was well enough to make the trip, if I kept him quiet and warm. By this time Teddy was getting used to seeing me around. His complete rejection and fear had progressed to a tolerant putting-up-with-me. On the train going home, he seemed in good spirits as he chuckled and played peek-a-boo and patty-cake with Donny. All the way home I told him about his Daddy and his two little sisters waiting for him, and I gave him snapshots of Carl and the girls.

When our train arrived in Chicago, we took the local north to Woodstock. Here friends met us, and drove us the remaining ten miles to Hebron. I carried my new son up the steps and stood him on our front porch, while Donny rang the doorbell.

Carl came out, kissed Donny and me, and then knelt down. "So this is Teddy! You know, that's a good name for you, son, because you look just like a little brown Teddy bear.

Teddy looked him over gravely. Then he scooted over to wrap his small brown arms around Carl's neck.

"Daddy!" he said.

At first Teddy refused to play with his two little sisters. While Laura and Susie dug in the sandbox, Teddy withdrew, his eyes like those of a wounded fawn. After a while he would run to a far corner of the yard, throw himself on his face and beat his head upon the ground, screaming. When I picked him up, he quieted immediately, clinging to me like a baby opossum to its mother. I would carry him indoors and rock him, singing folk songs and lullabies, and he would be outwardly calm for another day. After about two weeks, Teddy stopped beating his head, gave up the hysterical tantrums. He joined the sandbox play with his sisters, becoming both their pal and their little guardian.

His first sentences were full of concern for them. As Susie would start down the long stairs, Teddy would rush to take her hand, cautioning, "Careful, Thu-thie. Careful, don't fall." If one of the little girls stumbled or hurt herself, Teddy was there first to help his sister to her feet. His arms would go around the small shoulders as he pulled a Kleenex from his pocket to dry the tears, consoling, "Too bad. Too, too bad. Blow, now."

Teddy was as different from his older brother as night is from day. Donny was the loud, rowdy, happy-go-lucky kind of boy who rackets through the house and never shuts a door behind him, who wouldn't be caught dead hanging up his clothes. Teddy was a neat and orderly little fellow, who preferred to put his things away systematically so he could find them when he wanted them. He would even stop to close a door or drawer that someone else, usually Donny, had left open.

Teddy was thing-conscious, with the scientific turn of mind that enjoys collecting and cataloguing, and finding out what makes things tick. We always had to check under any car parked in our yard before it was driven away, to make sure that Teddy wasn't under it. He would lie under an automobile for an hour without moving anything but his dark eyes, just trying to figure out how the gears made the car run.

Donny was essentially people-conscious. He had no interest in things, except as they related to people. He was supremely interested in finding out what makes people tick. One day we drove past a cornfield where an airplane had crashed. Teddy was full of questions: Why was it smashed? What happened to the motors? Why couldn't he land on the wheels? How did they fix a broken plane?

Donny had only one question: *"Was anybody hurt?"*

Although Teddy's conscious self had become happy and adjusted within the first few weeks, his subconscious was still hurt, still puzzled and frightened, from his boarding-house experience. An emotional wound is deep and must heal from the inside out; it takes a long time, and sometimes the scar is always there. We knew, because of Teddy's nightmares. He would go to sleep with a smile on his little brown face, his Teddy bear in his arms. Two or three times a night he would scream out in his sleep. His crib was in the room next to mine, so I could rush to take him in my arms.

"Teddy," I'd whisper softly. "Don't cry. Mama's right here." He would be all right the minute I woke him; even with his face wet with tears, he didn't know he had been crying.

As the months went by, the nightmares came only a few times a week, and eventually the time came when the emotional wounds in Teddy's subconscious seemed to be completely healed. He never cried out in his sleep any more. When he was nearly three, I heard Laura tell him, "Sometimes when I in bed, sleeping, I got pictures in my eyes. Pretty pictures."

"That's dreams," Teddy said. "Me, too, but always bad ones."

"Always bad?"

Teddy nodded. "Bad animals scare me, lots of bad things."

A year later the children were talking about dreams again.

"I had a bad dream," Susie reported to the rest. She had been frightened by a large, stray dog the day before. "I had a dream that a giant big dog chased me and tried to bite pieces out of me, but I climbed a tree."

"I don't have any dreams," Teddy said, "except once in a while. When I dream, I have good dreams, and sometimes I laugh."

. . .

"There's only one trouble with Teddy," Donny said when he was five years old.

"What's that?" I asked.

"He's not big enough," Donny said. "He's just exactly the right size of the girls, and there still isn't nobody the right size of me."

I promised Donny I would think about it. The more I thought about it, the more I felt I ought to write some more letters. This time I didn't tell Donny I was writing, because I didn't want him disappointed if I could not find a boy his size. And I didn't tell Carl. Why should he be all stirred up for nothing, if I didn't find a boy?

I didn't find a boy, but I did get a letter that stirred us up. It was from the agency which had written before, about the Mexican-Indian girl named Rita.

"So you still haven't found a boy the size of your Donny?" the letter began. "We are sorry that we do not have a five-year-old boy of any kind, for adoption. Little Rita is still here, though. She is nearly a year and a half now, and still nobody wants to adopt her. Since our agency is only equipped to care for infants under a year old, and since she shows signs of being slightly retarded, the only place left for her to go is our state institution for the feeble-minded."

I met tremendous opposition all the way around, trying to bring her into our family.

First Carl balked. "No!" he hollered. "I'm going in circles now, to find enough time for studies and church work. We can barely scrape along with four children already, and you want to bring another one home. For the last time, *no!*"

Then the church stepped in to add its two cents' worth. The church year was up, and the official board offered Carl the pulpit for another year — *on condition that we have no more children.* I doubt if the board members knew we were thrashing over talk about another adoption; but we had adopted three in two years, and I suppose they just thought we didn't know how to stop once we got started. Racial prejudice was not involved, because the congregation had accepted all of our youngsters with real affection. The main issue was that Carl had little enough time for the church, and an expanding family might hinder his work.

Carl wasn't the least interested in having any more, but the ultimatum made him stubborn. It was the principle of the thing, he informed the board. "Having children is a private matter, between a man and wife, and God." He added his sincere regrets that, under the circumstances, he would not be serving them the following year.

The members of the board held another meeting and decided that the number of our children was not their rightful business. They unanimously asked Carl to return for another year, no strings attached. Any additions to our family would be solely up to the discretion of Carl, our Maker, and me.

I was jubilant. "Now can we drive over and get Rita?"

"I'm being pushed," Carl complained. But the next week he drove us to the agency in the next state.

"This little girl does seem retarded," the agency director admitted, when we arrived. "She has started to toddle, but there is no inclination to begin to talk, feed herself, use the toilet chair, or any other such things other children her age begin to do." Before she brought Rita down from the nursery she warned, "Don't be alarmed if she wails when she sees you. She seems to be quite fearful of strangers."

She was not afraid with us. Carl and I took turns holding her on our laps, and she clung shyly, black eyes shining. She had a creamy-beige complexion, and sweeping black lashes that matched her patent-leather hair.

"Pretty baby," Teddy said, patting Rita. "We take this baby home, okay?"

Laura looked dubious, a hint of jealousy sparking in her almond eyes, but Susie agreed with Teddy. "Nice baby," she lisped. "I sink we *need* zis baby."

At first, I was afraid that Rita, nearly a year younger than the two-year-old "triplets," would have trouble holding her own. The first morning after we brought her home, Rita gathered blocks to make a tower. Laura, Susie, and Teddy put their heads together in a conspiracy in another corner of the room, obviously hatching up some plot, along with much pointing at Rita and giggling behind hands. The huddle over, Laura ambled across the room, snatched one of Rita's blocks, and ran off with it. Susan followed, pilfering another. Then Teddy tiptoed over, his eyes dancing with mischief, and reached for the top of Rita's tower.

Rita was ready for him. She grabbed a long block and promptly clonked Teddy on the head. A new respect was established for the newcomer, and she was accepted into the fold.

After less than a month, Rita was no longer backward. She did everything other children her age did, and she jabbered continually, talking as well as the older three. All she had needed, to make progress, was the love and security of a family all her own.

My next opposition on Rita came from the state welfare department, which had to approve the out-of-state adoption before the final petition could be granted in our local superior court. The state social worker who came to see us was already familiar with our family; she had supervised the adoptions of Laura, Susan and Teddy.

"I don't like the reports on this latest one you've taken," she said, as she sat in our living room. "I see that the agency had thought to send her to a state home for feeble-minded children."

"But that was only because nobody wanted to adopt her," I pointed out. "There was no other place for her to go."

The social worker pulled Rita's case history from her brief case. "Yes, but there was good reason for sending her there. According to the test reports made on her, just before you took her, she wasn't too bright. In fact, she registered too low to be tested. You and your husband will have problems enough, when you adopt children who are different from you in racial background. Now must you take one that is mentally retarded in the bargain?"

"She's not the least bit mentally retarded, now," I said. "She was just lost and lonely in the institutional surroundings where she spent her first year. She didn't have any reason to *try* to do things, then."

"I'm only trying to consider your best welfare," she said,

"and the best welfare of Rita, too. Here you have Teddy, Laura, and Susan, just a little older than Rita, all bright, all sharp competition during Rita's formative years. Look at Susie, who is nearest Rita's age." She checked her notes. "Susie not only belongs to the dominant race, but also has beautiful blue eyes and blonde hair. How will poor little Rita feel, when the neighbor girls invite Susie to their birthday parties, their dances and slumber parties, and Rita isn't asked? And later, when Susie has dates, and Rita hasn't?"

"You haven't seen Rita," I said, "or you wouldn't worry."

"Nevertheless," she said, tapping her pencil on her notes, "the facts are here before you. You have to face the facts."

Just then I heard some of the children waking from their naps, so I excused myself. Laura and Teddy were still asleep, but I dressed Susie and Rita, and they started down the stairs. Susie was still in her painfully shy stage. When she saw a visitor in the living room, she scooted behind the couch like a frightened rabbit.

Rita came in singing, like a petite, ebony-haired princess, not the least ruffled to find a stranger there. Poised and happy, she pranced over to the social worker as if she owned the place. She leaned against the lady's lap, grinned her utterly bewitching smile, and flirted through her long, curling black lashes. They exchanged names, but Rita couldn't stand still for long. She never has.

Dancing around the room on toes as twinkling as a minia-ture Pavlova, she gathered treasured toys to heap in our visitor's lap. She swept down the playroom slide backwards and did a couple of graceful somersaults. Then she flitted out through the back of the house, and returned with a glass jar containing some ladybugs.

"She's a budding entomologist," I explained.

Rita climbed into the lady's lap, her black eyes sparkling and beautiful, her creamy-brown face lighted with her vivacity. "You like my baby bugs?" she asked. "I keeps them in a bopple, den I puts them in the *gar*-den."

She hopped down and raced out to the back yard, her patent-leather hair bobbing on her shoulders. Susie crept from her hiding place, gave one frightened look, and sped after Rita.

"Well," I said, "what do you think?"

The social worker looked thoughtful. "I was just thinking about Susie, growing up with Rita." She turned toward me, her face concerned. "Does Susie show any particular talents? When she's older, if she could have piano, or dancing lessons — do you know what I mean?"

"Yes," I said. "I know what you mean."

CHAPTER 5

Snow Country

UNTIL I was eighteen, I had lived most of my life in the Chicago suburb of Park Ridge, and never thought of the midwestern climate as a hardship. Since then I had lived ten years in Southern California, and that had spoiled me.

It was Carl's first experience in snow country, and he loved it. He had never owned an overcoat; now he couldn't afford one, and said it didn't matter. It worried the good ladies of our church to see their young pastor striding down the wintry streets, his thin raincoat flapping in the icy wind, his almost-bald head distressingly bare. One neighbor brought me a heavy overcoat which had become too small for her husband, and begged me to get Carl to wear it. He packed it in a box for overseas relief.

"They need it over there more than I do." Carl was always concerned about others, but never about himself.

I tried to be philosophical about the weather the way Carl was, but more often I was like a nervous hen who has just hatched chicks. So many tiny children under my feet, a balky furnace which worked only on week ends when Carl was home, and the times we got snowed in, were all periodically frustrating.

Any day, summer or winter, was a good day for the children to drop trinkets down through the furnace grating; but this game gained momentum with the first chill of autumn, and reached new highs during the long, cooped-up days until spring. The heat from our furnace was caught in an outer shell, which funneled up from the basement to a large register set in the living-room floor. The holes in the grating of the register were the right size to allow about half of the children's toys to go through, which they soon did. In spite of all I could do, every loose button, coin, toy, wheel, pin, pencil, spoon, or trinket that little fingers could find, eventually wound up in that secret and inaccessible place between the inner and outer shells of the furnace. It was a rare game, more fun than mailing letters or playing drop-the-clothespin-in-the-bottle.

The worst things they ever stuffed down the furnace were the balloons. Somebody had given us a huge box of balloons which, with frugality, should have provided fun for ten years. One freezing morning I gave each child a brightly colored balloon to play with, so they would be amused and stay out of mischief while I went to the basement to wrestle with the furnace. It took sweat, tears, and the last of my patience to get the fire going, but by the time I left the basement and started back upstairs, it was really roaring.

When I opened the door into the kitchen, black smoke billowed from the living room. A searing stench hit my nostrils and burned my eyes.

"Where's the fire?" I yelled, my heart pounding as I

stumbled into the living room and started sweeping little children into my arms.

Susie was sitting near the register, weeping bitter tears. "Ba-woon all gone, mine," she sobbed, pointing toward the furnace. "All ba-woons all gone."

The smoke was all originating from the register, so I set my armload of children down. Then I noticed that the big balloon box had been snitched from its hiding place, and was lying on the floor, completely empty. I rushed to the register and knelt down, almost burning the skin from my knees. As I peered with smarting eyes through the smoke, I could make out darkish puddles of bubbling rubber stuck to the glowing red top of the furnace. There was no way to reach the mess, or clean it up.

Donny started toward the kitchen. "I'll get a pan of cold water to pour on."

The acrid smoke continued to sting my eyes and tears were streaming down my cheeks. "Don't bother! It might crack the furnace open." I blew my nose with a loud honk.

Donny reappeared in the doorway. "You shouldn't cry about it," he said. "Those balloons aren't any good now, I don't think."

"You don't think, period," I muttered, and dashed for the front door and the windows, throwing them open. A sixty-mile gale, fresh from the Arctic, blew in, sweeping snow all over the place.

"First you let the house get too cold," Donny observed, "then you get it too hot, and then you get it too cold again. Daddy doesn't."

None of the smoke had gone out, but snow had come in.

I closed the door and windows. The smoke poured out of the register faster than ever, and the room was an oven again.

"This stuff doesn't smell good," Donny said. "Why don't you turn off the fire in the furnace for a while?"

"Why doesn't somebody turn off the mischief inside of you, for a while?" I groaned. I plunked Donny into a big chair, lined the four younger ones in a row on the couch, and gave each a picture book. "Now everybody read, until Mama comes back."

"Me can't read," Rita piped up.

"None of you can," I said. "Just look at the pictures."

Back in the basement, I shook down the coals, piled the fire with ashes. I did everything I'd watched Carl do when he wanted to control the temperature, but it was no use. The furnace rocked with heat like a thing possessed. Finally I gave up and dragged back upstairs. There I found Donny had borrowed a box of rolled-oats cereal from the kitchen, and had sprinkled it over the puddles of melted snow on the floor. Coughing and choking, the children were stirring the oats with their fingers and shaping crumbly little patties.

"We finished our books," Donny explained.

"We make tookies," Susie lisped.

"Oh, no!" I sputtered, wiping my streaming eyes. It was worse than living in a tire factory. "Did you kids have to *waste* all that perfectly good oatmeal?"

"No waste," Donny said. "We can bake them on the register. Look, it's so nice and hot — "

"No, no, *NO!*" I croaked hoarsely. "Merciful heavens, no! I don't want to see any of you children put *one more thing* on, in, under, through, or on top of that furnace register. *Do you understand?*"

"Yes, Mother," Donny said.

"Yes, Muzzer," Teddy, Laura, Susie, and Rita echoed solemnly.

They were true to their word. They *didn't* let me *see* them. But the next day I missed my fountain pen, a loose handle from the kitchen drawer, and a button I had laid out to sew back on my good coat.

In most of the winter activities, however, Donny felt singularly left out.

"We got to find a boy the right size of me," he complained. "These little kids just aren't old enough to play any real games. They just stand around and talk about the same old things, over and over. They sound like a bunch of church ladies."

The subjects of junior-level conversation, while limited, showed no signs of wearing out. One never-failing topic was the rehashing of the time Rita fell out of the window. She tumbled less than two feet and landed in a cushioning bush, but was so startled she screamed as if she had dropped into the Grand Canyon. Six months later, in the dead of winter, the topic was still as fresh as if it had happened an hour before.

"Laura," Teddy would begin, "Rita fall out the window, did you know that?"

"Oh. Rita fall out the window?"

"Yeah, Rita she fall out the window."

Laura would turn eagerly to Susie to pass along this

perennial tidbit. "Susie, Teddy say Rita fall out the window."

Susie's blue eyes would open wide, as if she had never heard this news before. "Rita fall out the window?"

"Yeah," Laura would marvel, pointing a chubby finger. "That Rita over there, she fall out the window."

So Susie would turn to Rita. "Rita, you fall out the window?"

"Yeah, me, I fall out the window. Hey Teddy, did you know I fall out the window, did you, hmmmm?"

At other times, Susie might be the one who would begin a favorite subject. "Do you like me, Teddy, hmmmm?" she would ask. "Do you like me?"

Teddy would mull this over, his brown face as serious as an Irish setter's, and finally reply, "Yes, I like you."

Susie would turn to Laura. "Lala, Teddy like me."

Laura, between Susie and Teddy all the time, her head turning back and forth to follow the conversational ball like a spectator at a tennis match, would ask in amazement, "He say that? Teddy say he like you?"

"Yeah, Teddy say he like me."

Then Rita would turn to Susie. "Thu-thie, you like me?"

Following a decent interval of thought, Susie would give a considered nod. "Yeah, I like you, Rita."

So Rita would say, "Hey, Teddy, Thu-thie tell me — "

This would go on, by the hour, by the day, through the long winter months, until I wondered where my sanity was when I used to say: *All I want out of life is a little family!*

More frustrating for me, and less so for Donny, were the

winter excursions outside. After days of howling blizzard
and subarctic weather, along came mornings when the sun
glittered with deceptive warmth on the snow. I remember
a morning typical of many, when the children crowded
along the window seat, noses pressed against the cold pane.
Bursting with energy, they asked if they could go out to
play.

"A splendid idea!" I said. The floors needed mopping
and waxing, and I might even have time to put some cup
custards in the oven, unimpeded.

Donny, old enough to manage his clothes with a minimum of help, could whoop it out to the snow in a few minutes. It took me a good half hour more to get Laura, Susan,
Teddy, and Rita encased in corduroy overalls, sweaters,
mufflers, ski pants, overshoes, jackets, mittens, and caps.
Then the inevitable happened, as I opened the back door
and stood shivering in the chill blast.

"Have to go to the baff-room," Susie sang out cheerfully.

"Me, too!" Teddy announced.

"Yeah," echoed Laura and Rita.

"Just a half hour ago — " I began, but in matters like this
the child always holds the trump card. Off came mittens,
hats, jackets, overshoes, ski pants, mufflers, sweaters, and
corduroy overalls. We all trooped solemnly upstairs; then
downstairs, and back on with all the wrappings. Two minutes after they went out, Donny was beating on the back
door.

"I want to come in. I'm cold."

I peeked through a crack. "Don't you want to play a
little more, so Mother can wax the floor?"

"I'm too cold," he said, so I let him in. Copycats all, the little children banged on the door like Donny.

"We cold, too," they insisted.

Everyone tracked across the partly waxed floor, dripping snow. By the time the little children had all their snow clothes peeled off, Donny discovered he was warm again, and dashed outside.

Teddy said, "Me wanna go outside again." His three sisters nodded in agreement.

I sighed and gathered together the heap of clothes. "Now hadn't we all better make another trip upstairs, first?" There was a loud and vigorous denial, so I began the stuffing and wrapping process once more.

They were just starting out the back door when Teddy piped up, "*Now* I hafta go to the baff-room, Mama."

"Me, too," proclaimed the Delphic chorus behind him.

The furnace was always running neck and neck with the children, in the race to see which could be more frustrating; but one time we had no heat for nearly two days, and for once it wasn't the furnace's fault.

A series of late-spring blizzards had piled the snow to record depths outside. The sunken, empty lot next door had filled in like a huge lake, and was frozen over. A sudden thaw followed, with leaden skies pouring down a torrent of rain. I remember the night I built up a roaring fire in the furnace, well banked to last until the next day, and how puzzled I was in the morning when I awoke to find the house like the Antarctic.

I put on my robe and slippers and hurried downstairs. As I opened the cellar door, I was frightened by the strange noises. There was a distinct sound of bottles clinking, and something gurgling.

"Is — is someone down there looking for me?" I quavered.

I had to force myself down the dimly lit wooden steps. There was no answer, only another ghostly *clink, clink* of the bottles. I swallowed hard, gooseflesh all over me and my knees knocking louder than the bottles. As I turned on the landing and started down the steps, I could see why the house was cold and why the bottles clinked. The basement was full of water. The water was over the bottom storage shelves where I kept my home-canned fruit and tomatoes. Empty bottles had washed off and were floating around on the surface of the water, clinking as they met. Over in the dim distance, the furnace sulked, cold and half drowned.

Now what would I do? Things always happened when Carl was away at school. The water kept rising and I had to move up another step. At that point I heard the thunder of little feet across the kitchen above me. The cellar door was flung open, and Donny, Teddy, Laura, Susie and Rita came tumbling down the stairs in their pajamas.

"Us couldn't find you," Susie said.

"Stop!" I shouted. "Don't fall in!"

"Fall in what?" asked Donny.

"The water," I said gloomily.

They came down with caution, sitting on the steps above me.

"Gosh," Donny said in awe, "our own swimming pool."

"Nobody's swimming in that," I said. "It's mucky, and it's ice cold."

"So am I," said Donny. "Why don't you light the furnace?"

"I don't think it burn," brown-faced Teddy said, dark eyes serious. "It's under the water."

"Let's bail it out," Donny said. "Shall I go upstairs and get some cups and a bucket?" The water was rising fast, and we all had to move up another step.

"It's coming in faster than we can bail," I said. The water had passed the middle storage shelves, and I was worrying about the top ones. Up there we had our camping stove and equipment, and the parts of a radio-phonograph Carl was assembling. "Mama has to think of some way to save those things," I told the children.

"What we need," Donny said, "is a boat. Could we use a dishpan for a boat?"

"Mama want Teddy go in a boat?" Teddy volunteered.

"Me no go," Susie said, shaking her blonde head.

"Me, no," Rita echoed, black hair swinging.

Laura eyed me warily, and retreated up to the landing. "Me no boat," she said, ready to evacuate to the kitchen, if necessary.

"No boat," I said. "Donny, please bring down Mama's rubber boots from the top step." I put them on, and they came barely to my calves. Gingerly I plunged one foot into the water and started down. I slipped on the slimy step, and the muddy, icy water poured into my boot, squishing around my bedroom slipper and bare foot. I was still a long way from the basement floor, so I returned to my perch. "No use," I reported. "Too deep to wade."

"Why don't you swim?" Donny asked brightly.

I shook my freezing foot. "This is enough for me. Let's go upstairs and get dressed."

I warmed the kitchen with the kerosene cookstove. We spent half the day returning to the basement, to watch the water rise. After I tucked the children to bed that night, I climbed into my own bed with a gnawing worry. The water was getting higher and higher. I half expected to awaken to find the house floating down the nearest river.

Carl returned the next day, called the proper places, and had the basement pumped out. A foot of muck remained on the floor and shelves. When Carl finally finished getting the place shoveled out and washed clean, he staggered upstairs to the bathroom and a hot tub, which I had filled with buckets of water heated on the stove.

"Nothing like a good flood," he philosophized, "to get a man to clean out his basement."

The snow swept down from the north in a howling blizzard, and everything froze solid outside for two weeks. Then another sudden thaw came. The house chilled, and there was the same ominous clink of bottles in the basement. I rushed, horrified, to the basement steps. The water was just over the bottom shelves again. This time I clenched my teeth, took off my shoes, wrapped my dress around my hips, and waded in. After same amateur sleuthing, I found the source of trouble.

"Horrible news, we're flooded again," I told Carl, when with chattering teeth I let him into the cold house the next day. "And did you notice that both times our basement filled up — *the lake next door disappeared?* I found a place in the wall, near that broken-down sink in the basement, where the water was pouring in like a burbling spring."

After the water had been pumped out again, Carl discovered the link between our basement and the disappearing lake next door. An underground channel had found its way from the thawed lake into an abandoned cistern next to our house which had been piped into the basement, so that the whole lake had deposited itself in our basement each time.

Carl filled the cistern with dirt, plugged the opening into our basement, and shoveled out the mud. This time he had no cheery Pollyanna comments about the value of having one's cellar flooded in order to get it cleaned.

These were all relatively minor irritations, however; it was a real crisis, one winter, that really gave me something to worry about.

I remember the Sunday night when Carl was packing up to go back to school and looking grave because a little boy in our Sunday school had just died of chicken pox.

"I thought chicken pox wasn't serious!" I exclaimed. "When Don had it, back in Cucamonga, he was scarcely sick."

"It usually is a mild disease, but this boy died of some very rare complications," Carl said. "Wasn't he in the same nursery class with Teddy and the girls?"

"Yes," I said. "Maybe if chicken pox is going around, I'd better keep them home next Sunday."

It was too late. The next morning, after Carl had left

early for school, I started dressing the children. As I took off Susie's pajamas, I saw that her tummy was peppered with red dots. It didn't bother Susie, who only looked at her rash with curious interest; but it bothered Laura, always sympathetic and supersensitive.

"Poor Susie," Laura whispered over and over, as she squatted down to inspect the rash at close hand. "Poor, poor Susie."

The next moment, her own pajamas off, she looked down to see her own red polka-dotted tummy. Huge tears rolled down her cheeks as she shrieked, "Poor me, poor *poor ME!*"

I tried to call the doctor, but a blizzard was blowing up outside, and the phone was dead. It was one of the old-fashioned, crank-type telephones and usually went dead in bad weather, which was the only time I really needed it. Long afterward, just before we moved, we found that squirrels had chewed through the cable and insulation. Every time it rained or snowed, moisture got in and short-circuited the wires, so the phone would be temporarily out.

I wasn't too worried at first. Teddy and Rita had the first faint pricklings of a rash, but all four tots seemed to be feeling well. Why should I be uneasy? The doctor hadn't even treated Donny. "Let me know if he scratches too much," was all the doctor had said, when Donny had had it. Why should Laura, Susie, Teddy and Rita have anything but mild cases, too? Still, I couldn't forget the neighbor boy, and the first uneasiness kept growing.

That night the little children refused their supper and were restless. I sponged them with baking soda and water, and they went right to sleep. In the morning I woke early, hearing them crying. All were feverish, itching so badly that they kept scratching their pox. The house was cold, like ice.

I hurried to the basement. Only a few shovelfuls of coal left in the bin! This was during the war, when coal was often hard to get, when shipments didn't come in on time and you sometimes went without. I had known we were low; Carl had reminded the coal company Saturday, but was only promised that some would be sent when the next carload arrived. I had been so concerned with the children, I hadn't realized until now how desperate our coal situation had grown.

After throwing in the last of our kindling, I piled on the precious bits of remaining coal and started the fire, knowing it couldn't last long. Upstairs, I jiggled the receiver again, but the telephone was still dead. The blizzard still howled around the house, wrapping us in a white, cold tomb. We were as isolated from the outer world, temporarily, as if we lived in the middle of Alaska.

The day was a nightmare. The fire in the furnace burned long enough to bring the temperature up a few meager degrees, then went out. By afternoon, with unprecedented use, the kerosene cookstove had gone out too, and it was half a mile to the nearest gas station where I could get kerosene. The house chilled down fast, and ice formed over the top of a pan of water on the sink.

Toward evening I began to get frantic. I was afraid to send little Donny out into the howling snowstorm for help, for fear he would get lost in the freezing, impenetrable whiteness and never come back. The other four wouldn't let me out of sight, crying hysterically when I left their rooms.

Donny and I were bundled in hats and overcoats and sweaters, but, even with our blue fingers, we were in a state of comfort compared to the small ones. If I kept them wrapped enough to be warm, their fevers and itching sent them into paroxysms of crying; if I uncovered them so I could relieve the itching with cool applications, the water almost froze on their bodies. I was afraid that if I didn't do anything, their fevers would keep rising and they would have their pox all infected, and that if I did try to cool them with wet cloths, I might give them pneumonia. I kept praying under my breath, "Please, God, help me keep my head." For the children's sake, I must keep cheerful.

Just as dark began to shut the swirling whiteness from the windows, I heard someone rattling at the front door. I stumbled down the stairs, thanking God that somebody had heard my prayers and stopped by. As I dashed toward the door, there was Carl. I fell in his arms. Never in my whole life was I so glad to see anyone.

Within a short time Carl was back with the doctor, some kerosene, and two buckets of coal.

The girls, the doctor said, had a severe case of pox, but should come along all right. It was Teddy who continued to grow worse, tossing with fever and delirium. When the doctor left, he told us he had done everything possible, and that we shouldn't worry; but I could see by the tiredness in his face that he was worried himself.

As soon as the front door closed, I clutched Carl's coat

front. "What did he tell you, while I was still upstairs? Tell me the truth! Teddy is very sick, like the boy that died, isn't he?"

Carl didn't hedge. He took my hands. His steady eyes, looking into mine, renewed my faltering faith and courage. "The crisis will come tonight. We'll know by morning."

"You didn't tell me, yet," I said, sagging against Carl's shoulder, drawing strength from his arms. "How did you happen to come home in the middle of the week? Just when I needed you?"

"That's why I came, I guess," he said. "I was in the college chapel after supper last night, and all of a sudden there came this intense feeling I should hurry home — something was wrong. I tried to phone, but the operator said a storm had the lines into Hebron down."

"I tried to call out. I thought it was just our own phone dead, the way it always is in bad weather."

"When I couldn't get you," Carl said, "I knew I must go home." Usually he made the trip in an hour and a half, but it took him eight hours just to reach Woodstock, after fighting drifts and blinding snow, and getting stalled behind abandoned cars and a wrecked truck. He could go no farther; the road into Hebron was completely snowed over with deep drifts. "I barged in on the Methodist minister at Woodstock," Carl finished, "and stayed there the rest of the night. This afternoon when the snowplow came through, I was the first car following it."

Teddy was restless and kept crying for me, in a weak, hoarse whisper. I wrapped him in a blanket and took him downstairs to the rocking chair. I rocked him most of the night, singing softly his favorite songs and hymns, and he finally fell into a troubled sleep. Gray morning was creeping through the windows when he stirred awake. His fever had broken, and I tucked him back in bed.

Donny joined us in holding hands at the breakfast table that morning. Carl and I had tears in our eyes as we sang the doxology, *"Praise God from whom all blessings flow . . ."*

CHAPTER 6

Taro

"MAMA," Donny asked, "do you think it's fair?"
"What?"

"All those four little kids," he said. "All the same size of each other and having so much fun. And *nobody* my size."

I kissed him. "We did try to find a bigger brother, you know."

"You could try again, couldn't you?" he pleaded.

It didn't seem like an impossible request. I was willing to go as high as six children, and even Carl wouldn't mind too much, once he got used to the idea. So I tried again.

Several weeks later, when Carl came back from school, I broached the subject. "Donny's still jealous of the fun that Teddy, Laura, Susie, and Rita have together."

Carl kept taking books out of his brief case. "Then why doesn't he join in the fun?"

"He gets tired of their baby games. He's so consistent in his wish for a boy his size, I think we ought to get one."

Carl slammed down a book. "Well *I* don't. So don't start writing any more letters."

"I already did."

Carl dropped into a chair and held his head in his hands.

"I tell her," he said, talking to himself, "I tell her and tell her, and she thinks I'm just talking for the exercise."

"Look, honey," I said, "I got a letter already this morning." I pulled it from my pocket and smoothed it open. "This orphanage isn't too far away. We could drive there and back, Sunday afternoon. She didn't say she had a boy, but she didn't say she didn't, either. She'd like to talk to us."

The next Sunday afternoon, one of the ladies in our congregation volunteered to baby-sit while Carl and I drove to the orphanage. When we arrived, the director showed us through the dormitories, dining hall, and grounds, then took us to her office.

"I was most interested in your willingness to take a child of any race," she said. "This is what I am wondering — while you are waiting to find a child for adoption, would you be interested in boarding a foster child?"

"I doubt it," Carl began. "You see we already — "

"At least we could think it over," I said quickly. The eager hope I had brought with me collapsed like a punctured balloon. A foster child, boarded for pay, is no substitute when you are wanting to adopt a child of your own, a child who takes the family name and all the legal rights of kinship.

"A foster child would be easier for you financially," the director said persuasively. "You wouldn't have to carry the full load of the child's expenses, as you must do when you adopt. If you took a foster child for temporary care, you would receive forty dollars a month, to cover his board and room."

"We'd really prefer to adopt," I said. "We could make out, financially. And a foster child would be so hard to give up — "

"But we don't have a single child, for adoption," she said. "Yet we do have a five-year-old boy who needs a temporary foster home. Our dormitories are full. You see, he is Japanese-Filipino, and most homes wouldn't accept such a child to board."

The orphanage director looked at me so expectantly, I couldn't let her down. So that was how Taro came to spend a year with us.

While Carl and I might have been equally dubious about the wisdom of bringing home a foster child, Donny was not. He whooped with delight when we brought home the chunky little boy with the round, Oriental face.

"Oh boy, oh *boy*," he crowed, jumping about the room like a cricket. "You're just the *right* size of me!"

Taro took a while to get adjusted to us. We weren't surprised, for tragedy had haunted his family ever since Pearl Harbor. Before the war, his Japanese father had been a truck farmer in California. He and his Filipino wife owned their own home and had three sons and a daughter; their oldest son was starting his first year of college, studying to be a doctor. When the war hit, they found themselves the objects of suspicion by jittery neighbors. Then, before there was time to adequately settle their affairs, they were herded into "relocation centers" along with all the other Japanese-Americans of the West Coast.

As if the ignominy of concentration-camp type of life

were not enough for Taro's America-loving father, steadily increasing trouble closed in. His ranch, leased to inept white farmers, who reaped the first crop and then neglected the land, was foreclosed; before the war was over he had lost both ranch and home. His oldest son volunteered for the 442nd Combat Team in the army and was killed in action, defending the freedom which his own family did not have. Even this did not end the chain of tragedy. Living in the drafty, cracker-box barracks which housed so many families without adequate privacy, the middle son developed rheumatic fever; when flu swept through the camp, both the boy and his mother, in weakened condition, died.

A year before the war ended, Taro's father was given the routine clearance by the FBI, so he could go to Chicago and work in a defense plant. There were only two children left in the family: little Taro, and his seven-year-old sister.

"Your daughter has a slight tonsil inflammation," the camp doctors told Taro's father, as the family was going through the red tape of being checked out of camp. "Nothing serious, but we advise a tonsillectomy before she leaves."

The father was reluctant, but he was persuaded that there would be no danger; she would be ready to leave the hospital the next day, and her susceptibility to colds would be reduced.

After his daughter entered the hospital, Taro's father never saw her again. Not alive, for the doctors reported regretfully that she had died on the operating table. It was undoubtedly one of those rare, unpredictable, and unavoidable accidents in an otherwise safe kind of operation; but these facts could have been of no comfort to the grief-laden father. He came to Chicago with Taro, the only surviving member of his family. Together they had lived in a small boardinghouse room; the father had taken his son every morning to an all-day nursery, worked from eight to five in a defense plant, picked up his son at night and returned to their cheerless room.

"Why won't Taro play with me?" Donny asked, the second day. "He just sits in a corner and sucks his thumb, and never says anything."

I put my arms around Donny and tried to explain. "Taro has lost so much, more than we can really understand," I said. "More than *he* can understand. We've just got to give him lots and lots of love and attention, so he can learn to be happy again."

In less than a month, Taro was a different boy, laughing, saucy, full of energy. He stopped sucking his thumb and brooding in corners, and entered into our family life like one of us, even calling Carl and me "Daddy" and "Mama."

Now that I had six children in the house, I was not as harassed and busy as I had been with five. Taro, nearly always working on some constructive project with sand, clay, blocks, or lumber and tools, was a good influence on Donny. Instead of being a ringleader in a perpetual round of mischief, Donny now found a companionable outlet for his superabundant energies by working along with Taro.

Taro's father continued his job in the Chicago defense plant. Every two weeks he took a bus to a neighboring town, where we met him with our car, bringing him home to spend Saturday night and Sunday with us. He was a small, stocky man, scarcely as tall as I; but his heart was as big as the whole outdoors.

"It is so good of you to come get me," he always said, in his gracious way, when we met his bus. "So good that you invite me to stay overnight, so I have a longer time with my boy."

How could this man, who had lost almost everything that was precious to him, have any capacity left for gratitude and thankfulness? But he did, with an abundance that made me feel humble. He was always bringing us little presents. Whenever he brought a new shirt, or bright-colored socks, or a new toy for Taro, he brought a twin gift for Donny.

Taro had the same stocky build, typically Japanese round face, and "slanted" eyes as his father. But Taro's oldest brother, who died an American hero, apparently looked more Filipino, like his mother.

On one of his visits, Taro's father was holding Teddy in his lap. "You remind me of my first-born son, when he was a small boy like you," he said, and then his voice seemed to get stuck in his throat.

"Tell me," Teddy said.

"He was brown, like you," Taro's father said, after a moment. "He had large, expressive brown eyes like you, too, only they turned up just a little at the corners. He — he looked very much like my dear wife."

Again he was unable to go on, until Teddy wiggled and asked, "Tell me a story, hmmm?"

"I'll tell you a story," he said, after another moment, and Donny, who always loved a story, moved in closer, blue eyes wide. "I'll tell you something my wife used to tell my first-born son, when he was a little brown boy like you. It is a Filipino legend, handed down from generation to generation among her people."

"What's ginger-ration?" Donny asked.

"Generation? Well, that's from father to son, father to — " He stopped, wiped his eyes, polished his glasses, and put them back slowly. Then he smiled at Teddy and Donny.

"Once upon a time, God created the sky and the earth. Then he put upon it all kinds of plants and animals to live."

"Snakes, too?" Teddy asked.

"Yes."

"Poison snakes, too?"

"Yes."

"Poison snakes!" Teddy shook his head. "I think God make a mistake."

"Perhaps, but more likely God has some good purpose in mind for everything he does, even if we don't always understand his purposes. Now God looked about at the plants and animals, and he liked what he had created. But he felt that something was missing.

"So he decided to create Man.

"He took clay and modeled a being in his own image. He put it into his divine oven to bake, and went about his other business. When he came back and opened the oven, he found his creation had burned black. Now God could not let his handiwork be wasted, so he stood this creature on its feet, breathed the breath of Life into him, and sent him on his way. Thus was born the Negro race.

"God took some more clay, modeled another being in his own image, and put it into his divine oven. This time he sat close by, to make sure it would not be burnt. After a few short minutes, he took it out. Alas! This man was under-done, and pasty white! Still, not wanting it to be wasted, God stood the creature up, breathed the breath of Life into him, and sent him on his way. Thus was born the white race.

"God made up his mind that his third try would be per-fect. He took more clay, molded it into his own image, and slipped it into the divine oven. This time he neither baked it for too long a time, nor too short. When he took it from the oven, it was a beautiful, warm-toned brown, and just exactly the way a man should be. With great pride he stood this final creation on its feet and breathed the breath of Life into him. And thus were born the Filipino people."

"I'll never forget that story," Donny said. "That was a real good story."

"When Teddy gets older, you'll have to tell it to him again," Taro's father said. "He's too young to remember it now."

"I will," Donny said. "I will."

The next month we had company. My youngest sister, Jane, came a few days before Thanksgiving to spend a week, while her husband went to California to see about a new job. Jane brought along her two boys, who were close in age to Taro and Donny. The four boys hit it off immediately and had wild and woolly times racing through our house.

When Carl came home Friday night, he stepped into a volley of that "Ack-ack-ack-ack" noise peculiar to boys.

"Hi, Daddy," Taro greeted him, pointing to Donny's blond cousins hiding in the bushes. "We're playing war, and Donny and me are the Americans, and those guys over there are the Japs!"

It was not incongruous to the children, for to their un-prejudiced eyes Taro looked as normal and American as the three blond boys. Only once, when Taro clowned at break-fast one morning, did the other boys ever put a race tag on him, and then only in jest. Taro had two fingers hooked into each corner of his mouth, stretching it wide in a gri-mace to show his teeth, as boys will do when making faces, and he had his eyes squinted almost shut. Donny's cousins didn't know that Taro was Japanese in ancestry, but they had seen the prevalent cartoons of the Japanese military in the newspapers, distorted sketches with huge, toothy grins. They both roared, thinking their jibe an original joke, funny because nothing could be farther from the truth.

"Hey, stop making that funny face," they shouted, doubled over with giggles. "*It makes you look like a Jap!*"

Taro's father had the Thanksgiving week end off, so he was invited to share Thanksgiving dinner with us. We ex-pected him to arrive the evening before, and telephone us when his bus arrived in the next town.

That evening, my sister Jane was baking some beautiful mince and pumpkin pies, and I was sorting cranberries. Carl, home that week to do church work, came into the kitchen from outside. He sniffed with anticipation and rubbed his cold hands.

"Smells good in here."

"Did you finish your calling?" I asked.

"Most of it," Carl said. "Has Taro's father phoned yet?"

"No." I glanced at the clock. "Seems like he should have, by now."

Carl snitched a bite of Jane's mincemeat. "Ummm, good. I have to run down the block and see the organist yet tonight. The call will probaby come while I'm gone. Just tell him to wait at that drugstore, and I'll be right over."

Jane put the last pies into the oven, and I finished the cranberries and put them on to cook. Carl came back.

"Did he phone?" he asked. "I can run over there for him now."

I stirred the cranberry sauce. "He hasn't called yet." The spoon slid slowly from my fingers and I looked at Carl, worried. "You don't think anything happened? He always calls before this."

"I'll go ahead and settle the four boys in bed," Carl said. "I'll tell Taro he can see his father in the morning."

"All right. Jane and I are going to make the stuffing. Teddy and the little girls are asleep already, so tell the big boys to be quiet upstairs."

"I'll read them a story when they're in their pajamas," Carl said. "Call me down as soon as the telephone rings."

The telephone didn't ring.

Jane and I finished the bread stuffing, put the pies and cranberry sauce out on the back porch to cool, and went into the living room to listen to Schubert's *Unfinished Symphony* on records. Our *Unfinished Symphony* was really unfinished now, because Donny had sat on the last record in the album.

Carl joined us. We all sat listening to the music, but with one ear waiting for the weak tinkle of our battery-crank telephone. It still didn't ring.

Then we heard the doorbell.

"We missed you, and hoped you were still coming," I said quickly, giving Taro's father a big smile as he stood under the dim yellow glow of the porch light. Then I gasped, as he limped into the brightness of the living room, a strange young man holding his arm.

Taro's father's face was battered, swollen, with a large bandage over one ear, his lip split in an ugly cut, and one eye almost closed.

First nobody knew what to say, and then everyone was talking at once. Later, from what the young stranger and Taro's father told us, we pieced together the story of a close brush with death. Coming north from Chicago, Taro's father gradually became aware of two men sitting behind him who kept muttering, making cracks about Japs and where they thought Japs ought to go. When he left the bus at his destination it was dusk; then he noticed that the two men had climbed from the bus behind him. Before he knew what they were doing, each had grabbed him by an elbow and whisked him past the lighted drugstore, around the corner to a dark alley.

Here they both jumped on him, cursing, kicking, punching, one breathing hard, "Let's give him a good one for my kid brother," the other puffing, "Let's finish him off. The only good Jap's a dead one."

Taken by surprise, Taro's father had gone down before the younger men, dazed and half unconscious. Then, suddenly, here was this brawny soldier landing blows right and left on the two assailants. His name, we found out, was Mike.

"I wish I could have roughed them up more than I did, before they got away," Mike told us ruefully, rubbing the knuckles of his big hand. "They made me so da—— Pardon, ladies, I forget my nice language when I meet such rotten skunks. It makes me so mad I can't see straight. A man's an American because of what he feels inside about his country. It burns me up to hear Americans of Japanese ancestry sneered at and called *Japs*. Plenty of those boys spilled good blood for our country. I know."

Mike stopped, looked around at us. It was awesome to see such a big man with tears in his eyes. Then he looked down at the floor and his voice was suddenly small for his size. "I know, because a Nisei boy saved my life. Over at Salerno. My life — my life, at the cost of his."

Mike had fought for freedom in Italy. Now that the war was finally over and he was home, he was still ready to fight for it.

"I don't know how I can ever thank Mike for what he did tonight," Taro's father said humbly.

"I wouldn't even have been around tonight," the soldier said, "here, or anywhere, if it hadn't been for an American boy of your ancestry." He turned to us, apologetically. "Those skunks really gave your friend a beating. I tried to get him to go to a doctor. I think he ought to have a stitch or two in that ear. He let us stop by our house and put a bandage over it, but he insisted he didn't want to keep you waiting. He wouldn't even stop to report it to the police."

We tried to get Mike to come in and sit down, but he told us he couldn't stay, his wife was waiting in their car. We asked him to bring her in, while we made a pot of hot cocoa. First he declined. When we urged, he started for the door.

"Maybe you would like to meet her, at that," he grinned. "You know I also wouldn't have been right there, at the right place, if it hadn't been for her. She'd been into Chicago for the day, on a shopping trip. Coming back in the bus, she was sitting a few seats back from those two thugs. She heard them muttering. When they tagged him off the bus, she became even more suspicious. I was parked in front of the drugstore to meet her, and here she comes flying out of the bus to our car and says to me, 'Hurry, Mike, follow those two guys!' " Mike winked at Taro's father. "I think I got me a pretty smart wife."

We helped Taro's father off with his coat, and then Mike was back at the door. "I want you to meet my wife, Cherry," he said proudly.

We did a double take at the beautiful, black-haired girl who clung with shyness to the hand of the big blond soldier. For Cherry was Japanese.

"After I was wounded and sent stateside, I looked up the family of this fellow who saved my life, and that was how I met Cherry." Mike grinned down at her. "Then they sent me to Denver to school to learn Japanese for work in the

Pacific. I thought she could help me." He laughed. "She couldn't even speak it. So I ended up trying to teach her, but I finally gave up!"

Mike and Cherry stayed for cocoa and graham crackers, and it was late when they left and we all went to bed. The next morning when Jane and I came down to the kitchen, there was Taro's father sitting with his head in his hands.

"Would you like some aspirin?" I asked. "Are you sure you shouldn't see a doctor?"

He managed a battered smile. "Thank you, that you are so concerned. No, my body feels stiff, but better, this morning. It is inside, now, where I am feeling bad." He looked up with so much sadness in his eyes that I had to swallow past a stickleburr in my throat. "That turkey," he said. "You remember, I told you I wanted to bring the turkey for the Thanksgiving dinner today? Well, Mike found my suitcase, but one of the fellows must have made away with the package with the turkey."

"Oh. *Oh!*" I was so relieved I started to laugh.

"Is funny?" he asked, incredulous.

"No," I assured him, wiping my eyes. "It's just that I'm so happy that it's nothing worse." I put my hand on the drooped shoulders. "It's no matter. You go spend your time with Taro. Jane and I will make out, honestly!"

There was no time to go out and buy a turkey, poof, just like that, even if the stores had been open — which they weren't. We wouldn't have had the money, anyway. Jane and I opened two cans of Spam, trimmed them to the general shape of a miniature trussed bird, molded drumsticks and wings on with the help of toothpicks, glazed the whole thing with a little brown sugar, and put it in to roast on a huge nest of seasoned stuffing.

"A beautiful bird, a wonderful dinner," Taro's father said at the table, later. "A wonderful family to take care of my boy while I work. A wonderful country in which to live." Then he added humbly, "I am very thankful."

As the year went by, we kept in touch with Mike and Cherry and saw more of them. Then Cherry found an opening for a worker on a large farm run by a candy company. All the workers on this particular farm were Japanese, and it would be possible for Taro to live with his father. Single men lived in a dormitory, and there were some small houses for the families. One young Japanese couple had two little boys near Taro's age.

"We would be happy to raise Taro with our boy, and board you both with our family," this couple told Taro's father, "if you want the job open here."

Taro's father came to talk it over with us. We hated to give up our lovable little foster boy, since he seemed like one of our own; but we knew it was best for both of them.

"You've said you miss farming," Carl said. "Wouldn't you be happier there, than shut up in a factory?"

He nodded. "But Taro is so happy here, with you."

"Too happy for his own good," I said gently. "If you didn't care about him, I'd say he'd be better off if you'd let us adopt him. But you do care, and he loves you. Seeing so little of him, weeks apart, is a big strain on you both. And then, being together so seldom, he might easily grow away from you. On the farm you could be together."

Taro's father smiled, and in his eyes was a hope for a new life. But we knew that Taro's going would leave a big hole in our own family. And we also knew that, with the governor off Donny's motor, things would not be so peaceful around our house any more.

CHAPTER 7

The Sorcerer's Apprentice

EARLY one summer day I decided I would transform the unfinished storeroom into a much-needed bedroom. Wallpaper had been bought for it, but Carl never had had the time to clean out the room and put it up, and I had felt the job would be too much for me to tackle alone.

On that day I awoke full of zing and vigor. I must have been under a spell, because I had the peculiar illusion that I could paper a dozen rooms that day, if I wanted to.

First I mixed a dishpan full of bread dough for our weekly batch of homemade whole-wheat bread, and set it to rising in the kitchen. Then I attacked the storeroom. It would make a good child's bedroom; although it was small, with sloping ceilings, it had a large window and was conveniently located at the end of the upstairs hall and right next to the bathroom. It had never been used, except as a catch-all for a dozen ministers' families before us. I carted old lumber, boxes of mildewed books, and other junk down the stairs, out to the converted garage-barn, and up the ladder steps to the unused hayloft above. After the cobwebs and dirt had been swept out, I unrolled the wallpaper down the upper hall, cut it into the proper lengths, and flipped the stack upside down over newspapers. Downstairs in the kitchen I mixed up a bucket of wallpaper paste. At last I was ready to begin.

The doorbell rang.

"Hello," I said, wiping my hands on my apron.

It was our neighbor, an elderly man from the "old country" who lived alone in a shack down the street. His faded overalls were tucked into high boots, and his frayed blue shirt was open at the neck. Although his nose wasn't overly huge, he reminded me of Jimmy Durante, with his wistful, crooked smile.

"Hullo," he said, and rolled his battered felt hat in his gnarled hands.

The children swarmed to the door from all directions to cluster around me.

"Where's the milk?" Donny asked. Our neighbor milked another neighbor's cow for half the milk, selling us what he couldn't use.

"I apologize, no milk. The cow she go dry. After she fresh again, I bring milk, okay?"

"That's fine," I said.

"How come the cow hasn't got any more milk?" Donny asked.

The old man knelt down to the children's level, and they crowded about him. "Well you see this Mama cow will pretty soon go out for walk in meadow. What nice surprise you think she gonna find in bushes?"

"Ice cream?" Teddy said.

"No, no! This Mama cow, she gonna find something she like better. She find *little* baby calf! Then, after she get her calf, she have more milk for all us peoples to drink."

"Oh," Donny said. He thought a moment, then lifted his round blue eyes. "When did you take her to see the *Daddy* cow?"

I saw the red flushing through the sunburn on the old man's grizzled neck. "Donny," I said quickly, "would you run out to the kitchen and see if that's a faucet running?"

"Don't hear any faucet running," Donny said. "Will the cow — "

"Donny! Mother asked you to go and see."

Donny went skipping off, and the old man fumbled with his hat and glanced shyly at me.

"What I really want to ask," he explained, pointing to our cherry tree, "is would you want me pick cherries? I pick for half of crop, you want that?"

"I would," I said. Our tree, which had borne a niggling yield the year before, was this year about to break under its load. The fruit was a tiny pie-cherry, too sour for eating out of hand, but excellent for canning. I knew that Carl could never get around to them.

"Okay," he smiled, replacing his comical hat on his white hair. "I get ladder and buckets."

Back in the kitchen I found Donny with dough and flour paste covering his arms beyond his elbows, and all over the front of him.

"I punched down your bread dough," Donny said. "It was puffing up and falling over the dishpan. I punched down the dough in the bucket, too, but it's all gooey."

I pulled my own hair to keep from pulling his. "Oh, Donny! That's paste for the wallpaper in that bucket." As

I scraped the goo from his clothes, washed him, and found a clean set of clothes, I wondered why I couldn't reason with a five-year-old. I soon found out.

"See how much work you're making?" I appealed. "I know you want to help Mama, and I appreciate it. But you should ask, first. How would you feel, when *you* are grown up, and then *your* little boy made a mess like this? Right when you were busy — "

"No bother," Donny said earnestly, his face untroubled. "I'd have my *wife* clean it up."

I lugged the paste bucket upstairs and began brushing paste on the back of the first wallpaper strip. It was evenly smeared when the doorbell rang again. I ran downstairs. The old man was standing outside the door with a shy smile and two buckets of cherries. I thanked him and emptied my fruit into a large kettle, returning his buckets to him. I started back to my job. All the way up the stairs were small, whitish footprints. In the upper hall the footprints were black, all down the length of pasted paper. I turned at the top of the stairs.

"Children!" I called.

Five heads poked around the corner from the downstairs playroom.

"Who walked all over Mama's pasted wallpaper?"

"Us had to go to the baff-room," Susie said.

"It's a nice day," I suggested. "Why don't you children all go play in the back yard, until Mama gets the wallpaper up?"

I rushed to put the first strip up, but it wouldn't stick around the edges, where the paste had dried. When I pulled it from the wall to repaste it, a piece stuck and left a hole in the middle of the paper. Again the doorbell rang. I flew downstairs, tripping over a pull-toy at the bottom of the steps.

"You hurry too fast," the old man sympathized through the screen door, as he held up his buckets, again full of cherries. "Shouldna hurry, I got lotsa time. I no hurry."

He exaggerated. It seemed he was picking our tree with a lightning speed that kept increasing in tempo. All my pots and pans were rapidly filling with cherries.

I detoured to the yard, to check on the children. They had been busy. From tin cans out of the trash barrel they had torn labels, and slapped them to the side of the house with a paste of mud.

"Pitty, hmmmm?" Susie asked, pointing to the uneven rows of gaily pictured tomatoes, beans, peas, and apple-sauce.

"But not *there!*" I pleaded. "Please, if you want to paste, I'll give you some scrapbooks. But good heavens, not on the walls!"

"You pasting on the walls," Laura pointed out.

After we gathered up the labels and washed off the side of the house, the children followed me back upstairs. The next time I ran down to answer the doorbell and dump cherries in the kitchen, the children tracked up and down again on the freshly pasted strip.

"Us all had to go baff-room," Rita explained.

In desperation I put all five of them into the big, old-fashioned bathroom, laid a chair on its side across the door-way, and handed in a box of assorted toys.

"How about staying in there like little angels?" I asked.

"You can watch Mama, or play with your toys, while I finish my job."

"Us wants to help," Susie said.

"Believe me," I said. "This is the best way you can help."

I brushed paste on a strip of ceiling paper, having decided it would be better to finish the top before I did the other sides to the room. Teetering on a board across two chairs, I tried to pound one end of the paper up with my dry smoothing brush, but the other end kept coming down. I shoved it back hard and my fist poked a hole through the damp paper. Then the first end plopped down in my face and wrapped around my neck. I lost my balance and fell with a loud crash.

Teddy, craning his neck around the bathroom door, called, "See, Mama? You should of let us help."

After a hot lunch, the children all took naps. They had been awake, and back playing in the bathroom, as I began on the last wall.

The doorbell was still ringing regularly. All afternoon I had protested to our neighbor that we really had plenty of cherries now, that he was welcome to the rest. He thought I was just being polite.

"Plenty cherries for me, already," he said with his disarming smile. "So many you can use, with all these little kids you got."

I felt like the Sorcerer's Apprentice, who, in the absence of his master, started a broom to fetching water — which it did, faster and faster, until the place was threatened with inundation. Like that apprentice, I felt vaguely responsible for starting the whole business, yet at my wit's end for the magic word which could stop it. Every time the old man hurried up our front steps with his heaping buckets, I remembered the symphonic scherzo which Paul Dukas wrote as a musical illustration to the old folk tale; the melody ran through my head like a stuck record.

I ran out of places to empty the prolific cherry buckets. All my pots and pans were full, the sink was full, and the bread was overflowing in the dishpan. When I went back upstairs, the water was overflowing in the washbowl and running down the hall on top of my wallpaper strips.

"No, no, no!" I shouted, as I waded through the bathroom to turn off the faucet.

"We were sailing boats," Donny said.

"You gave us boats," Susie said. "In that toy box, boats."

I mopped up the water and went doggedly on with my papering. Just three more strips, and I would be through.

The doorbell rang again. There was no counter space left in the kitchen, no empty pans, no boxes. I dumped the cherries on the floor under the kitchen table, and dragged back upstairs. The children were busy. Donny was cutting pictures from the middle of the next wallpaper strip, and Teddy and Laura were pasting them in one of Carl's books. Rita was stirring the paste, slopping it all over the floor, and Susie was doing finger painting on the woodwork. When they saw me coming, they scrambled back over the chair into the bathroom and turned up innocent faces.

"You said we could paste in a book," Donny argued.

The doorbell rang in the middle of my clean-up.

The busy bucket-bearer looked sad. "So sorry, but all picked, now. Not one cherry left on tree."

I wanted to jump in the air and kick my heels, but I was

too tired. I emptied those last buckets of cherries on the kitchen floor and thanked my neighbor profusely. The deluge was over!

I finished cleaning up the mess upstairs, put up the last strip of paper, and surveyed the new bedroom. It was depressing beyond words. Although I had worked like a dog all day, the room looked terrible. It looked like the kind of wallpapering job that Donny might have done. I led the children downstairs, fed them supper out of cans, and stared gloomily at the surrounding avalanche of cherries. Donny and Teddy took their wagon to ask the lady across the vacant lot for the loan of her wash-boiler, for the hot-water canning. I made sugar syrup and laboriously began to pit the cherries with a knife. By the children's bedtime, one lone quart jar was ready to process.

After I had my offspring tucked into bed, I stared in frustration at the ripe fruit spilling over the kitchen. It would take me from then until Carl graduated from seminary to pit that many pigmy cherries. I decided to throw them into jars, seeds and all. The first panfuls had to be washed in the bathtub upstairs, since the sink was full of cherries and the dishpan full of dough.

At five-thirty the next morning I had taken my last loaf of bread from the oven and lifted the last gleaming jar of canned cherries from the steaming boiler. I was too weary to go to bed, so I just staggered to the couch and flopped, the way I had done during those long months when Susie and Laura were on night bottles.

At six-thirty the children piled downstairs in their pajamas, shouting happily for their breakfast.

At seven-thirty the front doorbell rang. It was the old man, with two full buckets of cherries.

"Why, I thought all our cherries were picked!" I gasped, horrified.

"Yes ma'am. But the nice lady around the block, I do odd jobs for her, and she say, take from her tree all cherries I want, she already take all she want."

What could I say, when he stood there so wistful, so happy because he thought he was making someone else happy? The deluge was on again, and it seemed as if all the cherry trees in Hebron were pouring their fruit into our kitchen.

The following day I was droopy from lack of sleep, but as I gazed at my loaded fruit shelves in the basement, and my newly papered room at the end of the upstairs hall, I felt almost smug with satisfaction. The room had turned out to be a far more professional job than I dreamed it could. The wrinkles had smoothed out, the patched holes and rips didn't show, and the dark paste smears had dried to invisibility.

When Carl came home from seminary that night, he took me into his arms. "How's my girl?" he asked. "Have you been working hard?"

"Oh, I did a bit of papering, and canned a few cherries," I said.

Things were never so bad as they seemed, when you looked back on them afterwards.

CHAPTER 8

All the Wrong Sizes

AFTER four years of college and three years of graduate study, Carl received his Bachelor of Divinity degree. We began packing clothes, dishes, books, and toys for
our journey back to California. Carl was to begin his full-
time ministry there, in the semirural town of Forestville.

Donny, perched on a packing box, asked, "Isn't it about
time?"

"Time for what?" I moved Donny to a chair and tried to
squeeze some jeans into the already-full box.

"Time to start looking again. For a boy the right size of
me."

"I'll tell you what you can look for," Carl said. "Go out
to the garage and see if you can find a box big enough to
hold all these galoshes and rubbers, will you?"

"But I'm after five now, and a boy the size of — "

"Well not right now," I told Donny. "They wouldn't
let us adopt a boy when we're right in the middle of moving. We'll have to wait until we get to our new house in
California. Now run and find a box for Daddy."

When Donny was gone, Carl said, "Now don't go putting ideas in the boy's head. When we get to Forestville, I
want to be free to throw myself into my work. Besides, I
understand the parsonage there isn't very big."

"We'll see," I hedged.

We made a parting visit to my parents at their home in nearby Aurora.

"I hope you folks intend to ease up on this rapid family growth," my father said, concerned. "With five children, don't you think you've already supplied your share of the grandchildren?"

"You shouldn't spread yourselves any thinner," Mother urged, "trying to manage any more."

"I can't make any promises," I said.

"*I* can," Carl said darkly.

We piled into our secondhand sedan, with our secondhand camping equipment, and started west. Hotels were out of our class, even auto courts. We camped at county parks, state parks, and national parks all the way across the country.

One night it was after dark, and there was no park near. We put up our tent in a grove of trees, off the highway and away from traffic noise. When the first express train came through about midnight, on an unexpected embankment twenty feet behind us, it sounded as if it thundered right through our tent. We spent the night lulling the five children back to sleep, after each train came hurtling through with earth-rattling roars, hissing steam, and screeching whistles.

In two weeks we arrived at San Francisco, headed north over the Golden Gate bridge to Santa Rosa, then turned west on the Russian River road toward the coast. We came over the last rolling hill late in the afternoon, and saw the scattering of stores and houses that formed the nucleus of

Forestville. The church rose from a hill, golden in the sunset, its cross silhouetted against a rose- and salmon-streaked sky.

We found the parsonage wedged between the back of the stucco church and a neighboring wooden Lodge Hall. The parsonage originally had been a tiny one-and-a-half story frame cottage, but had grown a bustle of additions in back, through the years.

I was the first of our family inside. A strange feeling it is, to walk into an old house, timeworn, with the imprints of former occupants left as in an old shoe. It was almost like standing outside of time to look around the empty rooms, the strange rooms, to see sunlight streaming through the windows in unaccustomed patterns, and to think, *someday this will all be so much a part of us, so familiar, that we can't ever see it again, clearly, as we do now. Someday we will be leaving it, instead of just moving in, and we will be leaving part of ourselves behind.*

The children broke my reveries. They flew delightedly about the house, exploring, racing through the kitchen, dining and living rooms, up the narrow, winding steps to the two postage-stamp bedrooms upstairs.

"Where's the baff-room?" they called down.

"It must be up there, near the bedrooms," I called back. It wasn't. We finally discovered it downstairs at the other end of the house, tacked to the kitchen as an afterthought. We also found a small study off the dining room.

"I'll see if I can't find myself a corner over in the church for my office," Carl said. "With five children, we'll need this for a bedroom."

Donny was counting on his fingers. "There'll be *six* children, when we go get that boy the size of me."

"Don't bother Daddy about that now," I whispered. "Wait till we get unpacked and settled, then we'll talk."

There was a knock at the back door. The front door, we soon learned, was only for strangers and salesmen. Three ladies came in, introducing themselves as members of our new congregation.

"We thought you'd be getting in about this time," one said. She stood a three-layer frosted cake on the table.

A second handed me a big bowl of salad. "We thought it might be easier, if you didn't have to cook on your first night."

The third lady smiled and put a large casserole on the stove. "I hope your children like spaghetti and meat balls." She was rewarded by a full round of cheers and deep, hungry sighs.

When the good people had gone, Carl put his arm around me. "I think I'm going to find my work most satisfying, here."

There were problems, of course. The first was adjustment of time schedules for Sunday church services. Carl had two churches, one at Forestville, the smaller ten miles away at Occidental. They had not been under the same minister before, and both were in the habit of holding morning worship at the traditional eleven o'clock hour. Each set of board members insisted that the hours could not be changed, or people would drop out of the congregation.

"I guess you're the one, honey," Carl told me.

"One for what?"

"To help out," he said. "You can be the other minister until we work this out. You can take the morning worship at Occidental, and I'll do Forestville."

"Oh," I gasped. "I couldn't do that. I'm no minister."

"You've filled the pulpit before."

"But that was different," I said. "That was emergency, when you were sick and there wasn't anybody else."

"This is emergency, too, and there isn't anybody else," he said. "Don't let it worry you. It's only temporary."

Temporary turned out to be nearly three months. I found myself submerged in home and church work. Not only were there a weekly sermon and an order of worship to plan, with appropriate hymns chosen, but the regular housework, cooking, and laundry to do. Each day was busy, but it was Sunday morning that was really hectic. Teddy had just celebrated his third birthday, Laura and Susie had several months to go before they were three, and Rita was not yet two. All were so young they had to be dressed for Sunday school; Donny always needed mismated clothes exchanged for the ones which originally had been laid out and crooked buttoning, twisted socks, and tangled shoestrings fixed. All this had to be accomplished after a hurried breakfast, so Carl could lead the Forestville Sunday school, while I jumped into the car to make it on time for the Occidental service.

Donny sometimes accompanied me to the Occidental church, and sat in the front row where I could keep an eye on him while I was preaching. One day, riding home along the road that wound intermittently through the sunshine of hillside cherry orchards and the shadows of giant redwood groves, Donny said, "Now?"

"Now what?"

"Now can we go look for a boy my size?"

"Heavens, not right now. I know I said I'd think about it after we got unpacked and settled — But Mama didn't know she'd have to help Daddy with the churches!" I smiled at him. "Wait until I don't have to preach any more, and then we'll talk to Daddy about it, okay?"

The two official boards finally agreed on a compromise, so Carl could preach at both churches.

"Now I can relax and enjoy just being a mother," I told Carl that first Sunday night after the change.

Just then Donny slippered into the room in his pajamas and hopped into Carl's lap. "Now can we talk, Daddy?" he asked.

"Talk about what?"

"Getting a boy just my size," Donny said. "School starts this week, and I'm going to be six years old, and I'm going to be in first grade, so that's the size boy we want."

Carl held his head. "Here we go again."

Donny leaped off Carl's lap and into mine. "Daddy said we can go! Daddy said we can go get a boy, hooray!"

"All *right*," Carl shouted above Donny's din. "All right, *one* more. But that's final, do you both hear? Right size or wrong size, we'll stop right there, with *one more*."

Every week I wrote letters to agencies, and Donny licked the stamps. It was just after Christmas when a letter came from an agency in the Pacific Northwest, saying, "We are sorry we do not have any older boys for adoption at this time. However we do have a little year-old boy named Timmy, who is in desperate need of a good home. Because he was born to a Mexican mother and a Japanese father, nobody seems to want him. Yet he is a bright and charming baby."

"That Timmy isn't the size of me," Donny said.

"No, he's even younger than Rita," I said. "But we can't leave him in the orphanage all unwanted, can we? He's been waiting all his short life for someone to come along and love him, and nobody ever came."

"Well, I guess we ought to get him," Donny said.

I hugged him. "Maybe a boy your size will move into the neighborhood," I said. "Or maybe — "

"Or nothing," Carl said. "Just remember what I told you. This is the end, *finis*, termination. In other words, this winds up our little family."

"You're right," I nodded. "I think six will really be all I can handle."

We decided to let three-year-old Teddy go with me, to be company to little Timmy on the way home. Carl drove us to San Francisco to catch our train. Going north through mountains, the train ran into violent snowstorms and snailed through drifts behind a snowplow. We were supposed to arrive in two days, but it took two days to get as far as Portland and another long day on a branch line to reach the orphanage. It was pitch dark, nearly ten at night, as we walked from the station into the swirling, icy black-and-whiteness. According to my original schedule, I would have arrived in the middle of the day, picked up Timmy, and started back on the afternoon train; now it was past bedtime at the orphanage, and there would not be another train out until the next afternoon.

What to do? I was in a strange town late at night, with no money to spare for a hotel room. In a phone booth I found the name of the local Methodist minister, screwed up my courage, and telephoned him with one of my few nickels. I felt as welcome as a stray bedbug when I told him a mother and her little boy were stranded here, and asked if he could shelter two waifs for the night.

"Bless you," he exclaimed. "Come right over."

He and his wife fixed us sandwiches and milk, then took us upstairs. After two and a half days, and two nights, of sitting in a chair car, the hot bath and soft bed were luxuries beyond imagining. The next morning the minister drove us to the orphanage to pick up our new boy.

Timmy, dressed for the blizzard in a red snowsuit, was a roly-poly little elf, as round and chubby as Laura had been at that age, with red apple cheeks and enormous, questioning brown eyes that had a pixie slant.

"You darling! How could anybody not want you?" I said. I knelt down and took him into my arms. "I'm your new Mama," I told him, "and this is your new brother, Teddy."

Timmy wasn't talking yet, and he was too young to comprehend most of what I said. But he looked us over quite soberly, and chuckled in his unusually deep baby voice.

On the train going back, we were off schedule again as

we plowed back through snow drifts that night, the next day, and most of the next night. We chugged into Portland, our junction station, two hours past midnight, very early on a Saturday morning. A taxi to a hotel was out. This station didn't close at night, like the one at the orphanage, so I looked around for a place to sleep.

Juggling our suitcase, a shopping bag of groceries, a box of toys, and the added bundle of Timmy's belongings, with Teddy clinging to my coat pocket with one hand and tight to Timmy's chubby fist with the other, I led the way to the ladies' waiting room in the station. Except for some long, thinly padded benches with high backs and sides, it was deserted. I tugged one bench around until it faced another, and settled the boys end to end on the wall bench, covering them with a baby blanket and our coats. Then I dropped on the facing bench and fell asleep. After the past night and a half cramped again in a chair-car seat, even that hard bench felt good.

At six I awoke when the cleaning woman came in to scrub floors. I got the children up and pushed the extra bench back to its place along the wall. We three sat cross-legged there, I with my feet out of the way for the floor mopping, and drank canned orange juice out of paper cups. Then we tiptoed over the clean, wet floor into the washroom to scrub off train smoke and change into clean clothes.

Refreshed, we returned to the outer waiting room to finish our breakfast. I opened a can of evaporated milk, poured each paper cup half full, and filled it with hot water from the washroom for our make-believe cocoa. While we sat there, nibbling on whole-wheat biscuits and dried prunes, the waiting room began to grow crowded. Ours was the last train which had been able to fight its way into this junction, and all scheduled departures were being canceled because of blizzards and bridges out. This meant that the morning train we had intended to catch, for the last leg of our journey home, was also canceled.

By midmorning the little boys were getting tired of the station, so I decided to take them uptown. I wanted to store the suitcase and bundles in a locker, but I knew I'd need that dime for streetcar fare. With all the assorted baggage clutched under my arms and Teddy holding fast to Timmy and my coat pocket, we went uptown and spent the rest of the morning in a department store, having a wonderful time riding the escalators and elevators up and down in the warm building.

After a lunch out of our sack, Teddy admitted he was sleepy. Timmy nodded, rubbing heavy eyes. We went out to the snowy street. Up the block I saw the Portland First Methodist Church, so we headed there. When I approached the associate minister in his office, asking if there might be a couch in the building where the little boys could nap, he was most obliging. He not only produced a couch in the Cradle Roll room, but also two cribs. I undressed the boys, scrubbed them in the adjoining washroom, and put them into the cribs for real naps. When they awoke, we ate a supper of canned baby-food liver soup and canned applesauce. Then I telephoned the railway station.

"All departures are still canceled," the information desk replied. "The first train south will not leave before tomorrow afternoon, at the earliest."

Marooned another day with no funds! I went to the associate minister and asked if we might stay in the church overnight. He protested.

"You couldn't possibly be comfortable here!" His hand reached for the telephone. "My wife and I have only a small apartment, but we have friends — "

"But we *really* don't mind staying in the church," I said, "as long as we're not in anyone's way. There are cribs here, and everything we need to be comfortable."

So the children played happily with the toys in the nursery while I prepared a bed for myself on the couch, which was even supplied with a pillow and a quilt. I washed diapers in the washbowl of the adjoining rest room, found some string, and hung up my wash. At bedtime, the boys weren't sleepy after such long naps that afternoon, so they tiptoed with me to the balcony which ran around the interior of the second floor of the church. We sat there in the dark, a boy cuddled in each of my arms, and enjoyed the festive gaiety of a wedding reception, in full swing below.

After the party had drifted away, the lights downstairs had all been turned off and the church locked up, we tiptoed back through the dark and quiet church to the nursery room. I dug into my almost-empty grocery sack for some graham crackers and canned grapefruit juice, which provided our version of punch and wedding cake. The boys feel asleep as soon as I tucked them into their cribs, with cracker crumbs outlining their dreamy smiles. I settled myself on the couch. The blizzard was moaning outside. There were ghostly steps squeaking down in the basement, strange sighs from the surrounding pitch-blackness, and spooky rattles up in the church garret. I pulled the quilt over my head and went to sleep.

Next day was Sunday. I took down our washing, dressed the boys for Sunday school, and gathered together our things. While I attended a young-adult class and the church service, Timmy and Teddy went to the nursery class. When I turned them over to their teacher, it was not the new baby, but three-year-old Teddy who hung back, afraid of all the strange children. Timmy, even then the master of any situation, at home anywhere and with anyone, took Teddy's hand encouragingly, patted it, and drew him over to the toy shelf.

That afternoon the trains started running again. We arrived home with no further delays or trouble. When we walked into the house, the children were overjoyed to see Teddy and me, and they welcomed Timmy with open arms.

All except Laura.

Before we had known that our latest would be a boy, when I was still writing letters, I had asked the children how they would like a new brother or sister. They had been enthusiastic. When Timmy arrived, however, it was another matter to Laura. Her sudden jealousy burst in a shower of bitter sparks from her brown almond eyes. She pinched him whenever she thought no one was looking; she complained loud and long, "I don't like that *brother-sister*. Let's throw that little old *brother-sister* away!"

In time she fell in love with him, as most people did on sight. There was something irresistible about his quick grin and basso-profundo chuckle, the disarming friendliness radiating from his round face and large, pixie-tilted brown eyes. He became the official greeter in our family, the first to shout "Hi!" to a stranger, even when "Hi" was the only word he could say.

Six months after Timmy joined the family, Carl returned from a trip on church business to San Francisco. He hugged me, looking like a little boy about to confess he has been swiping green apples.

"What have you been up to?" I asked suspiciously.

"How would you like to adopt another boy?"

"You darling!" I said. "Donny still complains about our always finding children the wrong sizes! I *thought* it was time we started looking again, but I didn't know how to broach — "

Carl hesitated. "Well, this boy I found out about, well, he happens to be younger — "

"You found one? How young?"

"As a matter of fact," Carl admitted, "he was just born."

I was disappointed. "Really, honey, that's too young."

"He'll grow. Just give him time, he'll grow."

"Let's not get silly," I said. "He'll never catch up with Donny, and you know it."

"But nobody wants him. He's Japanese and Burmese and Korean, and the agency just doesn't have anyone on their waiting list who is asking for that kind of baby. I thought you couldn't resist giving a home to a child that nobody wanted."

"I couldn't, before. But there comes a *limit*," I said. "I'd be willing to squeeze in one more, just so Donny could have his brother the right size. *But no more babies! I've raised my share of babies.*"

Carl pulled papers from his pocket. "I've already been interviewed by the agency. I've given them all the references of the other agencies — "

"I'm *tired* of seeing dirty baby bottles gathering on the sink, and diapers always on the line — "

"We can go down to San Francisco," Carl went on, waving the papers. "We can look at him in the hospital. If we like him we can bring him home, simple as that."

"It's not as simple as that. I don't — "

"Once we see him you'll feel sorry for him. So helpless, without a friend in the world — You'll change your mind."

"I won't change my mind," I said stubbornly, "because I've already changed my last diaper. And made my last formula. The *diapers* I've washed so far would make a pile from here to the *moon*. And that is exactly where I'm going, if anyone brings a wailing, wet-bottomed baby into this house."

"Listen," Carl said. "You've done more than your share of the choosing, so far. It's time *I* got a chance to choose us a child, for a change." He started out of the room, whistling. Several children came in and asked, "Where you going, Daddy?"

"Going crazy, I guess," Carl said.

"Me go, too," Timmy demanded.

"Me, too," I called after Carl. "And I'll bet I get there before you do."

Laura looked around, frowning. "Who's going to stay here with us kids?"

"We're not going anywhere, princess," Carl said, kissing her. "We're just teasing each other."

"Oh," Laura said.

"Except your mother," Carl said. "She just said she might take a trip to the moon."

"Me, too?" Timmy hollered.

When we went to fetch home our new baby, the children came along. At the hospital we left Donny, Laura, Susan, Teddy, Rita, and Timmy in the waiting room, dancing up and down like sand fleas, while Carl and I took the elevator to the maternity floor. The head nurse was still out to supper, so we perched on a bench in the corridor, swinging our feet. Mothers-to-be paced in and out of their rooms, robes stretched to lap over tummies, and slippered up and down the corridor with varying degrees of patience and impatience. A white-coated worker pushed by us, his bucket on rollers, mopping the floors. We held our feet up in the air and Carl said, "I've always been away at school, before, so I never got to watch my other babies grow up from day to day. This is going to be fun."

"The more the merrier," I said.

"Do you feel any different, now you are about to become the mother of seven?"

"My feelings are mixed," I said. "What do you suppose he'll look like?"

Another couple joined us on the bench, the husband holding his wife's arm as if she were made of porcelain. "Are you just leaving with your baby, too?" the girl asked.

"Yes," I said. "What's yours, boy or girl?"

"Girl," she said. "We're naming her Linda Lee. What's yours?"

"Boy," I said. "His name will be Alexander Paul, but we'll call him Alex, for short."

"Who knows!" the girl said, laughing in her happiness. "They might even grow up and meet on a blind date. They could marry, and never realize their parents brought them home at the same time from the same hospital!"

"Who knows?" I said. "Stranger things have happened."

A nurse opened a door, accompanied by a background chorus of wails. "Reverend and Mrs. Doss?" she called.

We stood up, Carl and I.

She took my package of baby clothes. "Would you like to come in and watch us dress your little boy?"

We followed her into the nursery and watched her pick up the infant making the most noise. All you could see were his tonsils, which were nearly as red as his face, and the slits of his tightly closed eyes. Under the damp fringe of black hair, his tiny face looked completely and unmistakably Oriental, although he was crying so hard you couldn't make out the details.

As Carl proudly bore our blue-bundled siren out into the hall, the nurse motioned the other couple to enter. Passing us, the young mother smiled. "Let me see my little girl's future date!"

I pulled back the corner of the blanket, and the girl's blue eyes widened. She stared at Carl and me, and again at our Alex. Then she rallied, covering her bewilderment with a tremulous smile.

"It's a wonderful world," Carl said, "isn't it?"

When we emerged from the elevators and sailed into the waiting room, the other six children raced over to us like noisy, joyful puppies, falling all over each other to see their wailing baby brother. "*Here* he is!" they shouted to passing nurses, other occupants of the waiting room, and anyone who would listen. "See, we *said* he was coming! Whoopee!"

There was no shushing the delighted children, and Alex was adding his share of the noise. The quickest way to restore peace and quiet to the hospital was to get out quick, with our whole family. We did.

Alex cried all the way home, in his basket, wedged in among his tightly packed sisters and brothers. Donny listened to the wails with growing concern, until he could stand it no longer.

"Mama!" he burst out indignantly. "If you don't stop and feed that baby, or *something*, he'll be dead before we get home."

Alex continued to cry most of his first night; then he suddenly decided he liked it with us, and rarely cried after that. He was an unusually amiable baby, cooing contentedly in his crib, watching us out of his mysterious, dark, "slanted" eyes. The children were thrilled with the adventure of a new baby in the house; everyone, that is, except Laura.

Donny volunteered to be the baby-buggy pusher. Susie offered to sing Alex songs.

"I play with baby," Timmy grinned. "Make baby happy."

"I'll find him a nice bug for a pet," Rita said. "But I'll keep it for him until he's older, and won't squush it."

"I'll hold the pins when you change his diaper," Teddy said, "so he won't get stuck."

"I hope he does get stucked," Laura muttered under her breath.

Eventually Laura's feminine and maternal self won out over her jealousy. The daily care of a tiny baby turned out to be full of fascinating details to be watched, and imitated with her dolls.

One afternoon Laura had her doll laid on a folded diaper on the couch. She pretended to give her doll a good dusting from an empty talcum-powder can, while the other small children stood watching.

"You shaking snow on dolly," Rita asked, "like Mama do Alex?"

Timmy chuckled. "*Not* snow. Dat's pepper."

"Pepper's black, silly," Susie said. "Maybe it's salt?"

"You all don't know *anything* about babies," Laura said with motherly dignity. "This here is *telephone* powder."

CHAPTER 9

Farmers in the Dell

WHEN we moved to Forestville, we were too busy to think about putting in a garden, especially with the extra church work at first, then the adoptions of Timmy and Alex.

Finally our budget stared me in the face and I knew that a garden was something more than just a nice thing to have. The time had come when it was a plain, unvarnished necessity.

"We'll simply *have* to raise part of our food," I told Carl, after adding up our grocery bills in a stunned silence. He was earning $2800 a year now. His income had been rising steadily, but the postwar cost of living had risen more steadily.

"Good idea," he murmured. He was working on a sermon.

"The salary doesn't go very far, for nine people."

He shook his head absently.

"The soil here must be rich, because the weeds come nearly to my shoulder. In fact they're so high I couldn't possibly spade them under, myself. So that's where you come in."

"Ummm," Carl murmured, crossing something out and writing furious notes on the next page.

"Everyone in Forestville is putting in a spring garden, already. You ought to get out with a spade, first thing in the morning."

"Sure," Carl said. "Can you remember exactly how that quotation from St. Francis of Assisi goes, something about where there is hatred let us sow love . . . ?"

"I could look it up in a book," I said. "Besides, it would be good exercise."

Carl looked up, puzzled. "Since when is reading a book good exercise?"

"I was talking about you digging us a garden. Where there is hunger, let us sow vegetables."

"Oh," Carl said. "Oh, the garden. Well, don't fret about it. I'll get to it, when I'm not so busy."

But Carl continued busy. Sunday services at two churches, pastoral calls in the homes, membership-training classes, evening discussion groups, choir practice, potluck dinners, church socials, committee meetings, official board meetings — was there no end? The weeds in the back yard continued to flourish, and so did our grocery bills.

"If you could just start the spading," I said wistfully, "I could be planting seeds."

"We'll dig the ground for you, Mama," Donny volunteered.

"Just give us a shubble," Teddy said.

"You children may use the shovels in the garage," I said. "But you couldn't possibly turn the ground over, if Mama can't."

The next time I looked, the children had a hole five feet deep beside my clothesline post, where the weeds had been

tromped down. The clothesline post gave a sigh and top-
pled in.

"But you children have to keep digging *sideways,* not
straight down, if you want a garden," I explained. "Anyway, I think this is too big a job for you."

"Anyway, we're tired of digging," Donny said, and they
all drifted off, leaving the shovels scattered in the weeds.

Like the little red hen, I decided to do it myself. After
my first back-cracking day, I had but one row turned
under, and planted to radishes. The next day I was inspired.
Instead of bothering to spade under the weeds between my
rows, I would skip along and just dig the actual rows
needed for planting. I planted a strip of carrots that day.
The next day, two feet down in the weeds, I spaded another
row and put in corn. During the succeeding two weeks I
planted more corn, three kinds of squash, bush beans, leaf
lettuce, Swiss chard, beets, and turnips. When all my seeds
were in, I dropped the spade, hoe, and garden gloves in the
corner of the garage, took my last soaking bath, stuck Band-
Aids on my blisters, and decided that if I ever looked at a
garden again it would be too soon.

A month later, Carl stopped in the middle of a beeline
to the church, and did a double take. At first glance, the
back yard seemed to be nothing more than the same old
weeds. Then he noticed, in the narrow ribbons of earth, in
the bottoms of the sunless weed canyons, long wavering
rows of pale sprouts.

"Mama's garden," Teddy explained.

"Purty, hmmm?" Timmy added.

"Pretty neglected," Carl sighed. Not able to bear the

sight of anything helpless, tiny, and in need, he returned to the house and changed into overalls. In a few days, the whole back yard was turned under and neatly weeded. We had a real garden at last.

Little brown Teddy was Carl's right-hand man in the garden. He liked to water the seedlings with his sprinkling can. One day he told Timmy, "I'm playing God. I'm making rain for all the thirsty plants to drink."

"How they drink?" Timmy asked. "I don't see they got any mouth."

"You don't unnerstand because you only two years old," Teddy said. "When you four years old like me, you unnerstand things."

But even Teddy found some things hard to understand. When trucking the weeds off to the compost heap in his wagon, he asked Carl, "Why you pull them out, Daddy?"

"They crowd out our vegetables," Carl told him. "They keep out the sun and hog all the water. They won't let our garden grow."

Teddy squatted back on his heels and shook his head. "I don't think God ought to make weeds. I think God make a mistake."

Donny was conspicuous by his absence when weeding was done.

"I'll dig him his own patch," Carl said. "Maybe planting his own garden will awake his interest."

Offered a choice of seeds, Donny chose popcorn. He planted it in a rocket burst of high enthusiasm, telling us how we would all enjoy bushels of hot, buttered popcorn that winter.

The family garden was watered by a large, central sprinkler, but Don's plot was off to itself.

"You'll have to bring the hose over there," Carl told him. "Your garden will need lots of water during the hot summer."

Donny watered his garden faithfully for three days, and then forgot it. Scorching heat, and no water, produced a sad row of very stunted cornstalks which bore no ears. Late that fall, in a cold November rain, Carl saw Donny in raincoat and boots, out in his garden sprinkling the yellowed stalks with the hose.

"What in the world are you doing?" Carl called from the window.

"I forgot to water my garden," Donny shouted. "I'm trying to make my popcorn grow."

Rita found our garden more intriguing than Donny did. When Carl was hoeing, she followed behind and collected the slugs that turned up. Carl thought she was helpfully dumping them into the incinerator, but actually she was collecting them in a tomato can for pets. While I was hanging up the wash in the side yard, Rita went upstairs to play. Half an hour later I heard her sobbing in the kitchen. I came in and took her in my arms.

"I guess something bite her," Timmy commented.

"What?"

"Dunno," Timmy said. "Something bited me and I squash him, and he got green guts."

"No," Rita sobbed, "that's not it. All my baby-snails-withouten-any-shells, they all gone. I leaved them here onna kitchen table in my can, and now they all runned away."

"Your *slugs?*" I stepped back, skidded on one, and my arms and legs flew up while the rest of me whammed down.

"Mama, quit," Rita squealed. "You walk on one, and now you sitting on one."

The slimy creatures had left silver trails winding all over the kitchen. We tracked them down, under the tabletop, shapelessly inching down the table legs, heading for stove, sink, and dining-room door. Rita grinned, forgot her tears, and gathered her pets back into the can. For two days I moved warily in the kitchen, never knowing what I might step on, or discover in my sugar bowl.

Our two floppy-eared cocker spaniels were almost as destructive to our garden as Rita's snails. They solemnly watched me plant a row of potato pieces, then dug them up and ate them. Dogs are not popularly supposed to be fond of vegetables, but ours were. Patsy, the humble little freckled blonde, would not have had the sense to snitch if big red Rufus had not shown her how. Rufus figured that if people could eat out of a garden, he could. He had always considered himself to be a people, anyway.

"See that Woo-fus?" Timmy pointed out one day. "That bad doggy eat up all our dinner."

There was Rufus, trotting delicately through the garden, stopping now to nimbly bite off a tender, green cucumber, next to detach the juiciest red tomato from the vine, and finishing with nibbles from the berry bushes. Patsy followed ten paces behind like a Chinese wife, following his example.

Since these uninvited guests in our garden were really part of the family, we didn't resent them. Not the way we did the parasitic rats which lived off the sweat of our hoe. When the unwelcome vermin moved into our house, we resented them even more. They migrated to us from the barn next door, a quaint, tumble-down structure on the opposite side of us from the Lodge Hall. When the barn was torn down in the interests of sanitation, the rats came over and took up housekeeping in our walls. We didn't realize we had new boarders sharing our roof at first. Walnuts began to disappear from a box on the back porch, but we didn't guess.

"You children might get sick," I said, "if you eat too many walnuts."

"We're not eating extra," Donny said. "Just the handful you give us every day, that's all."

We harvested a bushel of small tomatoes, which I stored on the back porch until I could can them as juice. These, too, quickly disappeared.

"You children are liable to get tummy-aches," I warned.

"Not eat many," Timmy said, his round face solemn. He counted on his fingers. "Only one, four, two."

This obvious understatement I attributed to an inability to count. But next a sack of wallpaper paste diminished, fast. The children looked blank. "Not us," they said patiently.

The next morning I went to the back porch to wash the dirty clothes, which I soaked overnight in the laundry tubs. A suspicious gray lump floated in the water. Carl fished it out by the tail.

"We have rats," he said. "I'll go buy some poison."

The next afternoon, Timmy burst from the bathroom, his pixie eyes almost round. "There's a *skirrel* in there!"

"Couldn't be a squirrel," Donny said. "Squirrels live in trees."

"Sure, really, honest," Timmy said breathlessly. "A real live squirrel. He chew a hole inna wall and poke his head out the hole, and he wiggle his *whiskers* at me."

Carl found a fresh hole in the wall beside the bathroom window. "That was no squirrel, Timmy," he said. "That was a rat." He went for a tin lid, to nail over the hole.

Donny was busy examining the hole, and Timmy tried to peek in, too. "What's a rat, Donny, what's a rat?"

"A rat?" Donny threw out his hands, searching for words. "Well, it's sort of like a mouse, only more."

Carl nailed on the lid, then put poison out under the house. It didn't seem to diminish the rat population, though, as the walls grew noisier and noisier every night. One pair of rats had an apartment about two feet left of the place where our stovepipe entered the dining-room wall. Nightly scuffles, with angry low squeaks and high piping squeals, indicated that the relationship was not too happy. Periodically one threw the other downstairs, with a bumpetty, bumpetty, bump all the way down between the studding, ending in a dull thud behind the baseboard.

The last straw came the morning I went to get Alex up from his basket in the corner of the living room. There was not only a new hole in the living-room wall, but fresh tracks around the baby's basket and across his blue blanket. I snatched up Alex and called for Carl.

"Put out some more poison," I cried. "This is too much!"

"This time I'm getting professional help," Carl said, reaching for the phone. "It was bad enough having them invade the garden. When they take over the house — !"

The exterminator arrived and did his job. That night, and every night afterward, it was quiet in the walls of the old parsonage. No more tails lashed on the thin wallboard. We heard no more squealing and patter of rodent feet, and we didn't even miss the quarrelsome couple which had lived two feet left of the stovepipe.

When I tried to be a farmer, I fared much worse with the chickens than with the garden. My poultry fiasco began when somebody gave us a fat red hen which Carl didn't have the heart to kill. We kept it for a pet and it laid an egg or two, then seemed to lose interest. The trap was sprung when I was passing through the Sears, Roebuck store in Santa Rosa, and was drawn into the farm department by the irresistible peeping of a new batch of baby chicks.

Wouldn't the children be thrilled with these, I thought.

A salesman appeared at my elbow, beaming. "Can I sell you some of this fine, healthy stock?"

"How would I raise them?" I laughed. "I haven't any incubator, or whatever it takes. And no extra money to buy one."

He pursed his lips. He was trying to be very helpful. "Perhaps you could borrow a good broody hen from a friend?"

"I already have a hen, but I don't know if she's broody," I said. "She looks like she's brooding about something."

He demonstrated. "Does she sit on the nest a lot, and go around *cluck-cluck-cluck-CLUU–UUCK*, like this?"

I looked at him, surprised that he would know. "That's exactly what she goes around saying."

The salesman beamed. "A good broody hen could raise at least eighteen for you, and no trouble with temperatures or thermostats. You'll have some fine pullets for egg-layers, and good eating from your fryers. Would you like eighteen?"

"All right," I said dubiously, showing my lack of sales resistance. "But what if the hen doesn't cooperate?"

"She'll take them," he assured me, counting eighteen yellow balls into a box with holes. "The trick is to put them under her at night, when she's asleep. In the morning she thinks she hatched them."

At home, I opened the box on the dining-room floor and my family clustered around, hollering for turns to hold a chirping ball of fluff. The children were enchanted, delighted, overjoyed.

The old hen was not.

In the chilly night, Donny carried the flashlight, I lugged the cheeping box, and we tiptoed out to her hangout in a corner of the tool shed. Slip the chicks under her while she was asleep? That was a joke. She was wide awake, waiting for us, her battle weapons sharpened, tall and straight on her nest, with her wattles whisking from side to side as she glared from one eye and then the other. Grabbing two chicks, I lifted her wing and shoved them under. One chick escaped, and both that chick and I got viciously pecked in a manner meant to draw blood.

"She's mean," Donny said. "I think we ought to cook her. With dumplings and gravy."

We huddled in the dark, hoping she would go to sleep, but we grew sleepy before she did. Every time I tried to outmaneuver her with a fast shove of another chick under her wing, she outmaneuvered me.

"I'm freezing," Donny complained. "Let's go to bed."

I gave up and left the one chick under the old battle-ax, hoping that he might bring out her mother-instinct by morning. We took the other seventeen rejected orphans back to the house, and I left their box overnight on the gas range. Would the pilot light be warm enough to keep them from dying?

In the morning we awoke to a chirping like a houseful of canaries. All seventeen in the box were popping with life, but the other chick was not so lucky. He had been brutally pecked, kicked out of the nest, and left to freeze.

"You're right," I told Donny. "She deserves to go into the pot for dinner, Sunday."

I rounded up enough scraps of fencing and wire and boards to build a back-yard sunning pen for my orphans. It was chick-tight, but not child-tight. Timmy trotted in for a visit and forgot to shut the gate on the way out. The baby chicks, in all their trusting innocence, fluttered out to see the world. The children dashed to the rescue, helping me round them up. The two flap-eared cockers helped too, but only a few puffs of yellow down remained of the six they retrieved.

Every night the remaining eleven had to be rounded up and put into their box over the pilot light on the stove. Curiously enough, they thrived. The children were delighted to see the white feathers sprouting on wings and tails.

Then came the day it rained.

"Hey, Mama," Timmy shouted. "All our chickies, they turning into baby ducks. They swimming!"

"Goodness gracious," I exclaimed. "They'll drown, they'll die of pneumonia!"

We put on raincoats and rescued our crop of future egg-layers from the puddle in their outdoor pen. In the house we took towels and dried their tiny feet and draggled feathers. I put them in their night box and stowed it up on the shelf over our old-fashioned, uninsulated hot-water heater, which was going and would keep them warm. An hour later I noticed that the door to the heater closet had been shut, in spite of my solemn warnings to everyone to see that it stayed open. I threw open the door, pulled down the box, and yanked off the lid. Steam rose from the overheated inside; half the chicks lay on the straw, horribly still, and the rest drooped on their legs, panting.

"Give them water," Donny said anxiously. "They look thirsty."

We dipped their beaks into a cup of cool water, then had to tip their heads back so the water would run down their throats. We fluffed their feathers and blew cool air in their faces, kept dribbling their beaks through more water and holding them up when they were too weak to stand. Eight of the eleven pulled through. The next day Rufus dug under their pen and brought the number down to four.

"You won't get any eggs from this batch," Carl said. "Your four survivors are all roosters."

"I've got a rooster egg," Timmy said. He pulled a large, smooth stone from his pocket.

"Roosters don't lay eggs, son," Carl said.

"If a *Easter bunny* can lay eggs," Timmy challenged, "a rooster could lay eggs, if he wanted to, I betcha."

"That nuisance of a Rufus," I muttered, glaring down at the red cocker, who had the impudence to stand in front of us wagging his stubby tail for approval. "If he only could have left those chicks alone, I might have had some laying hens out of all my work and worry."

"Rufus does have his faults," Carl admitted, "but he loves the kids. You know, he's a pretty good dog, down underneath."

Our son bent over on his sturdy legs and inspected the underside of Rufus. "I think he looks better on the top," Timmy said.

Our little illusion that we were farmers in the dell might have been maintained, if it weren't for the Lodge Hall being in our dell, too. This brought city sophistication, noise, glamor, and secondhand parties into our otherwise quiet existence.

At night, the children could watch the festivities going on in the lighted Lodge Hall across the narrow side yard. Unfortunately, these fascinating doings began after the children's bedtime. Whenever things quieted down so I could coax them to leave their windows and go back to bed, the music would flare out again in a *tum, te-tum, te-tum, te-tum* that crashed down the scales with the irresistible appeal of a Pied Piper's flute. The children would leap out of bed and dance like elves and fairies in a moonlit ring, scattering only when my feet were heard on the stairs.

"That's what *they're* doing, marching all around," Donny explained. "Only they don't have fun, like us. They don't laugh."

The secondhand entertainment would have been bearable, if it had not been for the secondhand refreshments that went with it. Soon after we moved to the parsonage, I heard the children playing tea party outside on the morning after one of the Lodge Hall doings.

"I got a piece of bun," came Laura's voice, distinctly.

"There's a wienie inside *my* bun," Teddy boasted.

"Who wants mustard?" Donny asked. "I got half a bottle."

"Look at all the beans on my plate," Susie piped up.

"I'll trade you a bite of this brown cake for a bite of your pink cake," Rita was wheedling.

The aura of reality was too great for mere make-believe. I hurried outside. Behind the Lodge Hall, on the edge by the parsonage yard, I found an oil drum overflowing with boxes and paper plates from last night's refreshments. The children were sitting in a circle under a tree nearby, delicately cleaning the remains from the party plates. I had a long, quiet talk with them about germs, sanitation, and nice manners; then we collected and burned the rubbish.

When parties were especially noisy, I usually remembered to grab a match and beat the children outside in the morning. The quieter parties became my downfall. The next morning I would hear through the kitchen window the high, childish voices.

"Good jello, hmmmm?"

"Mine's soupy, but I got a cherry floating."

"I like this cake with the little white worms on top."

"That's coconut. I'll swap for some of this."

Clutching my head, I would dash out with a match. They couldn't really be hungry, as this usually happened after a breakfast that would fell a lumberjack. The challenge of a picnic, plus the irresistible lure of a grab-bag, drew like a magnet. It was the kind of fun they never forgot. Even last week, several years after we moved from Forestville, I overheard them reminiscing.

"Remember at our Forestville house?" Teddy asked. "Where they had that big barrel, and every once in a while it was full of *perfeckly* good food people just threw away?"

"We took our plates around behind the church and hid in the bushes," Rita said, "so Mama wouldn't burn them up."

"Once Daddy looked out the church window and saw us," Timmy giggled, "and spanked all our bottoms."

"Yeah," Laura drooled. "Once I had cherry pie with mustard."

"Mama kept saying there was germs in that food," Susie said. "But I never saw any."

"Yeah," Donny said dreamily. "Those were the days."

CHAPTER 10

Growing Pains

OUR Forestville house was uncomfortably over-crowded. We were too many fish for the fish bowl when we moved there; with Timmy and baby Alex added to the family, there wasn't room to flip around. So Donny had the perfect solution.

"What we need around here," he began, "is a boy — "

"We have a boy," Carl interrupted. "As a matter of fact, at my last count we had *four* boys, to say nothing of three girls."

"I'm not talking about girls," Donny protested. "What we need is a boy — "

"The RIGHT SIZE OF *ME*!" Teddy, Laura, Susan, and Rita shouted, as they stood on the stairs in their pajamas.

"No," Donny said, tears misting his blue eyes. "*You* all got each other the size of, but it's me who needs somebody the size of."

"Alex hasn't got nobody," Teddy said.

"Alex is too young to care." Donny turned his head and his voice choked. "But me, I'm lonesome, and I care."

"You've found a lot of friends in the second grade," Carl pointed out. "And I'll bet none of the boys you know has a brother just his exact size."

"One boy is twins, and he's the happiest boys I know," Donny said. "Besides, nobody my size lives close enough to play with."

I kissed all the children and started them up the stairs. "Bedtime, now. We can talk about this another night."

"We got room," Donny said. "I could squeeze over and let him have half my bed."

"You go off to sleep," I said, "and forget it for now. Mother and Daddy will talk about it later."

When the children were all tucked in, Carl said, "What's there to talk about? It's out of the question, and you know it."

"Getting another boy? When you first told me about Alex, I thought another baby was out of the question. See how wrong I was?" I grinned and chucked him under the chin. "Now maybe *you* could be wrong."

"Sure," Carl hollered. "Just ask anybody, and they'd tell you I was a piker with only seven children. Get eight children, and *then* I can do a good job in the church — make more calls — preach better sermons — get more adult discussion groups going — "

"Now that you bring it up," I agreed, "it might help a little that way, too. Donny's at loose ends, always keeping the household in an uproar with his mischief. If he had a boy his size, like when we had Taro — "

Carl went through the motions of tearing his hair, which wasn't long enough to tear. "Oh, fine," he raved. "I'm already swamped with responsibilities, so you know how to lighten the load. Just take on another responsibility. That makes sense."

"People need more than just sense," I said indignantly. "They need hearts, loving hearts. And it isn't just our welfare I'm thinking about, or Donny's. Somewhere there's a lonely kid whom nobody wants. I've got a *feeling* he's somewhere, just waiting for our letter to come, saying we want him."

Carl pulled me down on the couch beside him. "I like your enthusiasm, Helen, and your big, unsensible, loving heart. But you'll have to face facts."

"When I die," I said clenching my fists, "I want to feel that the world is even a slightly better place, because I lived in it. Is that conceited?"

"Not particularly. That's the way I feel, the way most people feel."

"Well, why should I even bother to clutter up the earth, unless I intend to do everything I can, within my ability? I don't mean just to do a few things that I can do without any sacrifice or trouble to myself, but *everything —* "

"Christian living takes on another dimension, besides just the quantity of things done," Carl said, unfolding my tense fingers. "There's a quality dimension, too. We might adopt twenty children, and then not have the time or money to really help any of them. I feel a tremendous responsibility toward the seven we have."

"Heavens, not twenty!" I said. "Only eight, that's plenty. One more, the size of Donny. We could manage one more if we wanted to — you know we could."

"I don't want to," Carl sighed, "but I will. This one, last time, I will."

I wrote letters again. We didn't hear of any children

needing adoption, but we were told about two little Indian children in a nearby town, who needed a boarding home immediately. It was arranged that they would come to our house for a week end visit, first.

Toby, the little boy, was the same age as Rita; his cousin, Rose-Marie, was almost as old as Donny. When they arrived, with pajamas and extra clothes in paper sacks, Donny was so delighted he bounced all over the house like a slap-happy kangaroo. When he calmed down long enough to tell Rose-Marie his plans for the week end, he discovered she had disappeared. He found her under the walnut tree in the side yard playing dolls with Laura and Susan. Toby had joined Rita and Timmy in a game of blocks in the living room.

Donny drifted disconsolately back to the yard, lonely as a cloud. He picked up a feather by the chicken pen and stuck it in his blond hair. His second grade was studying Indians at school, so his mental image of a teepee was undoubtedly more authentic than the shaky structure he decided to build of sticks and old canvas. He fastened his feather more securely with a red strip of cloth around his head, and began whooping around a make-believe council fire. The girls left their dolls and came over to investigate the racket.

"This is my teepee," Donny explained, blue eyes earnest. He touched his makeshift war-bonnet. "I'm an Indian, an honest-to-gosh Indian."

"Oh," the Indian girl said, fascinated. She ran into the house, her jet-black pigtails and ruffled gingham dress flying behind her. She came back, pulling her little copper-faced cousin by the sleeve of his cowboy shirt. "Hurry up, Toby," she hollered. "Come on out and see an Indian, a real, live, honest-to-gosh Indian."

Even Carl was won over by Toby and Rose-Marie. Although red tape kept them as county wards at present, they might in the near future be legally free for permanent adoption. In the meantime, they needed a home which would care for them. Before we could do this, our home had to be licensed by the county as a foster boarding home. Having your own children, either natural or adopted, didn't automatically qualify you to be foster parents, also.

When the county welfare worker came to inspect our house, she didn't have to bother with a tape measure. She merely handed us a mimeographed list of requirements for a county boarding-home license, specifying the number of cubic feet of air space needed in each child's bedroom, the number of square feet of window space in proportion to floor space, and other miscellaneous rules such as single beds for each child, only two children to the room, the type of plumbing and heating required, and so forth, for three closely typed pages.

"We can easily see," she told us, "your house does not have even adequate bedroom space for the seven children you already have, much less for the two more you want."

"If we could add on another room somewhere," I pleaded, "would our house pass inspection?"

"It would depend on the size of the room. You could fill out a new application, after making any changes." She shrugged. "There's the matter of bathrooms, too. You should have at least two baths, with a proposed family of eleven. I couldn't be happy about your present situation of only *one* bathroom, and so *far* away from the bedrooms."

I couldn't be happy about our present situation of only one bathroom, and so far away from the bedrooms, either; but there wasn't much I could do about it. It was a long trek downstairs, and through many dark rooms, with sleepy children at night. The location was embarrassing, too — right off the kitchen and but one short step from the back door which received all our visitors.

One afternoon, after a hard workout in the garden, I was taking a blissful soak in the tub when Timmy flung open the door.

"Here she is," he said over his shoulder, "in here."

I couldn't blame Timmy. After all, the man had knocked on the back door and been quite specific when he asked, "Where is your mother, sonny?"

Another time Carl had forgotten that a church committee was meeting at our house. I was taking a bath when I heard people start knocking at the back door. There I was, trapped with nothing but a sheer nightgown at hand. I should have tapped on the door right then and shouted, "Hey, Carl, will you get me my bathrobe?" I didn't, because I didn't know it was a meeting and I thought the visitors would soon be gone. When the minutes had dragged into an hour, I was too embarrassed to make my predicament known. The men in the committee had parked around the kitchen table, right outside the bathroom door, and I was trapped like a coon in a tree.

Carl got caught once, too. There was a middle-aged spinster in our parish who had taken a great fancy to Alex.

I couldn't blame her for that, as Alex was both handsome and lovable. He was like an Oriental doll, with a cheerful round face that was almost more concave than convex, ivory-tan skin, and intriguing black eyes that crinkled into slits when he laughed. Alex's friend began dropping in regularly about ten every morning, to watch Alex splash and chortle in the tub.

At this time of day, Carl usually was busy in his church office. One morning our whole family got a late start. We had been up until midnight with a young-adult discussion group the night before; Carl continued to stay up until the wee hours of two or three, to make out some church reports. At ten in the morning, I was still upstairs making beds. Carl was in his shorts, shaving, when the bathroom door flew open.

"Yoo-hooo! Is my favorite boy in here?" our daily visitor caroled out, as usual.

"Try another door," Carl said, his face as red as his beard gets to be, when it grows out, and shut the door firmly in her face.

An extra bathroom upstairs would have been a blessing, but there was absolutely no extra room up there.

"Besides, this house isn't worth adding on to," Carl said, working his foot out of a hole where the front porch had just given way beneath him. We were out there trying to figure how we might add another bedroom to the house.

"Couldn't we at least enclose this with some of that plastic screening?" I asked. "You know, like they use to let sunshine into chicken houses?"

Carl took two more steps and another dry-rotted board gave way. He pulled his shoe from the hole and moved gingerly around the porch. "It's a good thing nobody uses the front door, here. I suppose the floor might stay in one piece, if I covered it with the linoleum rug from the dining-room floor. . . ."

After two months of sparetime work, using plastic screen and scrap lumber from the pile behind the garage, Carl had a new front entrance and an extra bedroom built from the old front porch. I papered the room with some cowboy paper found at a paint-store remnant sale, and finally the room was ready to show the county welfare worker.

She checked the area of bedroom space and shook her head. "Your house still has a long way to go, to reach even minimum standards, and there's also the lack of adequate bathroom facilities."

After she left, I threw up my hands. "All I wanted to do was to help two little kids. With all these investigations, I begin to feel as if I were wanted by the FBI."

"You'd better start worrying about the seven children you've already got," Carl said. "Leave well enough alone. And leave me alone, too, so I can get more church work done."

In June, Carl attended the annual conference at Stockton. When he returned, he threw his arms around me. "Start packing, Helen. At least your housing worries are solved. The bishop has sent us to Boonville. It's supposed to have one of the few *big* country parsonages in the California-Nevada Conference!"

Our new church was in an isolated valley, not far from

Forestville, but accessible only by a narrow, winding road through unspoiled and almost uninhabited mountain scenery. Originally an area of pioneer sheep ranches that sprawled up into the hills and mountainous hinterland, it was now equally dependent upon lumbering as a local industry. After a recent boom, sawmills had sprung up around Boonville like toadstools after a rain.

Our new parish was a remnant out of the Old West, with dates on the gravestones going back to the gold-rush days. You never saw high-heeled shoes, fancy hats, or gloves worn on the street, unless by someone who had just come into the valley — or who was on the way out. As a matter of fact, there was only one main street, with partial sidewalks, and a general store which sold everything from woodsmen's tin helmets to cheese, yard goods, and fish hooks. Most of the women who had the figure for it, and some who didn't, wore jeans as the traditional shopping costume. It was friendly and informal, and I loved it.

I loved our new parsonage, too. There were only two bedrooms downstairs, but there was a large, unfinished area with a half-bath upstairs, and there was a back porch big enough to divide into two extra bedrooms. I did a twirl around our new living room and landed in Carl's arms.

"They can't object to our taking those two little Indians now," I said.

But the two little Indians had already found a temporary home with an Indian family. This family was also interested in adopting the children, if they should become free. Since Carl had already given the go-ahead on Toby and Rose-

Marie, I decided I had better get some letters out immediately and find a substitute child, before he changed his mind about a family increase.

A week later an air-mail letter arrived from Hawaii.

"We are sorry we do not have an older boy to be your eighth child," the agency wrote. "However we do have two little half-sisters who badly need an adoptive home. Even here in liberal Hawaii, it is quite difficult to find homes for children of mixed race. Elaine, five years old, is Japanese and Balinese on her father's side, and her mother was French-Irish. Diane, a year and a half younger, has the same French-Irish mother, but is Chinese, Hawaiian, East Indian, and Malayan on her father's side. Although they are lovable youngsters, they have been up for adoption ever since the younger one was born."

I showed Carl the letter. "It seems as if God meant for us to take both of them."

"All right," Carl said. "Shove the responsibility for this off onto God."

"You were willing to take two Indian children. What's wrong with taking in two little Hawaiian children? They need a home just as much. Even more, now."

"I don't know where we're going to sleep nine children, even in this house," Carl said. "I suppose we could divide up the upstairs and the back porch. Maybe I can get Dad to help."

It was lucky that Carl was the son of a carpenter. His folks stopped work on their new home in Santa Rosa, to come up and help with our remodeling. They were staying with us when the agency sent photographs of our daughters-to-be, so we could recognize them when we met them at the plane.

"Aren't they pretty?" I said to Carl. "Look at those lovely Balinese eyes Elaine has. And Diane looks like a Hawaiian doll."

Carl nodded, and passed the pictures on to his father. "They look like Dosses, too. What do you know!"

"And just what *does* a Doss look like, any more?" his father wanted to know.

When we finished the remodeling, we had four small bedrooms upstairs, papered in blue for the girls, with bunk beds built in under the eaves. Alex had a circus-patterned nursery at one end of the back porch. The larger addition to the back porch was transformed into a double-bunk room for Donny, with cowboy and Indian wallpaper.

The children were bursting with excitement on the morning we were to leave for San Francisco, to meet Diane's and Elaine's plane from Hawaii. We planned on an early start, so we might spend a few hours at the zoo in Golden Gate park; but by the time we finished breakfast, made the beds, did the dishes, hurriedly swept up the last of the lumber scraps and sawdust, and gathered together the hundred and one odds and ends needed for a trip with small children, it was almost lunchtime.

"Won't it be easier," I suggested, "to eat our picnic lunch right here at home, and let the children have short naps before we leave? Then they wouldn't be so cross by late tonight."

By the time naps were over, and everyone was washed

and dressed again, it was midafternoon. We piled into our station wagon and headed down the road toward San Francisco.

"When we had just one, it took us an hour to get ready to go anywhere," Carl said. "Now with seven children, it takes us seven hours. How long will it take when we have nine?"

"Just be glad you don't have a dozen," I said.

"Don't worry," Carl said. "We won't."

We arrived at the airport with an hour to spare, so we took our time, escorting the children to the rest rooms, watching people buy tickets, savoring the excitement and bustle of arrivals and departures. Two minutes before plane time, we showed the number of the plane to a guard, asking at which gate we should wait.

"You've got the wrong airport, folks," he told us. "That there plane arrives at the *other* one, two miles up the road."

We streaked out of there, Carl carrying Alex and holding Timmy by one hand, Teddy hanging on his coattails. I ran after them, holding Rita and Susie by their hands, Laura holding fast to Susie. We whizzed up to the door of the other airport building, and the girls tumbled out of the car with me; Carl and the boys drove on to park. The girls panting behind, I charged up the steps, through the glass doors, across the circular waiting room, and out the glass doors to the back. I prayed we would not be too late, so the girls would not be even more alone and frightened than they must already be.

First I saw the travelers swarming down the ramp from the alighted silver plane. Then I saw our girls.

I recognized them right away. Elaine, with her silky-straight brown hair swinging, looked around and around with expressive brown eyes that slanted up at the corners. Little Diane, who had wavy brown hair and olive skin, hung to Elaine's hand as someone adrift at sea might clutch a life raft. Even without the pictures, I would have known them, in their spanking-new matched coats, garlanded with leis. I would have known them by the way they stood so lonely and lost in the crowd, their dark eyes searching, searching.

I knelt to their level. "Hello, Diane. Hello, Elaine. I'm your new mother."

They hesitated, their eyes meeting like two startled fawns. Then Elaine smiled shyly and dimples flashed in her cheeks as she said, "Hello, Mommy. I'm Elaine."

Diane threw her arms around me, and the searching look was gone from her eyes. "Are you really our very *own* Mommy?" she asked, with a slight lisp. "Really and always?"

"Really and always," I assured them both with a big hug. "Now would you like to meet your new sisters?"

I had just introduced Laura, Susan, and Rita, when Carl and the boys rushed up. After another exchange of names, the children stood back and studied each other, with the frank, unabashed stares of childhood.

Some of the other lei-decked passengers came by, and Elaine called out excitedly, "We've got a Mommy *and* a Daddy now!"

"Plenty sisters, too," Diane added. "And plenty brothers!"

Falling asleep in the car with the rest of the children on the way home, the two new girls were too tired to be homesick that night. The next day, as long as the sun was up, they were too busy getting acquainted with their new house and family for nostalgia to knock them low; but when dark and bedtime came, tears flooded in a wild hurricane. Hysterical, they screamed for their "Other-Mother," the elderly lady who had boarded them during their long orphan years while the agency was seeking an adoptive home.

"We'll take turns," Carl said. "You rock one, and I'll rock the other."

Finally they cried themselves to sleep. The next day they settled into the routine of our family life, apparently content; but that night, after going off to sleep peacefully, Diane awoke sobbing, "Mommy, Mommy!" When I hurried to her side and gathered her into my arms, she explained tearfully, "I was crying for my *Other*-Mother."

The next week she awoke in the middle of the night again, crying out, "Mommy, Mommy!" as before. I went to her, took her into my arms, and she smiled at me through her tears. "I wanted *you*, Mommy. I got scared, and I wanted you to come hug me some more."

There was one unexpected complication to the adjustment of the two girls to our family. Laura, always a bit jealous of newcomers, and formerly the undisputed Queen Mother of the younger set, developed a bitter feud with the regal-minded Elaine, who had been the reigning favorite in her Hawaiian boarding home. The two would-be leaders spat and clawed like two fighting cats. They couldn't meet in a hallway, or eat across the table from each other, without drawing sparks. Each kept running to Carl and me, bearing tall and spiteful tales against the other.

"That mean old Elaine," chubby Laura would tattle, huge tears rolling down her face, "she tried to take a great, big bite out of me!"

"She hurt me first!" Elaine would accuse, her dark, up-tilted eyes flashing through her tears. "I don't *like* that girl."

The routine of the medical shots didn't help. Every time we adopted children, the state welfare department required that we all be X-rayed and have blood tests.

"But surely those little children don't need to be stuck again?" I asked the social worker. "We just had it done when we got Timmy and Alex. You know our family hasn't contracted anything since then."

She checked her case history on our family, a folder that was beginning to bulge. "I'm afraid we must. See, it's been over a year since the last record of tests, and according to law, there must be new tests within the year the children are adopted."

We made an appointment with our doctor. Psychologists warn that such trips must not be sprung upon innocent children without due advance preparation; this works well for all our children except Laura.

"Tomorrow is the day we go to the doctor for our blood tests and X rays," I announced cheerfully one morning.

"Will that doctor stick a needle in us?" Laura asked, instantly suspicious.

"Well, yes, the needle will make a bit of a prick, but — "

"Why do we have to get a needle stuck in us?" Laura wailed, retreating.

"So we won't get dippy-theria," Teddy said.

"So your face won't get locked up if you step onna nail," Susie added.

"We don't need that kind of shots," Donny said warily, joining Laura. "We had that kind this summer already."

"This isn't the same thing," I explained. "This time the doctor just takes out a tiny sample of blood to make a test. This shows that we're all healthy."

"Like we all hadda have before we could take Timmy and Teddy to the judge?" Donny asked.

Insight lighted Laura's round face, then a black curtain came down as she wheeled and pointed an accusing finger at Elaine. "She's why we have to go to the doctor." Her chin quivered. "I don't like that girl. I wish you'd send that girl back on the airplane."

The rest of the children took the matter philosophically, dismissing it from their minds as they dashed out to play. Not Laura. Like many grownups, she was not one to put off worrying until tomorrow, if she could worry just as well today. She followed me around like a forlorn puppy, sometimes wistful, sometimes defiant.

"Do we really have to ever'body have shots?" she whispered. Then she was shouting. "That old doctor can't have any of my blood. I need it all *myself*."

I took her in my lap again. "Goodness, don't keep thinking about it," I smiled, stroking her shining brown hair. "Sure, you'll get a little prick, but it's over so soon that you'll forget it right away. You remember how it was?"

Laura remembered all too well. She couldn't get it out of her mind. She found a sharp pin and followed Elaine around

with a gleam in her eye; when Elaine taunted her and disappeared, Laura decided to play doctor with her dolls,
jabbing them all viciously in their rubber arms. Even this
was not release enough for her tension. With all her doll
clothes packed in a small cardboard suitcase, she put on her
coat, tucked her favorite doll under her arm, and announced
she was running away.

"I'm going to find a better house, where the doctor won't
stick little girls with needles," she said. "And where there
aren't any mean old girls getting off airplanes to come live
with you."

The frying hamburgers smelled so good, and we were
having tapicoa pudding for dessert, so Laura finally decided
to stay and put up with us. But, after dinner she doubled
over and held her hand over her stomach, rolling her eyes.

"I think I'm getting sick. I think I'll just have to stay
home in bed all day tomorrow."

"Maybe some germs ate your healthy up," Susie said.

"Maybe the doctor will stick a getting-well shot in your
bottom," Elaine said vindictively. "And stick the blood test
in your arm, *too*."

Laura's hand flew off her stomach and she straightened
up. "Probably just ate too much," she said with dignity.
"I've still got my healthy."

The next morning Laura suggested that she stay home.
"I'd probably scream, and it might scare the other children," she hinted delicately.

At the doctor's, the waiting room was stuffed like a
Thanksgiving turkey by the time all of our children climbed
into chairs and reached for magazines. Laura, disdaining

the diversion of literature or pictures, began to whimper immediately. When the doctor opened the inner door, Rita, encouraged by Laura's now open sobs, hung back with wide fearful eyes, while the rest marched in. Always curious, Teddy stood with his short-tilted brown nose against the glass case full of shining scissors, knives and gadgets, completely fascinated. We put him on the table first, because he set such a good example. Although we tried to turn his attention away before the prick, with his scientific mind he had to see exactly how it was done; he winced when the needle went in, but didn't cry. When he was set down, he walked back to continue his study of the instrument cabinet.

We hoped to do Laura last, since she was such a bad example, but her sobs were so loud and poignant, we agreed to get her misery over with quickly. Laura's reaction was the opposite of the rest. She was howling when she went up on the table, but the minute the needle went into her arm, she stopped. When she was set down, she icily withdrew to a stool in the corner, crossed her chubby legs with a lady-like smoothing of her short skirt over her knees, and sat with the haughty look of a queen whose toes have been trod upon by a commoner.

"This does it," I sighed to Carl that afternoon. "Before, we did everything possible to break up this feud between Laura and Elaine. Now, with the added fuel of the shots, I wonder how many years it will be before we can even get them to civil speaking terms?"

They fooled us. That night they came to us, arms twined lovingly about each other, asking if they could share the same room and let Diane move in with Rita or Susie.

We were stunned, as if looking at a mirage. Yet it was obviously the real thing. They pressed each other with gifts of their own favorite dolls and possessions, and went everywhere hand in hand. To this day, we have never found out what caused this small miracle. Did ever-sensitive Laura feel sorry for Elaine when she, too, suffered the needle? Did they reach some kind of spontaneous pact? We could only guess, and then give up. At the time, we were too overjoyed to take any chances of destroying this beautiful thing by inquisitive prying.

A long time later, when the friendship was as solid and secure as the mountains rising behind our house, we asked them what made them decide to stop fighting each other, and be friends.

They looked at us as if we were senile, losing mind as well as memory.

"*Us* fight?" Elaine asked incredulously.

"We're the best friends in the whole world," Laura said. "I liked Elaine the minute she got off that airplane."

CHAPTER 11

The Sky Lark

DONNY isn't mechanically minded, not the way little Teddy is. Still, one summer day when Donny was eight, he had an inspiration.

"Hey, kids," he hollered. "I'm going to build an airplane!"

"A real airplane?" Timmy wanted to know. "A really, really airplane?"

"Sure," Donny said. He hunted up some paper and pencil, climbed up by the dining-room table and started drawing plans, filling his papers with sketches. "This has got to be planned just right," he murmured. "If you want things to work, you've got to plan them right."

"You mean it'll really fly?" Rita asked.

"Why not?" Donny said. "Now you little kids stay back and don't bother me. I've got a lot of work to do."

When the planning stage was over, he stuffed the papers into the hip pocket of his jeans. His brothers and sisters followed him outside, where he began to assemble his materials. He found some apple boxes stacked behind the garage, some lumber on the scrap pile, some discarded wheels from an old doll buggy. He kept running back to the house asking for "some string, please, good *sturdy* string," "some wire about as long as from here to there," and "some good, tough nails that won't bend when I hit them."

The younger children scurried around, hunting up required parts, asking endless questions.

"Can people ride in it?" Rita wanted to know.

"Of course," Donny said, hammering.

The children started jumping up and down, clamoring for turns to ride. "All right," Donny conceded, "I'll give each one of you a ride."

"How many can go at once?" Teddy asked.

"Well, it all depends," Donny said, "on the size I make it."

"Make it big enough for all of us to ride at once," little Timmy hollered.

"Yes, yes!" Teddy, Rita, Elaine, Laura, Susan, and Diane echoed, while Alex, who didn't talk yet, jumped up and down in the general excitement.

"All right," Donny agreed. "I'll make it big enough for everybody."

"Where will we fly?" Teddy wanted to know.

"Let's fly over the ocean and say hello to my Other-Mother," Diane said.

"Okay," Don said. "We'll take our first trip to Hawaii."

A destination picked, everyone began preparations for the trip. Diane had a new dress she wanted to take back to show the Other-Mother. Laura had a doll that would cry if it were left behind, some doll clothes to be packed, and a supply of her fanciest handkerchiefs to be tucked in her purse.

"Is Mama going?" Timmy asked.

"We'll take her next time," Donny whispered. "This time we're going to be *care*-free."

"The lady on *our* plane gave us food to eat," Elaine hinted.

"We'll pack up some sandwiches," Don said. "We can eat those while we're up in the air."

"How about when we get there?" Teddy asked. "We'll be hungry again."

"Don't worry," Diane said. "We'll eat pineapples. And pick bananas off the trees."

"And coconuts," Donny said learnedly. "And we'll all drink coconut milk."

"How will we get them open?" Timmy asked.

"We'll get a hatchet," Susie said, "and hatch them open. Don't worry."

When noontime came, the pilot and his passengers settled on an unglamorous glass of ordinary cow's milk to tide them over, and decided to eat the sandwiches they had packed. The made a picnic out of it, sitting in a big circle under the aromatic bay tree.

Timmy, staring intently at his sandwich, murmured, "Hey, there's a bug on my lettuce."

"Couldn't be," Donny said, "I washed it good. I'll have to train one of you to be my navigator."

"I want to be the alligator," Diane said.

"There is too a bug on my lettuce," Timmy said.

"Not alligator," Donny said. "Navigator."

"There is too a bug," Timmy insisted.

"It's probably just a speck of dirt," Donny said. "I guess I'll have to read the maps myself, because I'm the only one who can read."

Timmy was still staring at his sandwich. "Well, it's *crawling*," he complained.

A number of changes had to be made during the afternoon. A heavy cardboard box, once used for shipping a chest of drawers, replaced the apple boxes for the cabin. "This will hold more people," Donny said, cutting out windows on the sides with my kitchen paring knife.

Rita looked at the contraption with a cautious skepticism. "I'm not going," she said. "It might get bust."

"Not a chance," Donny assured her. "Not the way I make it."

"Yeah," Rita said, tossing back her jet hair, "but what if the bottom falls out, right when we're over the ocean?"

"Don't worry so much. I'm making it properly sturdy."

"I don't trust it," Rita decided, starting away on her slim, brown legs that never seemed to touch the ground. "I'm going to catch me some grasser-hoppers." Suddenly she jumped back. "Hey, what's this bug? Hey, Donny, what's this bug? Is it poison?" Her fingers were poised to catch it if it weren't.

"That's a dragon fly," Donny said.

Timmy, studying the insect, said, "What does it drag? I don't see it draggin' anything."

"What do you kids want to monkey around with dragon flies for?" Donny said. "You just stick around me, and you can fly better than any little old bug."

"When we're going over the ocean, I'm not going to look

out the windows," Susie said. "I don't want to get dizzy and fall out. I can't swim."

Teddy said, "Hadn't we better practice a little bit, before we try such a long trip?"

"We might," Donny said. "If we get through early to-night, we might fly straight up in the air and *hoover* around over the house for a day or two, first."

Late that afternoon, Teddy canceled his reservation. "You haven't got any motor in it," he said, his brown face screwed up as he squatted down to view the assembly. "I don't see how it's going to work."

"It's going to work, isn't it kids?" Donny said.

The rest of the loyal passengers, minus Rita who had gone off bug hunting, gave loud cheers of approval.

"Anyway," Teddy said, "I think I'll stay home. I got some other things to do."

"Hey, you can't back out now," Donny begged, scratching his blond head. "I'm *depending* on you."

"What for?" Teddy's large brown eyes were wary.

"To help me fly it."

"How?"

"Well, I was going to have you sit in the middle, and flap the wings," Donny said. "I was going to get Timmy to sit behind you and work the tail part."

"That's not the way airplanes fly," Teddy said. "They have motors, and the motors make the propellers go round."

"Not *this* airplane," Donny said. "It's going to fly like a *bird*. Birds don't have motors. They flap their wings."

"I'll be your ground crew," Teddy compromised. "I'll

help you take off, and I'll signal you in, when you come home."

When it grew dark, the children didn't want to come in to supper.

"We'll be leaving pretty soon," Diane said.

"Mama, why don't you pack us some sammitches to eat on the plane, for our supper?" Laura wheedled, dimples in her round cheeks, her arm and Elaine's mutually around each other's waists.

"Mama's dinner smells good," said Elaine, more to Laura than to me. "I think we all ought to go in and eat one last dinner with Mama, before we go. We might not be seeing her for a while."

"You might miss the take-off," Donny warned, "if you're in the house when I get the plane finished."

"Why don't you all come in," I suggested. "You could eat a hearty meal now, and finish the plane in the morning when it's light."

"Well," Donny admitted, "I still *do* have a lot of work to do on it."

"Besides," I added, bringing the strength of my adult reasoning to bear on the subject, "you'll all need a good sleep before you go. There won't be room for all of you to lie down and sleep on the plane."

"That's right," Elaine pointed out. "It takes lots and lots of hours to fly across the water to our Other-House."

So everyone came in, ate the hearty supper, and scooted off to bed, chattering about the fun they were going to have on the trip. A storm blew up in the night, and the play yard turned into a lake. Donny's cardboard fuselage disintegrated amidst the debris of boards, nails, string, wire, and doll-buggy wheels. In the morning the children ran to the windows and pressed their noses against the glass, staring out at the rain. Some of the smaller ones looked disconsolate.

"Well," Donny said, with a philosophical shrug. "It's a good thing it fell apart now, and not when we were about a thousand miles up in the sky."

"Are you going to build another one, Donny?" all the kids wanted to know.

"Oh, sure," Don said. "Maybe I'll wait till next year when I'm older, and I can learn how to make a more *durable* one out of metal."

"Yeah," someone sighed.

"That is," Donny added, with a trace of wistfulness, "if I don't have too much sense by then."

CHAPTER 12

All God's Children

OUR children never thought of themselves as looking particularly different from each other. One day, when Donny was eight and Alex a year old, Donny crouched on the floor to encourage his little brother to walk. Alex reached out both hands, took a hesitating step, and tumbled into Donny's arms. The high-pitched baby giggle interlaced with the hearty boy-sized chuckle, then Donny looked up at me, blue eyes wide and sincere under his thatch of blond hair.

"Mama," he said, glancing fondly at the Oriental ivory face beside him, at the black appleseed eyes that crinkle into slits when Alex laughs, "if he was seven years older, and if I had black hair, everybody would think that him and me was twins!"

They felt that much alike, our children, and often they took it for granted that this alikeness would show. Naturally they could see that there were minor and inconsequential variations, that Rita had "the blackest, shiniest hair," that Teddy could toast browner in the sun than the rest, but persons bearing such unearned distinctions were polite enough not to gloat. There are only two times I can remember when differences within our family seemed to be of any concern, and then, each time, it was only because a small child developed a sudden fear that a minor dissimilarity might be a physical handicap to the bearer. Once Teddy looked into the mirror at his own brown eyes and then studied Donny, solicitude puckering his face like a walnut.

"Donny," he asked, "how can you *see* out of blue eyes?"

Also there was the early-winter day when Timmy watched Carl trim brown spots from apples with the point of a knife.

"Why you do that, Daddy?" he asked.

"Bad spots," Carl said.

Later I noticed Timmy staring at me, his usually frolicking brown eyes now worried. "Daddy gonna cut pieces out of you?"

"Heavens, no," I laughed. "What made you say that?"

His fingers slid gently over the freckles on my arm. "Bad spots," he said.

It is the outsiders who imagine that our family is made up of incompatible opposites. Those who have never ventured beyond the white bars of their self-imposed social cages too often take for granted that a different color skin on the outside makes for a different kind of being, not of necessity completely human, on the inside. Granting the usual personality range found in any blood-related, racially identical family, some strangers go far beyond this and expect to find amongst *us* the lamb lying down uneasily with the lion.

Even college graduates with a supposed cultural breadth have made boners, each of which would have been hilariously funny if it were not such a pathetic exposé of the boner-maker, and, indirectly, the boner-maker's society.

Otherwise well-educated persons are always asking if it was hard to teach our children to speak English, and I have lost track of the number who have asked, even when Alex was still on Pablum and a nursing bottle, if we had to feed him chop suey!

One day a woman teacher sat in our dining room, watching our children eat. The younger ones, on nursery chairs and homemade stools made of orange crates, sat around a large table cut down to their size. All the children were shoveling in their food with the usual gusto, except Rita, who is so full of bounce and mischief she cannot sit still even at mealtimes. She kept cavorting about, doing everything except turn cartwheels on her wooden box, shiny black hair swinging, obsidian eyes dancing.

"Sit up and eat, Rita," I said.

Rita turned right-side-up, pulling a mournful cloak over her brown Mexican face. Rita clouds up like a quick summer rain when she is reprimanded.

"How can you expect her to be interested in something so foreign to her nature as lamb stew?" the teacher asked. "Don't you realize she craves *chili* beans and hot *tamales?*"

I didn't hurt the good lady's feelings by pointing out that when I did cook beans, Rita was the only one who didn't want chili in them. An American baby raised in a Mexican peon's hut would talk and act in a typically south-of-the-border way, while a baby of any nationality or race growing up in an American-culture home would be as completely American as hot dogs and ice cream.

Some of the skeptical find it hard to believe that people

of all races are born with the same kind of vocal chords for speech, the same kind of taste buds in the tongue, the same type of digestive apparatus capable of assimilating a wide variety of foods. Differences between national or racial groups are mostly just differences in culture. It is not heredity but a cultural pattern that makes the British love their royalty, the Chinese reverence their scholars, and the Eskimos relish partially decomposed and frozen raw fish. Cultural mores, not genes, determine the language we speak, our notions as to the wearing of a sarong, a kilt, or a stuffy business suit, and whether or not we think it polite to belch after a meal.

We try to explain these things, whenever we think the backs of the misinformed are strong enough to bear the truth; but the boners go marching on. One afternoon a businessman was talking to Carl at our front door. Rita whizzed down the driveway sloping from the church to the road, made too sharp a turn and flew off her trike, landing square on her nose.

"Wow," Carl said, poised to take off at the first wail from down below. "My daughter took quite a spill."

But there was no wail. Teddy was beside her in an instant, helping Rita brush herself off. They giggled as both hopped back on their tricycles and sped off around the circle drive again.

Carl relaxed and smiled. "I thought she was going to yell her head off from that bump. She's a tough little kid, though, and a good sport."

The man shrugged. "Actually, coming from such primitive stock, she couldn't possibly have felt it the way a *Caucasian* would have. I doubt if her nerve ends are very highly developed."

Primitive nerve ends! Our children don't need the studious anthropologists and ethnologists to tell them that such fantastic notions are hogwash, because they already know that people are more alike than different; nor do they need the proof of microscopes and IQ tests and statistics covering years of careful research, to believe that modern science finds no race superior to any other.

These scientific ideas are not new. Nearly two thousand years ago, the same thing was said in a different language, "God hath made of one blood all nations of men, for to dwell on the face of the earth." East may be East and West may be West, but the twain *can* meet and get along with each other, when each looks the other in the face and admits the truth we find in the Bible: God is the Father of all mankind; we are all God's children, and all men are brothers.

Why do people refuse to believe this, singling out certain portions of their fellow men to hate, to discriminate against, even to persecute?

First, prejudice is a contagious disease, as easily caught as measles, the babe from his parents, the school child from his playmates, the adult from his fellow workers and neighbors. To compound the social tragedy, prejudice once caught is hard to cure, since it unwittingly serves a number of morbid purposes. When a man is picked on by his boss, he can slam home and take it out on his family, and frequently does; however, a more socially approved outlet is to turn around and release the feelings of hate and anger on those of a minority racial group. If denied certain yearned-for opportunities and privileges, there is a devilish quirk within man which gives him perverse satisfaction in seeing that at least one segment of the population enjoys even less opportunities and privileges than he.

If a person feels socially or mentally inferior, has a persecuted feeling that society is crushing down on him, it is easy to bolster waning self-confidence by convincing himself, "At least there are whole *groups* of people socially, mentally, economically inferior to me." Worse yet, he will try to keep minority groups in a deprived and subjugated position, to prove what his ego wants to believe.

Psychologists and psychiatrists have long told us that bottled-up feelings of aggression and anger can be dynamite to the happiness and well-being of the individual who refuses to recognize real causes behind his maladjustments. Multiply these fearful and emotionally tense individuals by thousands, by even millions, and you have social dynamite. If people can't fight their personal frustrations directly, let out their angers in socially healthy ways, they will fight something else. Hostility will be exploded in any area where society permits it; there is no choice. If these virulent emotions were not released, they would destroy the individual from inside.

War has always been a socially glorified outlet for pent-up angers and frustrations of whole peoples. In America, our Negroes have provided another scapegoat, and so we have had race riots, Jim Crowism, and the Ku Klux Klan. On the West Coast first the Chinese, then the Japanese, provided another handy outlet for our inner tensions, and we have had discrimination in jobs and housing, an Orientals Exclusion Act, and the "relocation centers" of World War II.

What can we do about it? There is no easy answer, no quick solution. Civil-rights legislation, while no cure, can alleviate some situations, like the clean slash of a surgeon's knife to cut away festering flesh. Education, through books, magazines, newspapers, and the public schools will help. But, in the long run, we can never eliminate race discrimination, as we can never eliminate war, until a controlling number of the world population is composed of more emotionally healthy and mature individuals.

If we can help our children to become emotionally mature, they as adults can add to the happiness of the world — rather than subtracting from it because of inner compulsions to hurt others.

Also, in the meantime, Carl and I must prepare our children to stand up in the face of prejudice. We know they will someday share the fate of many Americans who, like Taro's father, are sometimes forced to live on the edge of danger because their skins are dark or their eyes "slant." Even harder to bear will be the daily hurts and petty discriminations, the snubs and innuendoes, the caustic remarks of the cruel or unthinking. Although our friends and neighbors and church congregations have leaned over backward to show affection to our dark-skinned youngsters, these halcyon days cannot last when adulthood approaches. The more secure and happy their childhood can be, the more they will be willing to try to understand, even pity, those who would hurt them. Above all, we will encourage them to develop one of the best defenses they can have — a sense of humor.

Teddy was the first of our children to be wounded by the barbs of prejudice. The incident caught us by surprise, because Carl and I did not foresee such a thing happening to any of our children until they were at least ready for high school. No occasion had ever suggested that a specific inoculation would be needed, at so tender an age, against the infection from such wounds; perhaps the complete acceptance of our children had lulled us into thinking the halcyon days might last longer than we first thought. Certainly, up until the day Teddy started first grade in Boonville, his playmates had been quite unconscious of color differences. Just a few weeks before school started, a little neighbor his age came running into our yard.

"Teddy," she gasped, "you know that house in back of us?"

Teddy nodded.

"Guess what! There's a Filipino moved in there, a real, brown *Filipino*. My mother told me. Her name is Tomasita, and I saw her. Do you wanna see a real Filipino?"

"Sure," Teddy hollered, his brown Filipino face popping with curiosity, and they ran off hand in hand to get a peek.

Since Boonville is a logging boom town, a large number of migrant families have crowded into the tiny shacks around the sawmills. Many have come from parts of the country where considerable resentment exists against Negroes; because of educational and cultural limitations, and the insecurity of their lives, some of these migrants were outspoken in their prejudice. It wasn't that the loggers and millhands didn't make substantial wages in season — they usually drove good cars or squandered unbelievable sums at the noisy bars — but they were restless and rootless in their work, and mere spurts of money cannot bring peace of mind.

Many of the local schoolchildren were from these lumbering shacks, and they mirrored, without thought, the prejudices expressed in their homes. We found this out when Teddy, Elaine, Laura, and Susan started to school. On that important first day, the four six-year-olds joined Donny at the bus stop in front of the church. They danced off to their new venture as eager as their fourth-grade brother; but it was different when they came home.

"How was school?" I asked. "And where's Teddy?"

"He's crying by the church," Laura said, tears of indignation in her eyes. "Those were real *mean* girls, and they shouldn't have said that to Teddy."

"Some girls we don't know called him names," Susie added. "They did it and *did* it."

"Out on the playground they kept yelling, 'Little *nigger-boy*, little *nigger-boy*,' till the teacher came out and made them stop," Elaine said.

I found Teddy under a bush at the far side of the church, sobbing his heart out. I sat down, took him into my lap, and dried the tears from his brown face. Running my fingers through his silky-straight dark hair I told him, "There's nothing wrong with being a Negro, and only very rude people call them 'nigger.' The trouble is, there are so many people think they hate Negroes, and usually it's because they are all mixed up inside and hurt about something. So it makes them feel like being mean. And then, because they are so mixed up, they think they hate anybody who has brown skin or different eyes, like you. When children shout names at other children, they just repeat things they heard rude and mixed-up grownups say."

"Oh," Teddy said.

"What these people don't know," I went on, "is that God made more dark-skinned people than any other kind! He made Filipinos — like you. And Negroes. And Hawaiians like Diane, and Orientals like little Alex." I hugged Teddy. "So I think God must *especially* love little brown children."

Teddy looked up, relieved. "I think I'll go play, now."

I took his hand. "Come in the house a minute, first. Mama wants to show you something."

We didn't have a globe, but I found a National Geographic map which showed the Philippines, far away in the blue Pacific Ocean. "Here is where some of your ancestors came from," I said, "and someday we hope our whole family can get on a big boat and sail all the way across this ocean, so we can visit there." Then we took out a picture book, telling about different peoples around the world, and found some familiar pictures of Filipino children. "Remember when we talked about these before?"

Teddy nodded, with a shy smile. "You said they looked like me. I guess I forgot."

"That's right. And now I'll tell you a secret *my* mother once told me, when I was little. If somebody calls you a name, and you cry, they have power over you. All they have to do is call you that name, and presto! They can see you cry! I'll tell you how to fool them."

His chocolate eyes were round. "How?"

"Laugh," I said. "Laugh right along with them, and make a big joke out of it. Then they'll either leave you alone, or else they'll make friends with you."

"What'll I say if they call me little nigger-boy again?"

"Just laugh, and say you guess they don't know very much. Tell them you're an honest-to-goodness, *real* American Filipino boy." Teddy knew a nursery song about a little brown Teddy bear. We sang it together. "Teach the other children that song, if you want. Tell them if they want to call you something, to call you brown Teddy bear."

When Donny arrived home later, on the next school bus, he was disturbed by the stories the first-grade girls babbled to him. To make sure that Teddy's ego was completely solaced, he gathered the children together in the yard, Teddy in the place of honor beside him. I could hear Don's high, earnest young voice through the open dining-room window.

"Would you kids like to hear a story a man told me when I was the size of Teddy?" he asked. "It's about how God made Filipino people, and all the rest of the people in the world."

There was a chorus of assent.

"Well," Donny began, "God was out in his kitchen making gingerbread men. He made their little eyes, put on a nose and a mouth, and stuck them in the oven. When he took his first batch out he looked at them and said, 'My golly, these got burnt!' So that's exactly how he happened to make Negroes."

"Didn't it hurt them to get burnt?" Timmy asked.

"Naw," Donny said. "Not the way God did it. He blew his breath on them, and they turned into real, live people, and he loved them anyhow. So then he decided he wouldn't make the same mistake. So he pulled his kitchen stool up and sat right by the oven door, and just baked the next ones a *little* bit." Donny paused and looked around solemnly. "That batch was half-baked, and that was me."

"Gosh," Diane said.

Donny put his arm around Teddy. "But now God caught on about how to do it, so he made Teddy and all the Filipino people last, and *they* were nice and brown, and just right!"

Teddy came home from school happy the next day.

"Everybody likes Teddy," Elaine reported.

"Yep," Laura nodded. "Teddy's the favorite."

"All the girls fight for turns to teeter-totter with him," Susie said.

The next week I saw the first-grade teacher at P.T.A. meeting.

"Your little Teddy is a charming boy," she said. "In spite of getting off to a hard start, he already has become one of the most popular boys in the room. And do you know what? I don't know how it started, but they all refer to him affectionately as *Teddy bear!*"

CHAPTER 13

Little Beaver and the War Orphan

THERE were two other children we almost adopted. One was an Indian boy named Little Beaver; the other was a European war orphan.

After Diane and Elaine joined our family, some of my query letters were still being passed from one orphanage director to another. One June morning the following year, the letter arrived about Little Beaver. That wasn't his real name; he had been the youngest in an Indian mission school, and the nickname given by the older boys had stuck.

"In most of his eleven years," the letter informed us, "this boy has not been able to make a good adjustment, due to unfortunate situations in his life. He has retreated within himself, become morose and a problem child. We have heard that you were looking for a boy of minority race to adopt. At present he is not free, although we hope to complete legal action sometime in the future which will put him in the adoptable category. In the meantime, we wondered if you would like to have him at your house for a summer-vacation visit? Even a short time spent away from the scene of his latest problems might give him a new start toward facing them."

When I hurled myself up the picturesque and rickety outside stairway to Carl's office above the little church kitchen, and waved the letter breathlessly under his nose, he just laughed.

"Silly girl," he said, reading it and pushing it aside for the plans he was drawing up for an Every-member Canvass. "You get the funniest ideas."

"Well, can we?" There was no answer, so I pleaded, "Well, can't we?"

Carl looked up as if he were surprised to see me still standing there. He made a vague motion, as if he were brushing away a disturbing fly. "Of course not." He frowned. "Didn't we agree to stop at nine?"

"But this is just for a short visit," I said. "If he becomes adoptable later, we can cross that bridge when we come to it. In the meantime, he's just a poor kid who needs a summer vacation."

"If I were sure it would end there," Carl sighed, looking around at the work he had stacked up to do, "I'd be out with a brass band to welcome the little fellow."

We met Little Beaver at the Ukiah airport; we didn't have a brass band, but our nine children made a noisy-enough substitute. He didn't look very little, either, although he did look uncertain and lonely as he stood beside the plane, clutching two cardboard suitcases.

Donny bounced up, full of welcome.

"I'm Donny," he said. "Gosh, you're a lot bigger than

me, aren't you? You get to sleep in my room, because I got two bunks. Do you hope someday you'll come back to stay, and be my brother? I sure do, boy, I sure do!"

Little Beaver only scowled.

On his first day with us, which happened to be Sunday, he announced that he had ten dollars in his wallet and was going downtown to buy a knife.

"I've been promising Donny a jackknife," Carl said. "Tell you what. You can save your money, and I'll buy you both one."

"Don't want any little old jackknife. I want to go down to the store and buy me a six-inch hunting knife."

"You can't shop today," I said with some relief. "All the stores are closed."

He acted as if he didn't believe me. He just stood there scuffing his toe in the gravel, his face a thundercloud.

"What do you need a long-bladed hunting knife for?" Carl asked gently. "Aren't you a bit young for that?"

"Maybe I'll decide to go hunting while I'm here. I ain't too young. *All* the guys at the mission got hunting knives, real long sharp ones, too."

"I'll give you a jackknife," Carl said, "and we'll see how you handle that, first."

"Wish I was back to the mission," he griped, "where they let a guy do a few things without asking."

Little Beaver did quite a few things without asking, anyway. One day a good-sized box of apples disappeared from the pantry, and that night I had two big boys groaning with stomach-aches. The cores had been neatly stored between their Sunday shirts in the drawer. The next day I smelled smoke coming from the boys' back-porch room, rushed in and found Little Beaver tearing pages out of Donny's good books, lighting them with matches snitched from the kitchen. Both boys had holes burned through bed sheets and blankets. Another five minutes and they would have burnt the house down.

The last straw was when the little children kept appearing with knives. I came around the corner of the house one day and found Timmy with a knife held experimentally across Alex's throat. I snatched the knife from him.

"Timmy!" I gasped. "What's got into you?"

"Li'l Beaver gived me the knife," Timmy said innocently. "He told me when I want something, stick it in the other guy's neck and say, 'Give it to me, or *elst!*'"

Later that night, I confessed to Carl, "I give up. We'll have to send him back right away. I wanted to give him a nice vacation — but I can't take it, and it's just too risky for the other children. I shudder to think what else he has up his sleeve."

"Tomorrow I'll have a talk with him," Carl said. "Let's see if we can't just keep a closer watch. As long as he's here, we ought to see if he can't have a summer to remember."

"For me, this will be a summer to remember," I said. "That's for sure."

"Just give him plenty of love while he's here," Carl said. "That's what he needs more than anything in the world. Plenty of uncritical love."

Carl went out to make some church calls in Boonville and Philo. I tucked the children into bed, then climbed into my own bed with some books I'd been wanting to read.

About an hour later I began to get a peculiar, uneasy feeling, and I couldn't keep my mind on my book. To reassure myself, I threw on robe and slippers and tiptoed out for another look into the big boys' room. The light was on and the room looked as if a tornado had whirled through it. The two bunks were empty. Little Beaver's two suitcases were gone, some of Don's clothes were missing, and a few of Little Beaver's least-liked clothes, including his Sunday suit, were strewn about the floor.

Running from the house, I called, "Donny! Don-ny, Little Bea-ver!" I tried to convince myself they were just playing some game. Had they decided to camp overnight in the tree-house? I climbed the swaying rope ship's ladder hanging from the wide-branched madroña. When my flashlight swept over the rough boards of the tree-house floor, I felt a chill that was more than the night air; I knew they had run away.

Where could they have gone, at that hour of the night? There was no police station to call. Boonville was little more than a wide place in the road, nothing but a few grocery stores, bars, and gas stations huddled on the highway which wound through the long, lonely valley. It was thirty miles by highway to Cloverdale, and nineteen miles over the rugged mountain road to Ukiah, with scarcely a house on either road — just barren hills and timbered mountains where deer and skunks roamed, and no telling what other wild life.

I kept calling, praying that Carl would hurry home. I didn't dare go far from the house and leave the other eight small children alone, yet with every passing minute my worry grew. While I shivered and called by the roadside, heavily loaded logging trucks went thundering past on night runs from the mills. If nothing else happened, what would keep the boys from getting run over on the narrow road? When our station wagon finally swung into the drive, I ran to it with relief.

"Carl! Donny ran away with Little Beaver!"

He was poised for action, yet calm, as he always was in an emergency. "How long have they been gone?"

"At least an hour by now. Maybe more."

"Now stop worrying," he said. "I'll go look. They can't have gone far. Perhaps they were intrigued by one of the bars downtown. Those places always have people and jazz and light spilling out. It might look good to a couple of lost boys, after wandering in the dark."

His car backed out in a spurt of gravel, then I saw his lights go slowly down the street toward town. Every hundred yards he stopped, put his head out of the window, and called. Finally his car was lost in the night. I paced up and down again, trying to probe the molasses dark with my flashlight, shouting the boys' names over and over until my throat hurt. The minutes crept by, each seeming like an hour, and a half hour like a whole night. Suddenly there was a noise down the drive.

"Mama?" It was Donny's familiar, high soprano. "Mama, Mama!"

My flashlight beam picked up two boys trudging toward the house, each dragging a bulging suitcase. I ran to them, gathering them both into my arms. "I'm so glad you came back. We missed you."

"I missed *you*," Donny said, hugging me. He was trying to act very grown-up and brave, but I could feel that his cheeks were wet, and he was trembling. "Little Beaver wanted me to go back to the mission with him, and so I said I'd go — just for a *visit*. We were going to take a short cut over the mountains, but we couldn't see, and there were all kinds of scary noises, and I was afraid there might be bears and lions!" He gave me a big kiss. "So I decided I'd rather stay home with you."

The phone was ringing, so we all hurried back to the house. As I picked up the receiver, I heard Carl's voice. "Helen? I'm going to call the county sheriff's office, then I'll — "

"Carl, Carl!" I cried, "they're here! Hurry home."

We all had hot cocoa to warm us before going to bed, and Carl talked to Little Beaver about running away.

"You don't need to run off in the night," Carl said. "If you decide you want to go back before your vacation is up, just come tell me. I'll buy you a plane ticket, or take you back myself, and that's a promise." With a resigned look at Donny and me, he turned to the boy kindly. "We even thought that if you liked it here with us, you might be able to come back next year — to stay."

Little Beaver squirmed and mumbled. He admitted he liked Carl and me, and Donny was okay, but he definitely didn't like anything else. California was too hot, and he'd rather live where it snowed. He hated going to church on Sundays, and he didn't want to be part of any old preacher's family. Neither did he like all the "little ole kids always hanging around," and he definitely didn't want to be in any family where he was the oldest.

"Up to the mission, I'm the youngest, and I get to do everything the big guys do," he informed us belligerently. "Carry knives, and everything."

However, he did have a compromise in mind that might work. Carl could give up being an old preacher, give the little kids away, and go up to the Pacific Northwest where Little Beaver had an uncle who was a chief. Carl could join the tribe and be a chief, too, and I could be his squaw. We'd live in a tepee and have free salmon-fishing rights on the Columbia, and he'd teach Donny how to be a good Indian.

I wasn't even tempted.

The rest of the month might have been a vacation for our problem-child visitor, but for me it had the nervous suspense of living beside an erratic time bomb. Finally it was time for Little Beaver to go back. Carl was elected delegate to the Methodist Town and Country Conference back in Iowa; he planned his train trip so he could detour north and drop the Indian boy off at the mission.

Little Beaver had actually learned how to smile, by the time he left. Waving good-by to the rest of us, he grinned and said, "You all come up and visit me, sometime, at the mission!"

Carl mailed me a letter while on the train.

"I'm having the dickens of a time trying to keep track of Little Beaver," he wrote. "He keeps trying to elude me. Every time he does, I find him at some souvenir counter in a train station, about to buy a couple of wicked-looking knives. So far, I think I've succeeded in getting him to save his money until he gets back."

A week later I had a letter from the superintendent at the mission.

"I thought you might be interested to know," he wrote, "that the Indian boy who spent his summer with you is making a wonderful adjustment since his return. His vacation has given him a new self-confidence and something to talk about with the other boys. He has begun to make real friends for the first time in his life. In view of his excellent adjustment now, I wonder if he is as much in need of adoption as we first thought? At his age, and being so self-consciously Indian, he might be better off to finish his teens here with us, where he can continue in an Indian atmosphere."

A postscript was added across the bottom. "You will be surprised and amused to know that his suitcases were found loaded with knives. We had to confiscate these weapons, since we have always had a rule here that our boys may not carry knives."

In the same mail I received a letter from a German woman doctor. I had written an article about our "International Family" in 1949, when we had only six children; it had appeared in the *Reader's Digest*, and had been reprinted in a number of the foreign editions of the *Digest*. The doctor had just run across one of these copies, and the *Reader's Digest* had forwarded her letter telling of her hopes that we might like to adopt a part-Negro war orphan.

"The child is pretty," she wrote, "with a medium-dark skin color, and wavy dark hair, not kinky. I think it is in America she should grow up, where there are other people of dark skins, like I read are children in your family. Over here, so different she is, people stare, and that is not good."

The child's mother had been German, blond and blue-eyed; the father was a Negro American soldier, who at one time had been stationed in the area. The child was being cared for by the orphanage which this doctor served.

Already, at four, little Gretchen knew she was different from the fair-complexioned children in the orphanage, and it worried her. "Wash me clean, so I will be white like you," she often pleaded with the nurses when they bathed her.

This last Christmas, the matron had asked Gretchen what she wanted most for Christmas, and the little girl had replied, "White stockings. White, not black ones, so my legs will look white."

When Carl returned from his conference, I showed him the letter. I was caught off guard, with an armload of unused arguments, when he surprisingly agreed we should take her.

I threw my arms around him. "You darling! With you, I never know what to expect! I thought this would be another knockdown, drag-out fight."

Carl admitted, "I've had a secret hankering to adopt a child with Negro blood." He laughed, and added, "See, I know better, but I get in a rut with the same old unscientific terms. As if *blood* could be Negro, or white, or any such nonsense."

"It never particularly mattered to me what race or color our children were," I said. "After we got them, they always seemed like Dosses."

"The same with me. On the other hand, I've been getting sick and tired of people saying, '*But you wouldn't take a child of Negro blood!*' You know, in all kinds of tones, according to whether they're conservative, or radical, or just curious."

"I know," I said. "Some people act very noble about our Oriental mixtures, but they draw the line there. So they exclaim in pure horror, 'Of course you wouldn't take a child of *Negro* blood?'"

"Yes, and then there are the liberal fanatics who act as if we had just gathered this family together as a cold-blooded social experiment, a sort of laboratory of racial relations. So they say accusingly, 'But I notice you *haven't* taken a child of *Negro* blood.'"

"Oh well, pooh," I said. "Let people talk. Somebody will object, no matter what we do."

"There's just one thing — " Carl began.

"What?"

"We're stopping with ten, after we bring Gretchen home. If you sprout one of those perennial ideas about adopting any more, we *will* have that knockdown, drag-out fight you were looking for."

A friend of ours, nicknamed "Mrs. Pickles" by the children, sometimes drove up to Boonville for a visit. We told her about our plans to adopt Gretchen, and proudly showed the snapshots which the doctor sent in her second letter.

"Isn't she a darling?" I said. "We are anxious to get her over here as soon as possible, so she can start learning English."

Mrs. Pickles looked at the photos suspiciously. "How do you know she's not part nigger? She looks pretty dark to me."

"She *is* half Negro," Carl said. "But she's also half white. So she ought to fit as well into our home as in any."

"Really, Carl, you can't be serious!" she exclaimed. "A nigger child? The good Lord made them to be slaves, and not on the same level with us."

"The good Lord didn't make them slaves," Carl corrected. "He created all men in His own image."

"They still come from slave stock."

"Here in America, many of them did," Carl said. "And that's probably where that inferiority myth started. Back in the Roman days, slaves were of all colors and races, according to the fortunes of war. The American slave owners had more sensitive consciences than the old Romans, and they sensed that slavery was morally wrong. Something had to be said to answer their critics — and their own uneasy consciences as well. So it was rationalized that it wasn't a sin to buy and sell blacks for work horses, since they were an inferior race, a sort of subhuman group, and therefore couldn't be considered as fellow human beings. This nonsense was repeated so constantly that people came to believe it. In fact many still do today, in spite of scientific proof that it is *not* true."

"Well, are you quite out of breath?" Mrs. Pickles yanked her knitting out of her bag. "When I want to be preached at, I'll go to church."

Carl shrugged, smiling. He was used to these verbal fencing matches; the two of them often went round and round on their differing interpretations of the Bible. "We Americans can't keep one tenth of our population in an inferior position, just because their ancestors were once enslaved," he reminded her, "and still be a healthy democracy. It isn't Christian and it isn't democratic, and most of us claim to be both."

"That's radical talk." She jabbed into her yarn with her knitting needle. "Real radical talk."

"But the whole idea of Christianity is radical," Carl said, looking at her earnestly. "And the whole idea of democracy is radical. Think how really radical it is to say that all men are created equal, and that all men are brothers — and that the individual is important! Everyone goes around crying about the dangers of Communism, but every time one of us steps on someone because of his color, we do as much harm to our country as if we were Communist saboteurs."

"You're wasting your breath," she sniffed. "I'm old enough to know what I know, and I'll believe what I want to believe. A person with honest convictions has to draw the line somewhere." She shook her knitting needle at Carl. "I'm not coming to visit with any pickaninnies. So if you bring the colored child into your family circle, you'll never see *me* back. And that's *that*!"

About that time we began to break the news to both our families.

"Just don't be bringing her visiting to my house," Carl's mother said. "No nigger will call *me* Grandma!"

My middle sister Lynn wrote, "If you think she'll fit happily in your family, I hope it works out. You'd better think of some way to break it to Mom and Dad gently."

My younger sister Jane wrote, "Why don't you wait until you actually get this German child into your home, before you write back to Illinois about this? If it doesn't work out for some reason, you can save the folks from possible grief. P.S. Your new daughter is welcome to call me Auntie!"

We had filled out the releases and affidavits and forms which the doctor sent us, and they had been air-mailed back to Germany, where they were approved and signed by the village magistrate. When we started writing to American authorities to get Gretchen a quota number, the red tape began to coil around our project and choke the life out of it. We tried to find an American agency which would act as the necessary intermediary in the adoption, but we got absolutely nowhere. The proceedings bogged down under the snarl of immigration quotas and visas and passports, as well as the continued lack of necessary approvals from American officials and agencies.

One day we showed some friends the snapshots of Gretchen.

"You know," one said, "this child doesn't look too strikingly Negro, if you weren't thinking of that. Why not try to pass her off for a dark Spanish girl, or Moorish, or something?"

"Why?" we asked.

"While I don't have prejudice myself," the friend said, "you'll have to admit that many do. Most white communities wouldn't accept a girl of Negro blood into the heart of their social doings, especially after she gets to be in her teens and close to marrying age. There isn't any Negro social group in this town, either. And even if you lived where there were Negroes, how do you know they'd accept her, white bringing-up and all?"

"It's a real problem," Carl admitted. "She might avoid some discrimination, if we labeled her as something else. But secrets have a way of leaking out. If we lied about that one thing, could our daughter trust us about anything else? And what feelings would that give her about her own ancestry? We're teaching our other children to be proud of their whole heritage. Have we the right to make her ashamed to be what she is?"

I agreed. "We'd have to be honest about it. After all, this little Gretchen owes just as much of her beauty, as much of her bright mind and budding talent, to her Negro father as to her white mother."

"It's difficult, in our society, to be half white and half Negro," Carl said. "Someday, if our democracy is to be strong, Negro ancestry will be just as acceptable to the majority as any other. In the meantime, as she grows up, we'll just have to help Gretchen understand the reasons why people nurse their prejudices, the same way we'll try to help all our children understand."

We never had the chance to help Gretchen understand, because we didn't get to adopt her.

Months passed and months passed. The red tape sprouted two new dragon heads for every one we slashed off.

"If we had the money to fly over there and pick her up directly," Carl said, "I'll bet we'd have her here in no time. Nobody explains the delay, but I suspect that much of this red tape is a cover-up. Some of the intermediaries probably object to placing a Negro child in a so-called 'white' home, and just haven't the courage to come out and say so."

The doctor began to worry about Gretchen's chances of

coming to the United States. She wrote, "If to America she is going, as soon as possible it should be, so she can learn the language before the time of starting to school."

Through mutual friends we learned of a warm-hearted young Negro couple who had a boy in second grade at school; this couple had talked of wanting to adopt a younger girl.

"Let's turn our information over to them, and see what they can do for Gretchen," Carl suggested. "You and I might never get her here to America. If it's really the racial angle that's holding things up, they might have better luck."

The Negro couple found red tape, too, but it gradually and miraculously unwound. After a short time they wrote, in a letter shining with quiet joy, that Gretchen had received her quota number; she would be on her way to America on the next plane which carried an extra stewardess.

Gretchen's stocking wasn't hanging beside our tree that Christmas, as we once hoped it would be. Still, we knew that she was hanging her stocking under another American Christmas tree, and that she wouldn't have to ask Santa Claus for white stockings any more. Now she had a father and a mother and a brother, all the same warm toast shade that she was, and she would know that her own color was just right for *her*.

CHAPTER 14

So This Is Life!

LIFE magazine heard about our family through some-one on the staff of the Santa Rosa *Press Democrat*, the newspaper for which I was Boonville correspondent. For the "Redwood Empire" section, I covered such Boonville happenings as auto accidents, school-board meetings, lodge initiations, and the annual Mendocino County Fair and Apple Show.

When Dick Pollard came up from the San Francisco office of *Life*, asking permission to do a picture story for his magazine, Carl and I said, "No."

The article I had written for *Reader's Digest*, back in 1949, had not affected the six children we had then; a pic-ture story in *Life*, we both felt, would be different. The attention of a writer and a photographer focused upon the children would be sure to make them self-conscious. It was enough of a goldfish bowl that they would have to grow up in a parsonage, under the critical eyes of the community.

While Mr. Pollard agreed that our motives were right in wanting to protect our family, he showed the instinctive psychology of a top newsman. He appealed to our sense of social responsibility.

"You believe in what you are doing," he argued, "and so

do I. The idea of the brotherhood of man needs to be preached to the widest possible audience, and as often as possible. Here is your chance to bring the philosophy behind your kind of life to the millions of *Life's* readers."

His enthusiasm was not faked. Recently he had finished some articles in which he had tried to explain the Orient to Americans, and vice versa.

"I wish you could realize how a general knowledge of your 'United Nations' family could help our country! Anti-American propaganda abroad emphasizes our intolerant side. If people in other countries could open a copy of *Life* and learn about your interracial family, they would see our better side, a glimpse of democracy in action."

Carl said, "But a *Life* article would reveal where we lived, wouldn't it? Helen was able to avoid that, in her article for the *Digest*."

Dick Pollard nodded. "We'd have to say that you lived in Boonville. We can't take pictures, and then be vague as to where we took them. Believe me, we have no desire to exploit your family. There would be no sensationalism, just a warm and sympathetic story that would take your ideas to the millions your pulpit can't reach."

Although we finally consented to the story, we still dreaded the ordeal of having our pictures taken. We expected the photographer to be a pompous, high-powered dynamo who would line us up brusquely for pose after pose, while the pot roast burned on the stove and Alex wailed from want of a nap. We thought he would thoroughly disrupt our household and depart in a flurry, leaving behind a litter of flash bulbs and bewildered children.

This didn't happen. On an appointed evening the next week, Dick Pollard again appeared at our front door; he introduced Wayne Miller, his photographer, a young father with several small children of his own. Our children piled into the living room to welcome our company. In five minutes Dick and Wayne were accepted as old friends, and the children were swarming over them like aphids on a rosebush. They were full of questions.

"Where's your mama?" Timmy asked.

This query comes early in any interview with a man, and refers to his wife, not mother. Both men explained that their wives were at home.

"My daddy preaches in a church," Teddy told Dick, "and calls on sick ladies. What do *you* do?"

"I write stories in an office, and I call on people, too."

"What you got in that bag?" Rita asked Wayne.

"Show us," Diane begged.

Wayne took out a Rolleiflex and two Contax miniatures for inspection all around.

"Cameras," Teddy said. "Why so many?"

"I like to take pictures."

"Take some of us!" they all shouted, as they do when I have our camera out.

"Tomorrow, maybe." Wayne showed them how he loaded his Rolleiflex with film, then said, "Tonight, how would you like to take pictures of each other?"

Everyone shouted, "Me first!"

"Calm down," Wayne said. "You'll each get a turn. We'll do it according to age. Alex first, then Timmy. Who's after that — Rita?"

"No, me," Diane said. "I'm bigger but I'm really *littler*."

"Younger," I said. "By four months, only."

"You all watch, now, how I do it." Wayne held the camera down so Alex could squint into the ground-glass view-finder. "When you get the picture you want in here, Alex, then push *here*. The flash bulb will make a big bright light, and then you'll have a picture."

Alex, just beginning to talk and usually shy as a woods creature around strangers, held the camera with a grin across his round, flat Oriental face, his black eyes happy and crinkled to slits. Wayne wasn't like most strangers who, with their patronizing attention, usually sent Alex scooting bashfully behind my skirts. Neither did he stoop to such meaningless questions as, "My, aren't you a nice little boy?" or try the third-degree with, "What's your name?" and "How old are you?" When the visitor's attention was focused upon an activity, the shy one could join the group with all his natural eagerness.

All had several turns with the camera. Everyone jumped about so much, I was sure the pictures would look like blurred snaps of whirling dervishes.

When the children finally were tucked into bed, I said to Wayne, with regret born of years of penny-pinching, "I'm afraid the children wasted a lot of film and flash bulbs."

"No waste," Wayne explained. "I did it on purpose. This should satisfy their curiosity about my cameras. Now I can be around them for several days, snapping candid pictures, without their being particularly aware of me."

The next morning, Saturday, was a warm slice out of Indian summer. It was the kind of day when you want to pack up a lunch and go on an outing, so we did. The children voted to invite their new friends, Wayne and Dick, who were staying at the local motel.

The valley narrowed as we headed west in our station wagon. We wound between towering redwood groves, and the children shouted in delight when they saw a deer standing shadowy and indistinct between the muted shafts of sunlight. The Navarro River was on our left, a quiet remnant of its roaring winter self.

"Let's go fishing, catch a fish," Timmy cried, pointing to the river.

"Can't you read?" Donny asked. "Those signs say *NO FISHING.*"

"How can I read?" Timmy said. "My teeth aren't falling out yet. You can't go to school until you're big enough to have your teeth falling out, your teeth."

"We can fish when we get to the ocean," Diane said. "Maybe we can catch a whale."

"Simple Simon caught a whale in a bucket," Susie said. "Our teacher said so."

"There's no whales in the ocean, are there, Donny?" Elaine asked.

"Sure there are," Donny said. "But you might have to swim out a ways, to get one."

After we left the forests behind, the road climbed toward barren, brown hills. Seeing the scattered sheep grazing there, the children all began singing, "Baa, Baa, Black Sheep," and "Mary Had a Little Lamb." We reached the top of the cliff, and the blue Pacific spread like infinity before us.

"The ocean, the ocean!" the children cried, springing from their seats in delight.

There was no place for a picnic here; the river's alluvial fan was muddy, and breakers crashed against high, rocky cliffs on either side. We turned north along the cliff-top road. Here the only live things were wheeling gulls, lonely sheep, and cypress trees which stretched wind-blown arms away from the sea. At Van Damme State Park, where the road dipped down to a sizable beach, we pulled in and parked.

The children spilled out like marbles from a bag. Fall comes early to the wild, rockbound coast of northern California, so our youngsters had the beach to themselves. They raced up and down the sand, shouted into the sea spray, dug for treasures, collected shells, waded in the chilly surf, and played jump rope with a long, rubbery, tubelike seaweed.

"Wonder what kind of seaweek that is?" Timmy murmured, squatting down on his chubby legs as he tried to peer inside a ten-foot length. "This seaweek looks like our gar-den hose."

Donny said pompously, trying to look very learned, "No wonder. I expect this is where garden hoses *come* from."

Soon ravenous, the children gathered in a circle and cleaned up the sandwiches in their individual paper-sack lunches, then polished off the assortment of fruit and boxes of animal crackers which Dick and Wayne brought.

By midafternoon, Alex's eyes had grown so heavy without his usual nap, he dropped peacefully in his tracks. I covered him with my sweater, shooed the older children farther down the beach, and let him sleep until he awoke, refreshed. The rest kept going with unabated energy, and only the lure of a hot supper at home could induce them to leave at dusk. That night, all were tucked to bed with sand and seaweed still in their hair, and smiles on their faces.

Sunday morning we were up early. Carl carried in wood and lighted the fires at the church, dusted the pulpit and the pews. After changing into his dark Sunday suit, he retreated to his study with his sermon notes. The children, too sleepy the night before for a thorough clean-up, were run through my assembly line in our one bathtub, each scrubbing topped by a vigorous shampoo.

Wayne Miller stopped by the house to ask if he might go early to both churches and replace the regular lights with photoflood bulbs. "The lighting would appear more natural," he explained, "and my picture-taking can be inconspicuous, so it won't interfere with the worship."

When the congregation filed in for Sunday school, and, an hour later, for church, people blinked and commented that the lights seemed somewhat brighter than usual, then forgot them. Wayne used his small cameras unobtrusively. The only reason he was noticed at all was because Boonville is a small town, and in a small town a stranger is as conspicuous as dirt on a small boy's face.

That night Wayne drove with us to Carl's second church at Philo, five miles up the valley. He snapped pictures of Carl's face, earnest and sometimes lighted with humor in the sermon, serene and compassionate in prayer; of the children, singing when they knew the hymns, wiggling when they didn't. Irrepressible Alex, who kept eluding my grasp, toddled full speed up and down the aisles during most of the service.

The next morning Wayne was at our house early enough to catch the children swinging their lunch boxes and sacks as they waited in front of the church. When the school bus came, he hopped aboard with the school children, visiting Don's fourth-grade class, then the first grade where Elaine, Laura, Susan, and "Teddy Bear" were working on their primers and word charts.

The following morning, Carl and I headed a ludicrous procession as we hiked downtown to do some local shopping. Alex bounced along between us, hanging to our hands; Rita, Diane, and Timmy danced around us and behind us; our two cockers trailed behind them, snuffling the ground ahead, occasionally looking back over their shoulders; next Wayne sauntered along, discreetly using his cameras; last came a newsman from the Santa Rosa *Press Democrat*, dodging about in the rear as he sought good camera angles to illustrate a story about *Life* magazine doing a story.

The formal, posed shot of the whole family was the only headache. Wayne decided to arrange us on the wide ship's ladder hanging from the shady madroña in our back yard. Carl and I sat with Timmy and Alex on the huge beam that anchored it across the bottom, while the rest of the family stood beside us or perched above, on the crisscrossed horizontal ropes. Carl had picked up the ship's ladder for three dollars in an Army-Navy surplus store, and our youngsters were always swarming over it; they used it for a jungle gym, a ladder to the tree-house, and a giant swing.

"This is just the thing," Wayne said happily, as he composed his picture. "An unusual background."

Much later, perspiring in a sudden burst of October sunshine, he wasn't so happy. When everyone was in place, Alex would have to scoot off to the bathroom; by the time he came back, someone else would beg to be excused. Some of the restless ones on the higher ropes moved around, and others below them were weeping huge tears and wailing, "She stepped on my *fingers*," or "Make him get off my hair!"

Donny, hanging upside down, finally rebelled. "I'm not staying up here any longer," he shouted.

Wayne wiped his forehead and ran fingers through his hair. He was beginning to look as if he had been up all night. "Just once more, Donny," he pleaded. "Everyone else is ready." But the rest were wiggling and fussing, too. "Look, if everybody would just give Wayne *one* nice smile, it would be all over."

"I'm tired," Laura said.

"I can't snap it now, you're all pouting," Wayne pointed out. "If everybody would just say 'peaches' all at once — "

In the middle of everyone else saying "peaches," Laura jumped down from the swing.

"I don't *want* my picture taken," she said with finality.

Wayne clapped his head. "Laura, honey, you can't do this to me!"

Laura turned her back and sat on the ground. Carl started to exert his parental authority, but Wayne shook his head.

"That's perfectly all right, Laura," he told her with dignity. "Only please move out of the way, so I can snap the picture without you."

Laura, who hates to be outsmarted, hopped back to her place and the camera clicked on a chorus of "peaches." When that picture was chosen to be blown up as the full-page lead picture in the article, Wayne's patience was rewarded. Ours, too, because at last we had a complete family portrait for our album.

It wasn't the only picture we added to our album, as a result of *Life's* visit to our house. After the article appeared in the November 12th issue for 1951, the editors sent us a folio of nearly eight hundred delightful candid snapshots of our family doings, along with numerous enlargements of the best shots.

We nursed a frail hope, when the magazine hit the stands, that if we didn't tell the children their pictures were in *Life* magazine, they would never know it. This bubble was pricked when Donny and I visited my sister Jane. No sooner had we come in the door, than Don's cousins pulled him across their living room.

"Look, Donny!" they both shouted. "We'll show you your picture in a magazine."

Don sighed. "Everywhere I go, people drag that out and show me those pictures. I'm getting tired of seeing those same old pictures. Can't we go out and play ball?"

Later, at home, I cautiously showed the younger children their photographs in *Life.* They weren't particularly impressed.

"These are just like pitchers in our album," Rita said.

Teddy cocked his head, studying them critically. "Yeah,

but these aren't so good. They're littler, and they're more blacker and sort of fuzzy. The big ones Wayne gave us are lots better."

"Here's me crying," Timmy chuckled. "That was when me and Diane was fighting, and we had to sit on the step together till we loved."

"There's us playing ring-around-the-rosie on the beach with Daddy," Elaine said. "Let's go out behind the church and play ring-around-the-rosie."

So they ran outside to play ring-around-the-rosie, and I decided I wouldn't be disturbed any more about the effect the magazine article might have upon the children.

There was something about *Life's* article that disturbed Carl, though.

" 'This Christmas the tenth and final Doss child, a Mexican boy, is expected to join us in Boonville, California,' it says here," Carl accused me, jabbing his finger at the article and glaring at me as if I had the tenth and final Doss child hidden in my pocket.

"I can't imagine where they got the Mexican part, because I didn't say exactly that," I said. "I guess I told Wayne and Dick about the eleven-year-old Indian boy we had this summer. And I probably mentioned that if we *could* find one the size of Donny, say about nine years old, we'd love to adopt him."

"How you do run on," Carl said dryly.

"Why Carl! If one turned up, you know, if we just *happened* to discover a boy Donny's right size — why, of course we'd take him. Wouldn't we?"

"Over my dead body," Carl said.

CHAPTER 15

Merry, Merry Christmas

OUR children begin preparing for Christmas soon after Thanksgiving. Christmas carols are sung at the tops of their little leather lungs all day long — while swinging, or bicycling, or making mud pies in the yard; even when they are in bed, long after everyone is supposed to be asleep, we hear strains of "Hark! the Herald Angels Sing" and "Away in a Manger" drifting out of each room in a high-soprano chorus. They wake up in the morning and pile downstairs to breakfast, hollering "Joy to the World."

The air is always full of secrets about who is making what, and for whom. Most of those in school create gifts for mother and father in their classrooms. How typical was that Christmas when our quads were in first grade! They went about giggling behind their hands, warning us that we would never guess what they were making because *they* would never tell.

"It's a surprise," Susie hinted mysteriously, shaking her blond head. "It's made out of clay, but you won't know what it is until you open it."

"Susie painted hers blue, but I painted mine green," Elaine said, her tip-tilted brown eyes shining. "You'll never know till Christmas!"

"You don't smoke," Teddy told us, "but you got to have something to put other people's ashes in when they come visiting. You'll never guess, and we're sure not going to tell you."

"Teddy painted his red, and I painted mine yellow," Laura said archly, wagging a chubby finger, "and are you ever going to get surprised!"

Sometimes they talked about what they wanted for themselves.

"I wish Santa Claus would bring me a *cyclo-peed-jiak*," Teddy said.

"A what?" Donny asked.

"*A cyclo-peed-jiak*," Teddy said. "So I could look up and see how they make things and do things, and how the world was made."

"Oh, you mean an encyclopedia," Donny said learnedly.

"Yeah, like one of my boy friends has at his house. I'd let everybody else look up things if they wanted, too."

"I wish I had a 'lectric train," Timmy said. "But if Santa would even just bring me even a hammer, and a little saw, and some nails, I'd make me a purty good train outa wood, I betcha."

"I hope I get my stocking full of suckers," Diane said, smacking her lips, "and bubble gum."

"Sugar candy and bubble gum makes holes in your teeth," Susie reminded her. "See, you and Elaine got holes in your teeth already. None of us other kids got holes."

"But candy tastes so dishes," Diane protested, her eyes as round as chocolate creams.

"Delicious," Donny corrected. "Daddy said that poison

syrup tastes delicious to little ants that don't know no better, too."

"God's kind of candy is dishes, and won't make teeth holes," Rita suggested to Diane. "Why don't you ask Santa for a stocking full of dates and dried *apercots?*"

"Yeah, and stuffed prunes and raisins," added Susie.

"And walnuts, too." Timmy rubbed his round tummy and chuckled. "And peanuts inside of shells. Oh, boy!"

"Boy, oh, boy!" Alex imitated, rubbing his own round tummy as he jumped up and down.

As Christmas came nearer, the tempo of excitement increased. The children got together in little huddles to discuss the mysteries of the season.

"Is there really and truly a real Santa Claus?" Elaine asked the rest.

"Of course," Timmy said. "I've saw him. Oncst I sat in his lap."

"A girl at Sunday school went down to San Francisco," Laura reported, "and she saw *five* Santas." She looked around solemnly. "All at once."

Teddy scratched his dark head. "Something's wrong there, all right."

Donny looked up from a book. He has the peculiar faculty of being able to absorb himself in his reading, and yet know what's being said when he wants to put an oar into the stream of conversation.

"Those are just Santa's helpers," he explained. "They dress up in Santa Claus suits all over the world, and help out."

"Where's the real Santa Claus?" Teddy asked.

"He's a spirit."

"Like God?"

"Sort of, you might say. Daddy says he's the spirit of giving. When he gets inside you, then you act like a Santa Claus, too."

"How can he get inside me," Timmy asked, "when he's bigger?"

"Well, anyhow," Susie said, "on the night before Christmas, we better leave out a glass of milk and some graham crackers again, like we did last year. Just in case his spirit's hungry."

A week before Christmas, Laura came to me, her grin showing a new gap. She held up a baby tooth, proudly.

"Here, Mama. Put this in a envelope, and send it to Santa Claus."

"Mama," Timmy asked, "why you allus tell the kids to give you their teeth, and you gonna send them to Santa Claus?"

This set me back a little, because none of the older children ever thought to question the method I had worked out for the disposal of baby teeth.

"You know, Timmy. That's so when *you* start losing *your* teeth, you let me send them to Santa Claus, and then he'll put an extra present in your stocking for every tooth you lost that year." I always figured I was safe in this promise, since the children wouldn't know how many little trinkets to expect in their stockings, anyway.

"Yes," Timmy pursued. "But what the gosh does Santa Clause *do* with all the teeth?"

I was caught in the snare of my own fiction. When I was

a girl, a baby tooth put under my pillow was replaced by a dime while I slept, although I did sometimes suffer a crushing disappointment when I forgot to mention my expectancy beforehand. Now that I had children of my own, but very few spare dimes, I had built up the tradition of putting the teeth into any spare envelope, and disposing of it in the round, pseudomailbox at the side of my desk. So far it had worked, made everyone concerned happy, and no one had ever been unintentionally disappointed. Yet now, when Timmy pinned me down, I saw that my unfinished myth had obvious holes in it.

"The teeth," Timmy repeated. "What for does he want all those teeth for?"

Teddy, imaginative little Teddy, saved both the day and the legend.

"Gosh, I'll bet I can guess what he wants them for. That's what Santa Claus's little elves use in his *doll* factory, up to the North Pole. That's what they use to make all the *doll's* teeth, I just betcha."

"Oh," Timmy said. "I didn't knowed that."

The children love the warm traditions of Santa and their own embroidering of the legends; they revel in the fun of tree decorating and the hanging up of stockings. On the night before Christmas they scurry off to bed, pulling the covers to their chins and shutting their eyes tight, hoping to hear the tinkle of reindeer bells.

Still, they do not forget that Christmas is basically a Christian celebration, the birthday of the Saviour.

One of the high points of the pre-Christmas week is

Carl's retelling of the story of the birth of Jesus, from Luke, with the children clustered at his feet. Another high point is the annual Christmas program at the church.

Lit by flickering candlelight and decorated with greens, the humblest country church becomes a reverent sanctuary. The choir sings some of the great anthems, and the Sunday school presents a tableau of Biblical scenes depicting the nativity. Our younger children sit in the front pew, scrubbed and starched, their dark eyes reflecting the shine of the candles. On such a night, even little Alex's eyes seem round. The older ones are in the tableau, as shepherds dressed in crude sandals and bathrobes, or Wise Men draped in discarded velveteen draperies and with striped towels around their heads. My own eyes are a bit misty, as I watch the tableau. I know the great wonder and the singing joy which the original Mary must have felt, upon being given a child to raise.

Also, as I sit in the fragrant and candlelit church, I usually remember another tableau, an outdoor-manger scene which we did at our first church, when Donny was a baby.

Carl had transformed the big, old-fashioned, front porch of our Cucamonga parsonage. By hanging his paint-splashed canvas drop-cloths across the front of the house and around the two ends of the porch, it had become a rock-walled stable. In the center of the porch was placed a crude, hay-filled wooden manger, where Donny lay as the Holy Babe, wrapped in swaddling clothes and spotlighted by a golden beam from above. I knelt by the manger, dressed in pale blue and white as Mary; Carl stood beside us, a regal Joseph in brown drapes and a glued-on brown beard.

Tethered on the porch with us was a small donkey named Pietro. On the lawn grazed some borrowed Persian sheep and lambs, the long-eared black variety which might have been equally at home on the hills of Biblical Palestine. Two laymen, complete with shepherd costumes and crooks, tended the sheep, while our choir sang Christmas carols which were amplified across the broad lawn to the watchers beyond the curb.

The floodlighted tableau lasted three hours at a time, for three nights in a row, during the week before Christmas. It was hard to stand still that long; it was even harder to keep warm when it was so cold, cold enough that smudge pots were kept smoking in the surrounding citrus groves to keep the oranges and lemons from freezing. Since we didn't have a smudge to keep *us* from freezing, we did the next best thing: I added flannelette pajamas, wool slacks, two sweaters, wool socks, and galoshes under my thin costume, and Carl wore his windbreaker and hiking boots under his.

Donny was warm enough, down in the hay with the swaddling sheets wrapped around his wool snowsuit, but he kept rebelling because he couldn't sit up and point at the cars which drove up and parked in a continual procession. I had to keep singing and stroking his head so he wouldn't let out a lusty yell. He also had a feud with Pietro, who insisted on chewing the hay from Donny's manger, and ignored the large amounts of hay piled in all the corners of the porch. Donny would try to kick the donkey in the nose with his swaddled foot, and the donkey retaliated by trying to nip his foot. The feud lasted all three nights.

The genial Italian who owned the donkey didn't come

for him until after New Year's. By that time, Donny and Pietro had overcome their earlier mistrust of each other. Pietro would trot obligingly around and around on the circumference of his tether, while Carl held little Donny, chuckling, on the donkey's back.

Although by next Christmas Donny was two, and a little big to look like a baby, we thought it would be nice to repeat our outdoor tableau. When we approached the owner of the donkey to see if we could borrow Pietro again, we found we were too late. Donny's old feuding friend had just been ground up and made into salami.

"My family, we lika that kinda salami best of all," he told us. "The donkey, she maka the best kind."

He offered to prove his point by making us a salami sandwich. We thanked him politely, and a bit sadly, excusing ourselves on the grounds that we really weren't hungry. In view of our memories of last Christmas, it just didn't seem right to eat Pietro.

The most unforgettable Christmas, embellished with fanfare and hullabaloo and an unexpected deluge of gifts, was when we were chosen the "Christmas Family of 1951" by a coast-to-coast radio program.

Since we almost never had time for the radio during the day, we didn't know about the NBC "Welcome Travelers" program, and its contest for letters to nominate families "best typifying the Christmas spirit the year around." One day in December there was a long-distance call from the producer of the program in Chicago. He explained the contest and told us a letter about our family had been chosen from thousands to be one of the ten which would be read over the air, competing for the grand prize. A lady in Michigan, a complete stranger to us, had written her letter from information garnered from the *Life* magazine article. Her nominating letter won a wrist watch for her, an apartment-sized food freezer for us.

We were surprised and happy about the freezer, but we did not give the program much thought after we hung up. Our friends were more excited.

"We were listening to the letter they read about you on the 'Welcome Travelers' radio program!" one after another called up to say. "Every day they're reading one of the top ten letters. We can hardly wait till they choose the grand-prize winner!"

We were too busy with our annual church Christmas plans to get very excited ourselves. Winning a big contest is the sort of thing you read about, but don't expect to happen to you.

Two weeks later, the producer of the "Welcome Travelers" program telephoned us again.

"Brace yourself," he said. "You have been chosen as our Christmas Family for this year. Three judges, Joe E. Brown, Cornelia Otis Skinner, and Wade Nichols, editor of *Redbook*, have picked the letter which was written about you."

It still didn't seem real.

"Our Christmas broadcast is to be made from your home," he continued, "and the gifts you have been awarded will be presented at that time. The trucks containing those gifts are starting west immediately, and out entire cast will fly out there to make a tape recording on December 21st.

The recording of our show will be released at our regular broadcasting hour on Christmas Day."

The night before the recording was to be made, after the children were in bed, Tommy Bartlett, Bob Cunningham, and the producer and staff writers, came to make final arrangements for the next day. Carl was needed to help the movers, and members of the show, set up the prizes and equipment. They wanted at least the children and me to be surprised, so we were to leave first thing in the morning and stay away until the show was ready.

It was ten in the morning when I piled the nine children into the station wagon, and none too soon. We were just turning out of the drive when I saw, through my rear-view mirror, two moving vans lumbering up the highway behind us. I distracted the children's attention to the bridge we were about to cross, and they didn't notice the trucks turning in beside the church.

We spent the morning at a friend's ranch. The nine youngsters had a joyous time, never suspecting that their house was being turned upside down to prepare a surprise for them. The only hint I gave was, "Wouldn't it be funny — if Santa Claus got his dates mixed up, and came early this year?" We had our picnic lunch, then Alex and Timmy took naps in the cottage while the rest whooped back to their play. At two o'clock Carl phoned.

"They decided they want you to come on home, so the first part of the broadcast can be done with us alone. They'll send a car back for the children in the next hour."

I told the children Daddy wanted me to go back. They all raised a clamor.

"So quick?" Rita asked. "We hardly been here, yet."

"We're having *so* much fun," Elaine added.

"You may stay another half hour or so," I promised, "if you'll come right home when we send a car back for you. Some of Daddy's friends will bring you home."

"We will, we will!" they chorused, and Alex bobbed his head like a chickadee.

I hardly knew our house, when I saw it. Crowds were milling around the church and our yard. The trucks were parked in front, plastered with signs reading, LOADED WITH PRESENTS FOR THE 1951 WELCOME TRAVELERS CHRISTMAS FAMILY! The house, white with new paint Carl had put on that summer, now looked like a Christmas package. Candy-red cellophane swags looped around the house and outlined the windows, there were green holly wreaths in the windows, and jolly little elves peeked from above the front windows and the porch light.

I made my way through the ring of bystanders and into the crowded, unfamiliar-looking house. The air was blue with cigarette smoke. The living room was jammed with large, bumpy objects covered with sheeting. In the dining room, our homely tables of different heights and all the nursery chairs and makeshift boxes were gone, and a blond-mahogany dinette table, with six chairs, stood in the center of our linoleum rug. A Westinghouse electric kitchen was temporarily parked around the dining-room walls, complete with refrigerator, range, dishwasher, automatic washing machine and drier. The window seat was filled with tape recorders and broadcasting equipment.

The general public had been kept outside, but the rooms were still crowded with reporters and photographers from newspapers and wire services. Wayne Miller was there with his cameras for *Life*. Besides all these were the members of the radio staff, the sound technicians, and the decorators imported up from San Francisco.

After a brief review of the questions that would be asked, the NBC microphone was brought upstairs to Carl's study in the church, where the first part of the program was recorded. Then Carl and I came down to stand in the living room by the lavishly decorated Christmas tree, which stood knee-deep in wrapped presents. Here we were interviewed again. We had just finished this second part of the broadcast when someone called, "Here come the kids!"

We saw them pile out of a car and stream through the gate. They were so entranced with their transformed, fairyland house, they didn't notice the people standing around.

"Oh, boy, Santa Claus *did* come early," Diane squealed, jumping up and down and clapping her hands.

"Oh, boy-o, boy-o, boy!" Alex cried, jumping up and down, spatting his small hands together.

I opened the front door. "Come in and see what Santa brought!"

They rushed in, twittering like a flock of birds, pointing at everything, heads turning round and round like little owls. From then on, once they were shown their presents and the unwrapping was begun, the radio staff merely had to stand by and record. The children were too excited to pay any attention to the microphone. Soon tissue paper and ribbons were flying everywhere, and the children were ooohing and aaahing over each item opened, whether for them or not.

"Gosh, pretty," Teddy said, as he opened a box of dresses.

"Oh, boy!" Diane exclaimed, as she unwrapped a package of boys' undershorts.

Donny tried on a pair of pants which were too big, even on top of his jeans, and out of the general hubbub the microphone picked up his plaintive, "Hey, Mama, my *pants* keep coming down." A minute later he hollered, "Gee, I bet I've opened a hundred presents!"

Alex found some transparent blocks with movable figures inside and contented himself with those, leaving further unwrapping to the rest. While the children were still busy under the tree, the announcer took Carl and me around, showing us the balance of the gifts in the house. Besides the time-saving appliances, there were two Hungerford mahogany bedroom sets, and a resplendent black Nash which we could see outside the dining-room window. In the china cupboard were arranged a set of Metlox pottery, and service for eight in Easterling silverware. Under the sheets in the living room were several pieces of a new living-room set, and some more things for the children: five wagons, five doll buggies, and six small bicycles.

The children, eager to rush outside with their new wheel toys, first agreed to sing, "Hark! the Herald Angels Sing" for Santa's genial helpers. They caroled in their sweet, soprano voices, all on key except chubby little Timmy, who plodded along at his own speed in his earnest, deep voice, just a little flat. Later, letters poured in from listeners from all parts of the United States, telling how whole families listened to the "Welcome Travelers" program on Christmas morning; many of the writers confessed they had to wipe their eyes after hearing the childish voices raised together in the familiar carol. Many noticed "one very small boy's voice, husky and a little off-key," and said they liked his singing best.

The recorded program faded out on the last strains of the carol; when it was over, willing hands helped the children take their wheel brigade outside. We had been afraid that the radio show might be confusing to the children, but they were having too good a time to be confused. They discovered several gym sets of swings and trapezes in their play yard, and like squirrels they spurted from swings to wagons to doll buggies, and went weaving about unsteadily on the unfamiliar medium of two-wheeled cycles.

Actually, it was Carl and I who were completely bewildered and overwhelmed by the number and magnitude of the gifts. It had happened with such Cinderella suddenness, we were not prepared for the avalanche of gifts. I expected the clock to strike midnight, and everything to disappear, at any moment.

By dark it was all over, and the last reporter, photographer, sound man, and Welcome Traveler had packed his gear like the Arabs, and as silently stolen away. Carl and I sank into the new chairs, exhausted, and looked at each other. The living room was knee-deep in crumpled tissue paper and ribbons. Open boxes spilled their contents all over the floor, and some of the new white underclothes and tee shirts were patterned with dark footprints. Discarded flash bulbs, bits of paper, and stamped-out cigarettes covered the floor in the dining room and kitchen.

"What a day!" I said.

"You didn't see the half of it," Carl said. "You should have been here when they were unloading everything, and setting things up, and putting things together. What a madhouse!"

"I can imagine."

"Just before the broadcast," Carl said, "I went into the bedroom to take off my overalls and change into my suit, and I was standing there with nothing on but my shorts when a lady reporter walked in and squealed, "Oh, excuse me, I thought the telephone was in here.""

I looked around the room at the unfamiliar new furniture. It was a great contrast to the wicker set that usually sat about the edges of our green linoleum rug.

"Where's all our old furniture, and stuff?"

"Oh, it's around," Carl said vaguely.

We called the children in, gave them sandwiches and hot cocoa and oranges, and sent them off to an early bed. "Where do we sleep, Mama?" they came back, asking.

I opened the doors of the downstairs bedrooms, but I couldn't get in. Desks, bookcases, books, filing cabinet, tables, lamps, beds, and dressers were piled on top of each other, halfway to the ceilings and jammed to the doors.

"There's part of our furniture," Carl said, "and stuff."

"Where do we sleep, Daddy?" the children asked.

"You girls can get in your rooms, upstairs," Carl said. "I'll fix up you little boys on the couch and the window seat, until Mama and I can get your rooms empty."

By midnight we had moved everything from the downstairs bedrooms into the dining room. We tucked the boys into their beds, and tumbled into our own, half asleep already. No sooner had I rolled over a time or two, and yawned twice, than the morning sun was coming in our window and the children were streaming in our door.

"Daddy, Mama," they hollered. "How do we get through the dining room, now?"

We slipped into jeans and tee shirts and joined the children in the downstairs hall, at the dining-room door.

"Well," Carl said, "we could all climb out of our bedroom window and go around, and come in the kitchen door."

"I can crawl under those tables," Timmy said.

"Me, too," Diane said.

The children all crawled through, weaving their way under tables, and between dressers and unconnected kitchen appliances. Carl and I got down on our hands and knees and followed the children.

"This is fun," Rita said. "Let's leave it this way."

"What do we eat on?" Elaine asked.

"Why don't we sit on the kitchen floor," Teddy said, "and eat breakfast like a picnic?"

We did. When we were through we piled the dirty dishes on the sink, and I said, "Now what?"

"Let's do the dishes in the new dishwasher," Donny said.

"In the first place, it's buried behind everything else in the dining room," Carl said. "In the second place, it's not connected."

"Connect it then," Donny suggested.

"In the third place," Carl continued, "there isn't room for it in this little kitchen until we remodel it, and I tear that old pantry wall down."

"We'll help!" the children volunteered in an eager chorus.

"In the fourth place," Carl finished, "the water hasn't drained out of the kitchen sink all winter. So, until we dig a new septic tank, how could the water drain out of a dishwasher, even if it was connected?"

Timmy stood staring at the choked-up dining room. "Santa Claus brought you too many things."

"Nothing we can't put to good use," I said. "Give us time, and Mama and Daddy will find a place for everything."

When we tired of eating on the kitchen floor, we moved half the things from the jammed-full dining room into the already overcrowded living room, leaving a narrow rabbit trail through to the front door. Our house was not wired for 220 current, so until the electric company could get around to installing the heavy-duty wire, we had to store the new electric stove and the clothes drier in the dining room. All winter, during the interminable rain, rain, rain of coastal northern California, I strung wash lines across my dining room, reaching over my unconnected electric clothes drier and stove to hang up the dripping sheets and diapers to dry over the gas heater.

"You know what I hope Santa Claus brings us next year?" Diane asked.

"What, dear?"

Diane threw out her arms. "A house as big as the sky."

"We could use one," I said.

CHAPTER 16

There Was an Old Woman

IN the late spring, Donny brought me a letter. "I decided I was too old to ask Santa Claus again, this last Christmas. So I thought I ought to do it directly."

"Do what directly?" I asked. I looked at the letter. "This begins, 'Dere Lady.' Does that mean me?"

"No, Mama," Donny said. "I wrote that to the lady who owns the orphanage."

"Which orphanage?"

"Any orphanage. Any place that's got boys to adopt, just the right size of me. You can read it."

The letter said, in a bold scrawl:

Dere Lady,
I would like a bother 9 years old, my father made me a room, it has a desk, a doubble desk, cowboy BunkBed, Cowboy and Indian wallpaper, two rugs a table some blocks a car and other toys so you see theres lots of room for a new bother.

Donald Doss

"Will you put it in a letter and send it for me?" Donny asked. "You see, I don't know any address."

That night I told Carl about the letters Donny and I had sent to an orphanage in the Rocky Mountain area.

"Ummmhmm," Carl said, from deep inside an editorial in the *Christian Century*. He hadn't tuned in on me yet; he was just nodding in an abstract way.

"Donny's letter was really cute," I said. "When he copied it over, I saved his original."

"That's nice," Carl murmured, turning a page, still nodding absently.

"He was asking for a brother, only he spelled it 'bother,' " I laughed. "When he gets one, he may find that a brother his size might be a bother, too. But if we can only find one, I'm sure it will be worth all the trouble. As the old saying goes, *the more the merrier!*"

The magazine lowered and Carl looked at me with a startled expression. "The more the *what?*"

"When Donny gets a brother," I explained.

"He's *got* brothers," Carl sputtered. "Brothers all over the house."

"No, the one he's hoping to get, just his size. We sent letters — "

The *Christian Century* hit the floor and Carl hit the ceiling.

"Letters? Letters?" he roared. "We've been through all this before."

"It does sound familiar," I agreed.

"We can't afford another child! Nine is all — "

We started going round and round at this point, and we were still going round and round a week later when our answer came from the orphanage.

"We are sorry to disappoint you and your Donald," the director wrote. "At the present time we have no older boys for adoption. I don't suppose you would be interested in a baby? We have here a seven-month-old Cheyenne-Blackfoot Indian boy, named Gregory. . . ."

Carl stopped arguing and looked interested. "Well, now, if you *must* have another boy, this one might be worth considering. Now that Alex is past two, I kind of miss not having a little baby around the house."

"Don't change the subject," I said. "I'm looking for a big boy, and not another baby."

"Sorry you took Alex?"

"What a silly question. Just the same, I can't stand the thought of more diapers, bottles again — "

Carl wouldn't let go of his brass ring, so we were back on the merry-go-round. After days and weeks of going in rhetorical circles, another letter arrived. It was the letter Donny and I had waited for all these years, the letter I was beginning to think never would come.

"Perhaps you won't be interested in our little Gregory," the director of the orphanage wrote, "when I tell you we now have a boy the age of your Donald. Richard is Chippewa Indian and Canadian on one side, Blackfoot Indian and Scottish-American on the other. He was nine years old this winter. Although Richard is not nearly so dark as little Gregory, he may be even more of a placement problem. Because he has had so little love or security, he has become uncooperative, sullen, and withdrawn."

"Another Little Beaver," Carl said.

"Y—you wouldn't *think* of turning this Richard down?" I gasped. "Would you?"

"I'm thinking quite definitely along those lines."

"After all these years of hunting, searching, just hoping to find a boy the size of Donny? A boy who needs us, and here we are, wanting him, too — "

"Look, Helen," Carl said, putting the letter away with an ominous finality. "In the first place, I've dedicated my life to my faith, and if I'm tied to the ball and chain of a big family, how can I serve? In the second place, we both have an obligation to the nine we already have. Bring home a problem child, and you're apt to throw the house into an uproar."

"But Donny wants — "

"Donny's too young to know what he wants. He's just as apt to end up bitterly jealous of a new, competitive brother."

Now I clutched the brass ring, and we were back for another long ride on the merry-go-round. Several weeks later, another letter came. It was from the same orphanage.

"If you are thinking of choosing between Gregory and Richard for your last child, you may not be interested in a girl who has come to us for permanent placement," the letter read. "Like Richard and your Donald, she is just nine years old. Her name is Dorothy, and she is a lovely and talented girl, with an artistic bent and a nice singing voice. Her mother was Welsh, English, and French. After the death of her parents, she lived with her maternal grandmother; when the grandmother died, she came here. No one was left who could give us data on the father's background; as nearly as we could guess, he was possibly Brazilian-Portuguese. Dorothy is a pretty child, with fair complexion, blue eyes, and curly, dark-auburn hair. In spite of Dorothy's charm, she will be difficult to place. Not only is part of her background unknown, but it is also at least partly 'foreign.' As one set of would-be parents objected, 'How could we be absolutely positive that she doesn't have some hidden Negro blood?' And they wouldn't take a chance."

"How ridiculous can people be?" Carl said. "I wouldn't mind if Dorothy actually were Negro, and dark. I've always been sorry we couldn't get Gretchen."

I threw my arms around Carl's neck. "Let's bring home all three! Richard, Dorothy, and the baby. Let's splurge, and not be so timid!"

Carl looked stricken. "*Three* more? All in one swoop? I've told you and told you — "

"Don't be so worried," I laughed, giving him a kiss that smothered his arguments. "Pooh, what's a few extra? As the old saying goes — "

"I *know*," Carl said. "The more the merrier." There was no conviction in his voice.

Donny went with me to bring back our three new children. He would not only provide company for Dorothy and Richard on the return trip, but he could be an advance-guard kind of friend, in helping them meet the strangeness and inevitable adjustments of a new home.

Carl drove us to the Sacramento station, where Don and I boarded the California Zephyr. We arrived at the orphanage two days later. First, the superintendent took us to see Richard.

Our new son looked like a typically American boy, with his straight brown hair and brown eyes, his light skin sprinkled with freckles; only his slightly high, flat cheek-bones revealed the Indian side of his ancestry. When I put my arm around him, he hung his head; but he looked more lonely than sullen. I knew he would be willing to give his love, when he knew it wouldn't be ignored or thrown back in his face.

If Richard had nothing to say, Donny more than made up for the lack. "Hey, Richard," he chattered, "did you get my two letters I wrote? Hey, wait till you see our room, wait till you see our bunk beds, do you want to sleep in the top or the bottom one? Hey, Richard, we got two dogs. One's Patsy and the other one's Rufus, and we got — "

They walked on out to the playground, shoulder to shoulder, while the superintendent took me to see Dorothy. I found her to be an unusually attractive girl, with fine dark eyebrows and curling dark lashes to frame her blue eyes. Not as tongue-tied as Richard, she shyly began to call me "Mama."

Dorothy accompanied us to the nursery, to see the baby who was to be her new brother. Gregory was a husky, brown-skinned little boy, pink on the palms of his hands and the soles of his feet, with silky-straight dark hair and enormous brown eyes. I picked him up and he was dumply, fitting into my arms as if he were made to be there. He poked at my eyes with his chubby finger and said, "Goo?" As I kissed him, the thought of more bottles and diapers didn't bother me at all, any more.

For Don, Richard, and Dorothy, the train ride home was a picnic, with no time for the games I had brought to amuse them. We rode upstairs under the transparent bubble top of the Vista-Dome chair car, and the nine-year-olds watched the stars go by overhead at night, counted deer in the mountains by day. They dashed downstairs for an endless supply of paper cups and drinking water. With their heads together, wavy yellow-blond hair contrasting with straight dark Indian hair and crisp curls of chestnut-brown, the three were as thick as pudding. They chattered and giggled as if they had always been brothers and sisters.

On our last morning, they had been crowding around while I handed out breakfast, begging, "Please, Mama, give us some more sweet rolls," and "Please, Mama, can we have our apples now?" I was giving the baby his bottle, and burping him with experienced pats at my shoulder, when the lady across the aisle engaged Donny in conversation.

"Are all of you brothers and sisters?" she asked, incredulous.

"Yep," Donny said, his mouth full of apple.

"The baby over there, too? He's your little brother?"

"Yep," Donny nodded.

"You certainly have a big family!"

"This is nothing," Donny said expansively, waving his apple. "You ought to see what we got back at *home*."

When tired, the three nine-year-olds curled up in their seats and slept, but I hardly dared to close my eyes for the whole trip. Gregory intermittently dozed and bounced in my lap; I was afraid that if I drifted to sleep, my arms might let him drop. Compounding my general weariness was a knifing pain in my back. I had sprained it severely, once, when I skidded on icy steps at Hebron, while carrying Laura and Susan from the buggy into the house. Now, on this trip, with the load of a heavy baby and bulky hand baggage, I had twisted my back again.

Carl met our train at Sacramento, and drove the tiring travelers home. By the time we came over the mountains to Santa Rosa, and along the winding valleys to Boonville, it was dark. Carl carried the baby and my luggage into the house. The two new nine-year-olds followed with lagging steps, dragging their own suitcases and looking around with apprehension at the strange surroundings. Donny bounced all over, greeting everyone with his usual volubility and unrestrained exuberance.

Carl kissed the whole family around, dumped the baby into my lap, and excused himself to take the baby sitter home. When the door shut behind him, complete pandemonium broke loose in our small living room. The eight younger children jumped up and down, yelling a welcoming "Mama, Mama!" They tried to swarm over my lap, shouting simultaneously about everything that had happened in my absence. Gregory, hungry and wet, frightened by the noise, started howling like the Duchess's baby in *Alice in Wonderland*.

Laura screamed in my ear, "Mama, hey Mama listen, will you curl our hair tonight, will you?"

Donny was leaping all over the house, flourishing his choice possessions to impress his new brother and sister; but Richard and Dorothy, so self-possessed and excursion-happy on the train, were suddenly overwhelmed with loneliness in the midst of the confusion.

"That big new boy is out crying in the hall," Rita shouted, over the din.

"That big new girl is out by the steps, crying," Diane reported three times, at the top of her lungs.

I groaned. Gregory had soaked through to my lap; Timmy, holding his nose, said frankly, "That new baby doesn't smell good."

"He needs clean diapers," I said. My back ached as if I had been freshly stabbed. "He's also hungry."

"So are we," Timmy said. "We haven't eat yet."

At that moment I would have traded the whole howling mob for a deserted island in the Pacific. I pulled up the corners of my face into a reasonable facsimile of a calm smile.

"Let's be more quiet, now, shall we? If you will give Mama a chance to take care of the *new* children first, then there'll be time to sit down quietly for talks, one at a time, later."

Nobody heard me, of course.

I gave Gregory a quick bath, put him into fresh diapers and a nightgown, and fixed him some formula. Carl arrived then, and gave the baby his bottle, while I turned my attention to the weeping Richard and Dorothy. After cuddling them both, I racked my brains to think of a diversion for their sudden loneliness.

"It's past suppertime," I said. "Would you two like to be my helpers?" With brighter faces under the tear streaks, they followed me into the kitchen. I found some carrots for

Dorothy to scrub, some oranges for Richard to peel and slice.

The rest of the children crowded into our Pullman-sized kitchen, demanding to know why they couldn't help, too. Many of them dragged out chairs to stand on, so they could reach the counters. I couldn't turn around without bumping into a chair or treading on small toes. Keyed up by the homecoming tension and excitement, the children pushed each other and quarreled, whining and fussing about everything. Suddenly I felt like the old woman who lived in a shoe and had so many children she didn't know what to do. I knew exactly how she felt when she gave them some broth without any bread, and spanked them all soundly and sent them to bed.

That night, after the twelve were finally fed and tucked into their cribs and cots and bunks, I tumbled into my own bed like a broken sack of wheat. I had pulled my happy little world down around my ears, and I felt as low and cheerless as a dungeon.

The next day I discovered that my troubles were just beginning.

Laura kept glaring at her own straight hair in the mirror, then went about telling everyone that Dorothy didn't deserve to have curly hair. "I wish Mama would send *that girl* back to the orphanage," she muttered in jealous spite.

Donny tried to boss Richard around in the high-handed way he sometimes bossed the younger children; Richard, after three patient warnings, finally took Donny down and pummeled him good. Donny came sobbing to complain about a microscopic bruise and a cut lip, proclaiming loud and long that he didn't want his new brother any more.

Even roly-poly, good-natured Gregory added to the troubles. It was on his medical record that he had suffered a cold that spring, with ear complications, but the nurse at the orphanage thought that the infection had cleared up. On the second night home, I had to walk the floor with him when he awoke screaming with earache, both ears discharging pus. The next morning our family doctor found Gregory's ears perforated and severely infected; the baby was put on around-the-clock doses of an antibiotic.

This was not the last link in our chain of trouble. On the following morning when the children came thundering into the dining room for breakfast, I noticed that several looked flushed. A closer inspection revealed rashes on the necks and chests of three children.

"Oh, no," I groaned. "Not *measles*, not now!"

It wasn't technically measles, but a kind of virus which attacks the glands and causes a skin rash. It was sweeping through the schools in the valley, and the children called it the "speckles." Most children would not suffer after-effects, the doctor told us, as long as they had sufficient rest; but babies, and occasional adults, might come down with very severe cases. We concentrated on protecting little Gregory, who needed all his resistance to fight the remaining infection in his ears.

Now I came to the full realization of the staggering number of children I had proposed to care for. As fast as two or three recuperated from the speckles, several more came down sick. I thought the siege would drag on into forever, would never be over. Night after night I went from one bed to another, holding wet cloths on feverish foreheads, soothing restless ones back to sleep.

The last straw was the stream of visitors.

The publicity from the *Life* magazine and the NBC "Welcome Travelers" show was beginning to bear some unpalatable fruit. People motoring through northern California would detour to our isolated, mountain-rimmed valley and knock on our door at all hours, just to have something to tell the folks back home.

One morning three strange ladies stood on the front step. "We read in the newspaper that the International Family had three new children," one gushed, "so we thought we'd drive up and look them over."

"I'm sorry," I said wearily, "but some of them have the measles now."

"That don't bother me," the spokesman said, as she pushed into our front room. "I've had everything."

Walking around the children, patting them on their heads, one said, "This one is kind of cute. Is he part Jap, or what?"

While we were eating lunch, two more strangers rang the bell. They were a middle-aged couple, the man with yellow false teeth that clicked, and the lady with a very large and slightly soiled bosom.

"We heard your family over the radio," the lady twittered, "and I vowed that if our vacation took us to California, we'd certainly look you up, so here we are!"

They strode on through to the dining room, stared at the toys on the floor, the piles of laundry waiting to be folded on the window seat, the rolls of dust in the corners on the floor, and at the children, who had stopped eating to watch.

The man started counting with his forefinger. "Let's see, is it nine you have?"

"Twelve now, some are sick. It's contagious," I added hopefully.

They weren't listening, but the children were. They were all ears.

"What a wonderful thing you and the Reverend are doing," the soiled bosom gushed, "to take in all these poor, neglected little orphans that nobody wanted, and give them food and shelter. The good Lord will certainly reward you with stars in your crown. Now I want you to tell me all their names, and what they *are. . . .*"

Emily Dickinson's lines went through my head:

> *How dreary to be somebody!*
> *How public, like a frog*
> *To tell your name the livelong day*
> *To an admiring bog!*

I tried to cut short my visitors' thoughtless prattle, and head them back toward the door, when the husband spoke up.

"Photography is my hobby."

I noticed for the first time the camera slung around his neck.

"Mind if I take a few souvenir snapshots of the kids? Thought you might sort of help me line 'em all up, outside."

"They're eating, now," I said through my teeth.

"No rush at all," he said with a generous wave of his

hand. "Me and the missus will sort of mosey around outside while we're waiting, and maybe get a few shots of the yard and the church. Take your time, we don't want to interfere with your *privacy*."

When the door was shut, I went back to the dining room. "Finish your lunch," I said. My head was whirring. "I want you all to hop in bed immediately, and take naps."

The older ones put up a wail.

"Remember what the doctor said about the speckles," I said. "It leaves you weak and cross for a while, and the naps build back your strength."

"But that man said — "

"The man came to see me, not you," I told them. "You get off to bed, and I'll talk to the man."

When our visitors bustled up to the door again, I managed a wan smile.

"I am honestly sorry that I have to disappoint you," I said, "but I'd be even more sorry if I let our children be spoiled by too much public attention. I'm afraid I can't let you take any pictures of them."

"But — but you said," the man sputtered, "at least I gathered — "

"It is a rather new rule," I admitted, "but, from now on, we can make no exceptions."

That evening, as I was slogging around the kitchen cooking supper, the vent plugged up in my pressure cooker and the emergency pressure valve blew out. Thick potato chowder was plastered over walls, counters, and stove, and dripped down from the ceiling to add to the soupy puddle on the floor. By the time I had the mess cleaned up and the children fed, my ears were ringing and my head was going around. I was helping the children into their pajamas when there were knocks on the front door again.

A couple stood there beaming.

"We made a long detour, just to swing around through your town and see your precious kiddies," the lady gushed. "My, what a wonderful thing, taking these poor little orph——"

"Yes, I do feel sorry for them," I interrupted. "They've got the *measles*."

It didn't stop them. The strangers shoved right in, and the children crowded around, in various stages of undress.

"This is a real sight," the man confided. "We never got to see the Dionne quints when we went to Canada, so we thought that this would make up for it."

"Won't you excuse me?" I said, swaying. "It really is past their bedtime." I herded the children off, while Carl chatted politely with the strangers, and sent them on their way.

When the children were in bed, I collapsed in Carl's arms. "I can't take any more," I wailed. "I'm going to blow up, just like the pressure cooker. The kids are driving me crazy. And the last straw is all the nutty sightseers who keep sticking their noses into our private lives. As if — as if we were running a circus sideshow — "

Carl patted my shoulder. "Don't let them get under your skin, honey. People may seem nosy, but they mean well. You've had a tough day."

The tears were running down my cheeks. "It's not just today. It's every day. Look at the dishes piled in the sink!

The laundry tub is full of wet diapers, the dirty-clothes baskets are overflowing, and the school children haven't any clean clothes left to wear. The ironing's piled up and all my cooking pots are too small for f-fourteen p-p-people — "

"There, there, it's nothing that can't be worked out with a little organization, now that the children are getting well. I'll see if I can arrange my time so I can help you some."

"No," I wept. "We can't fix it that easy. You were right all along, when you said that nine were enough to take care of. I'm a blind, headstrong, know-it-all fool."

Carl hugged me. "That's what I like about you. You'll rush in where angels fear to tread."

"Carl, I'm serious. I've made a terrible mess of our lives. How can I put us back the way we were, so — so peaceful, before I brought all the extra children home? And what's to happen to Richard and Dorothy and Gregory, after we take them back?"

"Take them back? How could we take them back?"

"B-but how can we manage if we don't?" I sobbed. "I feel like I'm at the end of my rope — "

Carl took his handkerchief to wipe the tears from my face, then pulled me toward the light. "Oh, boy! No wonder."

"No wonder what?"

"That you're so feverish and down in the mouth." He turned me toward a mirror. I looked and saw the rash climbing up my neck, spreading over my cheeks.

"You've got the speckles," Carl said.

· · ·

After three days the rash went down, but the gland infection had left me so weak I could hardly lift my arms. I felt as if I had gone through the washing-machine wringer.

"You just rest and get well," Carl said. "At the end of the month, go down to the University of Redlands for summer school. What you need is a vacation."

"But Carl," I wheezed, "I can't go off and leave you."

"Don't worry about me, because it will be good for me to spend my vacation with the kids. That way, I can still preach on Sundays, too, and we won't have to close the church down. You and the children made it possible for me to go to college. Do you mind, now, if we all send you?"

"But honey," I groaned. "It's much different now. We've got *twelve* children."

Carl laughed at me. "As you have often said, *the more the merrier!*"

CHAPTER 17

Daddy Sends Mother to College

AT the University of Redlands, the dean of women assigned me to a room in one of the dormitories. I strolled about the campus, registered for classes, bought textbooks. I was a college student again, carefree, with nothing to do but study, eat, and sleep.

I enjoyed my courses. One was in sociology, on the races of man and their origin. Tying in closely with this was a workshop on intercultural education. Both could help me understand the backgrounds and problems of my own family.

Equally stimulating was a course in the writing and production of plays. In my homework for this class, I had to write an original one-act play. What should I write about? I began and discarded a wastebasket full of false starts. Finally I remembered an old writing dictum, iterated and reiterated to beginners: *Write about what you know best.* So I invented a young minister and his wife who had just gone to live in their first parsonage, and evolved a comedy about the problems which might be typical of any spirited girl in a rural parish. The first birth pangs were over, and my play began to be born.

School kept me so busy, at first, I didn't have time to worry about how Carl was making out at home. When I did steal time to think about it, I was petrified. Had I taken leave of my senses, to leave an unexperienced man to cope with a hectic household of twelve child-size bombshells?

Carl's first letters weren't too reassuring.

"We now have several sets of pink sheets," he wrote. "Why didn't you warn me that Alex's red overalls would fade?"

And, "I seem to have lost the formula for Gregory's bottle. Isn't it time he started drinking out of a cup, anyway?"

After the first Sunday night he wrote, "I was proud of our twelve today. Got them up, Richard helped me fix hot oatmeal and oranges for breakfast, and all were in Sunday school by ten. During church, they sat like angels in the front pew, where I could keep my parental eye on them, and Dorothy held the littlest angel on her lap.

"When lunch was over, we all took naps. Took one myself, since I'd been up late the night before, finishing my sermon in the peaceful quiet. Later, we hiked down to the river, Alex riding astride my shoulders and Gregory in my arms. After a supper of milk and jelly sandwiches, we dressed for the evening services at Philo. At the very last minute, when we were all ready to go, I noticed that Alex's hair was slicked down, shiny as patent leather. You know how Alex's short 'butch' usually stands up straight like a brush — well, I thought maybe he had just imitated the big boys, by slicking his hair down with water. Then I saw the red jelly on his clean collar. I soon discovered that he had used the same for pomade; the jelly jar, left on the table, was cleaned out. What didn't go on his hair, I suspect he ate. Was he one sweet mess!"

It bothered me, those sandwiches the children were eating. When I had been sick in bed, the stand-by for every meal had been sandwiches, often supplemented with canned beans. This might pass for an occasional meal, but I pictured the children bowlegged with rickets and malnutrition after half a summer on such a diet. I felt especially conscience-stricken because I was enjoying such bountiful meals at the university cafeteria. My place was back at home with my family, cleaning house, caring for my children, cooking them balanced meals.

I began to worry, and my worry slipped into my letters. Carl attempted to put my mind at ease.

"Don't judge by the emergency meals you've seen me throw together," he wrote. "Didn't I tell you about how when I was fourteen, I spent a whole summer on a building job where Dad was foreman? We had to camp out, because it was up in the mountains back of San Diego. I was a carpenter's helper, and the crew also elected me to be the cook. I'm a cook from away back."

A few doubts still lingered, even after Carl began to include some of his menus in his letters. "I use your chart from the Department of Agriculture, and every day, in fact nearly every meal, we have something from each of the *'Basic Seven'* food groups. Tonight we had pork liver smothered with onions; potatoes, steamed in their jackets; green beans and yellow squash from our garden. For dessert and salad combined, I shredded two heads of cabbage, added some raisins, and topped it with chopped walnuts from our own tree. I tossed it with a fruit-juice dressing I'd made, and this dish was such a hit with the children that they cleaned it up and yelled for more."

Another day: "Tindall's gave me a box of lamb necks, shanks, and ribs, which were trimmed from meat used at a lodge barbeque. I cooked lamb stew for supper, along with potatoes, onions, carrots, and turnips from the garden. We ate the turnip tops as cooked greens, and we have enough lamb scraps saved in the freezer for another couple of meals."

Carl even did some experimenting.

"Yesterday I bought some garbanzos, then discovered we had no recipe for cooking them. I figured they should be soaked overnight like any dried beans, which I did. Then I cooked them with some ham bones, added chopped onions, seasoned them with curry powder and a little Worcestershire sauce. The children stood up and cheered. Richard claimed they tasted like wienies."

These meals just sounded too good to be true, but my last, lingering doubt was dispelled when I received a long newsy letter from Dorothy. After an extended account of the family activities, she bragged on her father's cooking.

"Some peepul in our church went surf fishing," she wrote in a neat hand. "They brought us a whole bucket of those little, bitty kind of fish. Daddy said they was nite fish. Daddy learned Richard how to clean out the insides and roll them in Corn Meal and fry them. He showed me how to steam potatoes in there skins, and how to make a toss salad. After supper, Daddy and Richard and me packed all the extra fish into empty paper milk bottles, and we froze them to eat later. Donny doesn't cook much. He rather to eat. But Daddy, he sure can cook good, and he's learning us how to cook, too."

If I no longer needed to be concerned about the family's diet, there were other things to chew my nails over, such as the possibility of accidents. True, we had raised children for ten years now, with no important accident outside of the foot Donny broke when he was four. Still, our luck seemed to be running out, because Carl reported two in one week. First Donny fell on a sharp garden stake, which narrowly missed his eye, and had to have several stitches through his eyebrow. Then little Alex tripped and crashed face down on a rock, knocking out five of his top teeth in front.

"Even these accidents had their brighter side," Carl wrote. "We can be thankful that the stick missed Donny's eye. And it's lucky that a younger child knocked his teeth out, and not an older one with permanent teeth. In another two or three years Alex can grow in his own perfect replacements."

It was a nervous strain, being a long-distance mother.

I finished writing my play, and it was chosen by the drama class to be the one produced. It was to be given by the class in a premier performance during the last week of summer school, with the rest of the college and the townspeople invited. Rehearsals were fun. It was exciting to watch characters, created on paper, coming to life on the stage. It was exciting, and yet I found it harder and harder to concentrate on my play, or any of my schoolwork. I felt I should have been at home, helping Carl bear the load of caring for our huge family, especially since it was my pressuring that had made our family so overgrown.

Had Carl ever asked for anything like this? All he ever wanted to do was to listen to the inner voice, to serve God through the church. Was this the thanks he was receiving for his long years of schooling, for specialized preparation at seminary, for his devoted ministry in small rural churches — to end up washing diapers, wiping dirty faces, and cooking Paul Bunyan-sized meals over a hot stove? It wasn't fair to Carl. *It wasn't fair.*

I would have to go ahead and finish summer school, because he would be unhappy if I quit in the middle. As soon as I got home, I must start making it up to him. I would run the household efficiently, get his meals on time, keep the children away so they wouldn't bother him. Also I could do his typing and other secretarial jobs, and dust the church for him. These things I could do, but even this would not be enough. Carl was being very noble and kind about these last three children. For my sake, he was putting on a good front of being glad, after all, that I had brought them home.

That still didn't make it fair. Nine were enough for a low-paid rural pastor to feed and worry about. As soon as the new ones could be prepared for the change, I would have to take them back.

At least the children seemed to be having a good vacation with their father. He often took them down to the shallow creek for a swim and a picnic. Several times he drove them to the ocean; these excursions were a big thrill to Dorothy and Richard, since they had never been to the coast before. On their last trip to the ocean, the older ones went fishing. Donny was so excited, he fell into the surf and had to be fished out himself.

The next morning, Carl asked Donny if he would like to write Mama about the fishing trip.

"Oh, yes!" Donny said. "Give me some paper with lines on it, so my words won't all run together."

Carl gave him a sheet of lined paper.

"Oh, one piece wouldn't be *nearly* enough," Donny said. "You'd better give me a whole tablet, because there's so much to tell."

Don took the tablet to his room. A little later Carl heard him whooping and hollering outside with the other children.

"Your letter finished already?" Carl called out the window.

"I'm playing berryman right now," Don explained. "I'll write it this afternoon, when I can think better."

That afternoon Don again retired dutifully to his room. The next time Carl saw him, Don was helping Dorothy make grass skirts for the girls to tuck into the waistbands of the sunsuit shorts.

"Now what?" Carl asked.

"I'm president of the Honolulu Grass Company," Don said. "I'm teaching the girls how to do the *hula-hula* to the tune of 'Yankee Doodle.' "

"I thought you were writing Mother a letter."

"Oh. Yes. Well, my pencil broke. Anyway, I thought

I'd do it in the morning, when I can think better. You see, there's so much to say."

Several days later I received Don's letter, written after the exertion of parental pressure. It said eloquently:

Dear Mom
    we went down to the beach. after lunch we went fishing. no fish.

                                        love Don

I was not worried when Carl took the children to the ocean, because it was fairly easy for one person to keep track of them on a semideserted beach. I did grow alarmed when Carl wrote that he wanted to take the gang to the zoo in San Francisco for a day. I couldn't concentrate on sociology or play production when I thought of our large and bouncy tribe running loose at the crowded zoo, with only Carl to watch them.

"Why don't you ask someone to go with you?" I airmailed back. "How about Tomasita? The two of you could manage our twelve, and her two, much easier than you could watch our twelve alone. You always need an extra adult along, to run down the stragglers and supervise visits to rest rooms."

Tomasita was a charming Filipino war bride who lived down the street from us. Her complexion was rich and dark, her hair black, but she was proud of her fair-skinned sons, Sonny and Stinky. Her American husband was a serviceman, then stationed in Japan.

Carl asked Tomasita if she and her boys would like to make a trip to the zoo.

"I'll fix a picnic," she said. "What fun!"

On the big morning, Carl was up early to feed the children and pack the needed things in the car. There were a box of snacks, and extra jackets and long jeans to wear on the four-hour trip home after dark. Extra diapers and pants were needed for Gregory, and paper sacks for Donny. Donny usually became carsick, and needed the sacks in case Carl couldn't find a quick place to stop after going around one too many curves.

Dawn was streaking the sky when Carl stopped at Tomasita's house and squeezed the children over to make room for three more passengers.

"It's starting out to be a nice day," Carl said.

A little later Donny exulted, "Look, we're practically to Cloverdale, and I never even used my sack!"

He didn't either. Just then a curve caught him in the pit of his stomach, and little Gregory got all of Donny's breakfast in his lap. Carl pulled into the first gas station, took Greg into the washroom, gave him a bath and shampoo in the wash basin, and dressed him in clean clothes.

"At least Donny picked someone who had an entire spare outfit along," Carl said cheerfully.

As the station wagon headed south into the traffic on Highway 101, the gay spirit of adventure returned. Our children sang, as they always do in the car, as they do anywhere when they are happy and not inhibited. When they passed a freight train they sang "The Little Red Caboose" and "I've Been Working on the Railroad." Blackbirds perched upon a fence brought to mind "Sing a Song of Sixpence." When the road swooped over a bridge, it was

"London Bridge Is Falling Down." In between songs inspired by the passing scene, they sang whatever came to their minds. They jumped without pause from "Fairest Lord Jesus" to "Jacob's Ladder" to "Santa Claus Is Coming to Town."

Intermittent with the songs was a running chatter, with a "Hey, Daddy, baby pigs!" and a "Hey, Daddy, see the airplane!"

Soon Tomasita's little boys were joining in the camaraderie, yelling, "Hey, Daddy, look over there," and "Hey, Daddy, when do we get to the zoo?"

After crossing the Golden Gate bridge, Carl drove Tomasita to the San Francisco house of her girl friend, whom she wanted to visit. He let out Tomasita and her boys, promising to be back in an hour for the picnic and the trip to the zoo. While waiting, he took the children to Fisherman's Wharf. They shouted at the quaint fishing boats, pressed small noses against the windows of entrancing restaurants, sniffed the fishy sea smells.

When Carl returned for Tomasita, he found three young Filipino women waiting for him on the sidewalk. Tomasita's girl friend, who was hugely pregnant, held a little Eurasian girl by the hand. This girl friend had another girl friend with her, a dark-eyed young woman with two small boys. Both Tomasita's girl friend, and the girl friend's girl friend, were married to American seamen; their children were all Eurasian mixtures, like Tomasita's and ours.

"My girl friend, she like to go to the zoo weeth us," Tomasita said. "And she's got another girl friend here. *She* like to go too, if there's room."

"There's room," Carl said, "if we all squeeze."

So they all squeezed, and Carl drove the gang to the picnic grounds at the Children's Village in Golden Gate Park.

"We want to go to the zoo, Daddy," the children hollered, when they finished their lunch. They all squeezed back into the car for the short trip down the ocean highway to the zoo.

"Now let's all stay together," Carl warned, as the seventeen assorted children streamed out of the car.

"Yes, Daddy," some of the bigger ones hollered.

"Yes, Daddy," all the smaller ones echoed, and they all promptly started running in different directions.

Carl rounded them up at the entrance again and held a council with the three mothers. "What we need is a sheep dog," he said.

During the council the children started yelling, "Let's find the lions!" and "Look over there!" and "Hey, there's a peanut stand!" They started off in every possible direction, and a few more. By the time they were rounded up and counted, three proved to be missing: Diane, Donny, and the little boy belonging to the girl friend's girl friend.

The distraught mother was frantic, her dark eyes trembling with tears.

Carl took charge of the situation. "No need to worry. All three of the lost ones are probably ahead of us on the path. If we move along rather rapidly, sooner or later we're bound to overtake them." He divided the remaining children in twos, buddy system. "Now everyone keep track of his buddy," he admonished.

Double file they started off, going just a little too fast to see the animals, hoping to catch up with the three lost children.

"It's a good thing I put red shirts on all of mine," Carl said. "Easier to keep track." Everyone was too busy searching the crowds for the two missing red shirts, and the cowboy shirt of the little boy belonging to the girl friend's girl friend, to really enjoy the zoo.

After three hours, Carl wiped his perspiring face with his handkerchief. "I think it might be faster if I took it alone for a while," he suggested. He settled the three exhausted young mothers on a shady spot of grass, where they could stretch the children for a rest; then he started the rounds again. Finally, at the other side of the zoo, he found Donny and the cowboy shirt at the monkey cages. Donny was holding the little boy's hand, pointing out the sights.

"Hi, Daddy," Donny said, as if he had been standing beside Carl all the time. "I've been showing this little boy the zoo, and I kept tight hold of his hand so he wouldn't get lost."

"You *were* lost," Carl said. "Have you seen Diane?"

"Nope," Donny said. "Maybe she's the one got lost."

"I eat popcorn," the little boy said.

"Yeah, I found a lot of popcorn and peanuts on the ground," Donny said. "I dusted it off real clean, and I divided it up with me and the little boy. *And* the monkeys," he added with a generous sweep of his hand.

Carl restored the lost child to the tearful embrace of his mother, asked Tomasita to keep a double watch on Donny, and started out again in search for Diane. As he swung past the playground, a white-haired old lady tapped him on the shoulder.

"Did you lose a little girl?"

"Yes!" Carl looked around, and there was Diane with a tear-streaked face and chocolate smeared around her mouth.

While Carl held Diane, the little old lady explained, "I found her nearly three hours ago. All she could tell me about her Daddy was that he was wearing a green shirt. So I've been stopping every man I see in a green shirt." She patted Diane's head. "The poor tyke's been crying most of the time. She was sure she would never see her Daddy again."

Diane had been consoled with candy bars and ice cream, but she had never gone beyond the ladies' comfort station at the playground. By the time Carl brought Diane back to the rest of the group, it was closing time, too late for everyone to go around for a real look at the zoo. As they filed out to the parking lot and packed themselves into the station wagon, the children hollered that they were hungry again. The girl friend of Tomasita, and the girl friend's girl friend, put their heads together, then called out to Carl that they wanted to treat everybody to dinner somewhere, as their contribution to the day.

"How would you like to go to Chinatown?" Carl asked. "I know a place there where our whole family can eat for a few dollars."

Everyone was thrilled with the idea, especially the three mothers. Carl swung over to Market Street and across through the middle of downtown San Francisco. As they rode, the children chattered about the zoo.

"Did you see any elephants?" Diane asked. "Did the bears beg for peanuts? What did the monkeys do?"

Unfortunately, the only ones who could answer her questions were Donny and the little boy. They had not been dragged along at a brisk pace, like the other children; they had been busy looking for animals, not red shirts.

In Chinatown, Carl parked. Passers-by gawked and traffic on Grant Street came to a standstill, when the station wagon disgorged a blond man, three black-haired young women with Oriental faces, and a seemingly endless stream of small children, nearly all of mixed Oriental-European ancestry.

When the party streamed into the small, upstairs Chinese restaurant, the scattered diners looked, and did a double take. The pert Chinese waitresses were staggered for a moment, then rallied and pushed five or six tables together. Plates of *chow mein* and *chow yoke* were ordered, with bowls of rice all around. There were sesame cookies, with fresh pots of tea, for dessert.

When the children were through, Carl went around helping the littlest ones down from their chairs. They were all hollering, "Where now, Daddy?" and "Do we have to go home, Daddy?"

Carl took the arm of the pregnant Filipino girl, going around the end of the table. They passed two sailors who were too astounded to drink their tea.

"What's that guy got, a harem?" the one with the weather-beaten face muttered, not trying to keep his voice down.

His young companion glared at Carl. "I wonder just who he thinks he is, anyway."

The three young women had reached an impasse on the question of who would pay the bill, each wanting the honor of treating the whole party by herself. After a whispered huddle, Carl finally arbitrated a compromise, whereby each girl would put two dollars into the pool, and Carl would pay the small balance. As they were leaving the dining room, all the Chinese cooks came out of the kitchen to see the enchanting-looking children, who were yelling with unsuppressed delight on the stairway, dashing out onto the balcony over the street, with hands and eyes into everything. The manager had let them have the run of the place, apparently tickled with their company.

Carl stopped at the cashier's desk to settle the bill, while the three Filipino mothers rounded up all the youngsters and shepherded them through the door. The children kept looking back, hollering, "Don't lose us, Daddy," and "Hurry up, Daddy!"

The manager, veiling a tremendous curiosity behind his Oriental mask of politeness, asked, "Which of the charming ladies is your wife?"

"My wife isn't here," Carl said. "She's going to college."

CHAPTER 18

The Full Quiver

SCHOOL, after marking time on slow feet all summer, finally ended in a tarantella of activity. My play, *The Tie That Binds*, was performed for two nights in the university Little Theater; my last final exam was taken, my clothes and books packed. I started home, carrying a bundle of mixed emotions with my luggage.

I was homesick, yet I dreaded going back. I had disrupted my family when I brought the last three home; now my heart wept because I knew it was up to me to reverse the process, and disrupt it again. The only thing that made it easier was knowing that our nine didn't seem to care too much for the three new ones. Perhaps, after the three went back to the orphanage, they wouldn't even be missed. Donny definitely resented Richard, Laura was jealous and spiteful about Dorothy. And it was inconceivable that any of them would miss Gregory, because a new baby in the house provides little more than unfair competition.

When I opened the parsonage door in Boonville and threw myself into the welcoming arms of my family, I felt like the prodigal son come home. *I love them*, I thought, looking around at my dancing, joyous, beloved children. I had to blink my eyes to see them through the undersea mistiness. They seemed to be mermaids flipping wildly about as they covered me with wet kisses.

I love them, all twelve of them! Dorothy and Richard were throwing their arms around me, too, as if they had always been my children; and little Gregory was bouncing up and down in his playpen with a smile clear across his broad, dark face, holding up fat little arms so I would pick him up.

"He acts as if he actually remembered you," Carl marveled. "He's been leery of strangers lately, never lets outsiders pick him up."

I kissed the baby, and decided I would keep my unhappy plans to myself. First, I rationalized, and I was good at rationalizing, I would get settled in the routine of home life, and then I could see what would be the best way to break the news. In the meantime, I would pretend that it was possible for us all to stay together. Dorothy and Richard should remember their last days here as being the happiest possible. If they ended with a happy experience with us, it would be easier for them to adjust in the next home that took them in. *If* another home was ever offered . . .

My first major task was to give haircuts.

"I took the whole gang downtown to the barbershop once while you were gone," Carl said. "Wow! Our family can eat for a week on what *that* cost. It's lucky you can do it for us."

"They all look like cocker spaniels," I laughed. "I can hardly tell the boys from the girls."

"After you get our hair cut, you can," Timmy assured me.

I put two low stools outside the back door, got out my scissors and clippers, and my home barbershop was ready for customers.

"Why don't you cut mine and Gregory's in a Mohawk?" Richard asked. "We're both real Indians."

"A Mohawk?"

"Yeah, like those college boys in the newspaper picture we saw," he grinned. "You know, shaved all over, except with a piece down the middle like a long toothbrush upside down."

"That might be interesting," I admitted. "What do you think we should do with Alex's? Shall we let it grow out in a long, braided queue? Or do you suggest we put a rice bowl on his head and cut around it?"

"No," Timmy said. "You ought to keep cutting Alex's hair short on top. He's got a natural-born *butcher* haircut."

As I clipped and trimmed, the hair piled up around me, blond, auburn, soft mole-brown, and shiny black; and the vari-colored snips blended together as they fell.

I soon discovered that I was wrong about the way our children felt about each other. My first night home, Laura came running up in her pajamas for her good-night kiss. Her straight brown hair was twisted into bunchy rolls.

"I sure like that Dorothy," Laura beamed, patting her head. "She puts my hair up in curlers any time I ask her. I'm sure glad you brought her home to be our big sister. I always wanted a big sister, and now I got one. She helps me fix clothes for my dolly, too."

The next day, while I was treadling my old-fashioned

sewing machine and catching up on the mending, Donny and Richard ran in, flushed from play. Don, bare from the waist up, flourished a row of turkey feathers held in place by a leather strap in his blond hair. His fair cheeks had streaks of red water-color paint.

"Hi, Mama, we're playing cowboy and Indian," he said, pointing to Richard, who wore a battered cowboy hat and a bandanna knotted at his neck. "Boy, are we ever having fun!"

"Yeah," Richard said, holding up a length of clothesline. "Here's my lasso. Watch out the window, Mama, and I'll show you some tricks I'm learning." He dashed out.

When we were alone, I told Don, "You seem to be happy with your new brother."

He looked astounded. "Well, gosh, why shouldn't I be?"

"That's a good question. Before I went to college, I seem to recall that you kept hollering for me to take him back."

"Well, gee. Like Daddy told me. When a guy goes out and picks a bunch of roses, he ought to *expect* a thorn or two. Richard's a real neat guy, boy."

And my "Indian" whooped out to rejoin the cowboy.

Gregory, far from being resented by the other children, was the family pet. He was still cutting his baby teeth, and they watched him as excitedly as any set of fond parents. If one of the children was feeding him his cereal or applesauce one morning, and the spoon clinked on a new tooth, you'd have thought it was somebody's birthday from all the gathering around and hullabaloo. The first time Greg pulled to his feet, the children cheered and laughed and praised him so much he giggled until he fell down. They encouraged him up again and again, until he learned to be steady on his feet; from then on, he was into everything.

Donny, as a baby, had explored his new world by putting as much of it into his mouth as he could. Gregory was different. Completely ignoring the world of taste, he turned all his attention to the fascinating world of sound. He never went around like a crawling vacuum sweeper, as Donny had, and never put a single thing into his mouth. Greg wanted to know but one thing: what does it *sound* like? He rapped his knuckles experimentally on everything, grinning as he listened attentively to the varying timbre of sound. His favorite toy was a tom-tom Carl had made out of a piece of old inner tube, stretched across a large-sized tomato-juice can. This amused the older children, and they taught him a song called, "Big Red Indian, Beats Upon His Drum." Gregory couldn't talk yet, but he could imitate the tune perfectly, singing a lilting da-da-da in place of the words.

I thought that at least Alex might feel jealousy toward Gregory, since his place as baby of the family had been usurped by this little newcomer. Apparently Alex was ready to grow up, and let someone else be baby for a change. He was as proud and possessive of the baby as were his older brothers and sisters.

"*My* baby," he often announced with a big grin, his eyes crinkled shut as he happily patted Gregory on his dark hair. "Mine!"

One day a parishioner came to visit. She admired Gregory, who crawled at our feet on the floor, knocking with his knuckles on the linoleum, the chair legs, the toes of our shoes.

"Isn't he a darling?" she cooed, leaning over to snatch him up for a kiss. Startled, Gregory scuttled into the next room and peeked out from under a dining-room chair with his round, brown eyes.

"Isn't he sweet?" she gushed, then turned to the children clustered in the dining-room doorway. She was teasing, as adults often do, but the children didn't know it. "I don't have any baby. You have so many children here, you surely wouldn't miss one. I think I'll take that baby home with me!"

They lost no time. Susie ran and held the front door open. Alex grabbed the lady's hat and purse from the table and dumped them into her lap, his small black eyes flashing fire.

"Bye, *bye*," he spit out, and it was more than a hint. It was a royal command.

The next time the parishioner came to call, Laura peeked through the curtains at the front door, and promptly turned the lock.

"It's that lady who wants to take Gregory away," she hissed to Teddy. "Run, lock the back door too. We just won't let her *in*."

Richard was nearsighted, so Carl drove him up the coast to Fort Bragg, to have him fitted for glasses. It was the best part of a day lost from his church work, and my conscience bothered me. *If the last three children were going back, the sooner they went back the better.* The longer they stayed, the more they seemed blood of my blood, flesh of my flesh, like the rest. It would be like cutting off a piece of myself, to see them go. . . .

That night, after the children were tucked into bed, Carl said, "Honey, we shouldn't put it off any longer."

I looked at him, and there was a lump of something·cold and heavy where my stomach was supposed to be. I knew what he was going to say.

"About those last three, I mean," he said.

I nodded, trying to keep my chin from quivering.

"The sooner we get it over with, the better I'll feel about it. I don't like it just dragging on and on like this."

I tried to think of Carl's needs, to concentrate on Carl's face so that I wouldn't see the faces of Dorothy, Richard, and little Gregory — so I wouldn't cry, and let Carl know how bad I felt.

It didn't work. All of my love for those three children welled up in my eyes, and the next minute I was in Carl's arms, sobbing.

"Why, honey," he exclaimed, surprised. "What in the world brought this on?" He patted my back helplessly.

"I — I suppose I'd get used to it, in time," I said in a shaky voice. "And I know it's better for everybody this way — "

Carl sat down and pulled me into his lap. He looked hurt, disturbed. "I had no idea you felt so strongly. I thought you might feel different about the new kids after you'd been away all summer. But if you're absolutely sure you don't want to adopt — "

"Adopt?" I popped upright in his lap. "Is that what you

were talking about doing, to adopt? Richard, and Dorothy, and Gregory?"

Carl looked at me, puzzled. "Who else, silly? What did you think I wanted to do with them? Take them back to the orphanage?"

"Well I, well I — " I grabbed his shoulders and tried to read his eyes. "I thought that was what you *really* wanted, to take them back. I thought you were just putting up a good front about liking them, just to be nice to me."

"I wouldn't set those three kids adrift," he said indignantly. "They're *wonderful* youngsters. I'm proud to call them my children. That's why I said I didn't want to put it off any longer, getting their adoptions started. I've been meaning to talk about it ever since you came home. But every time I brought up the subject of the new children, the conversation seemed to get sidetracked to something else."

"Call up the lawyer," I told him happily. "Let's get the court wheels moving."

While we were waiting out our probationary period, the children started to school, then Halloween and Thanksgiving came and went, and it was Christmas again.

My mother and father, back in Illinois, sent out Christmas gifts to the children. They also wrote a letter saying how much they looked forward to a trip west the next summer, so they could get acquainted with their northern-California grandchildren.

On Christmas day, after we had our stockings and our tree at home, we drove down to Santa Rosa for a family get-together at the home of Carl's parents. Carl's father, who had become quite fond of little Gregory that summer, delighted in giving his papoose grandson a horsy-ride on his knee. He had also taken quite a shine to Richard; as a carpenter and a fine craftsman, he was pleased to find a boy who also had a knack with tools — Richard was forever whittling and working with wood.

As Carl and I watched, the baby crawled off his grandfather's knee and headed for the piano. Carl's father pulled Timmy up on his lap and started telling him a story.

"That tickles me," Carl said. "When I was a boy, my dad used to say that you could never trust a Jap, and the only good Mexican was a dead one. And Timmy is both. I guess that shows that anyone can change his ideas for the better."

The other youngsters were crowding around their grandfather's chair. Out in the kitchen, Dorothy and her grandmother were talking chummily together. I whispered back, "You know, I believe they like our children just as much as if they were natural grandchildren. And when my own folks come out for their visit this summer, I'll bet they'll feel the same way."

"Why shouldn't they?" Carl smiled. "Maybe once these were children that nobody wanted, but not any more. Anybody would want them, now."

"You know," I said, "I don't think there really is such a thing as an unwanted child. Anybody in the whole world could have the bad luck to be in a particular place where he didn't happen to be wanted. But somewhere else in the world, there are always those who would love him."

Carl nodded. "There's the job that needs to be done. To help the ones needing love to find people who have it."

Just before we gathered the children together for our trip back to Boonville, I overheard Teddy and our girls talking to one of their young cousins.

"I like your baby brother," the cousin said.

"Us, too," Teddy said.

"Guess what?" the cousin said.

"What?" Susie asked.

"We're going to get a new baby, too."

"Oh."

A respectful and awed silence followed this announcement, then Laura asked, "Is your mother going to the orphanage, and adopt him?"

The cousin was taken aback. "Well, no. She's just going to go to the hospital and have him borned."

Again the silence, then came Laura's consoling voice. "Well, don't feel bad. I expect she'll really get to love him, just the same."

And all our children nodded.

I had a bonus present that came unexpectedly. The week after Christmas the children came running into the house, bursting with excitement.

"The 'lectricity men came," Timmy shouted. "They're putting up a new *telephone* pole in our yard."

After having been postponed for financial reasons, then waiting its turn on the crewmen's schedule, the 220 heavy-duty wiring at last was coming to our house. Carl remodeled the kitchen, installed our electric range, automatic clothes drier, and dishwasher. A new septic tank had been dug, and the water now drained out of the sink instead of overflowing. The church even installed an electric hot-water heater, so I now had automatic hot water.

"Never was a woman so fortunate," I told Carl. "With all these labor-saving machines, I don't work as hard with twelve children as I did back in Hebron, when I had three."

Another tremendous help was Carl's getting up and cooking breakfast in the mornings. "I got used to doing it when you were at college," he told me, "and I sort of like to keep my hand in things."

Now, with Carl cooking the morning meal, with my breakfast dishes, my daily washing, and housecleaning done by noon, I was practically a lady of leisure. The three smallest boys took naps after lunch, the other nine children were still at school, and I had my afternoons free to work on a college extension course. Carl thought it would be nice if I finished my senior year and got my bachelor of arts degree, as long as I was so close to it. He thought it would be a good example to the children.

When grade school let out, I had plenty of time to talk with the children, and still get a casserole or stew finished for supper, along with a gallon or two of tossed salad. In the evenings I took care of the family mending, while the children sat at Carl's feet and listened to stories, or while we all sang. Our family was always singing.

I was singing, too, when our lawyer phoned and told us that our probationary waiting period was up, and a court date set for the adoption hearings.

The night before the important day, Carl and I went around tucking the children into their cribs and beds and bunks. Hair like ripe wheat, hair shining like polished chestnuts, and hair as jet as the night sky outside, was flung quietly against white sheets. Donny was asleep in his top bunk, one arm hanging over down toward the bottom bunk, where at last he had a boy the right size of him. Richard had gone to sleep, his face peaceful, with his glasses on; Carl removed them gently and put them on the dresser.

Timmy was relaxed, a roly-poly Puck caught in his own enchantment. In the bed beside him, Teddy was a slim brown pixie curled under an imaginary mushroom, snoring with his lips parted. Alex and Greg were each sleeping softly in their cribs, more like dolls than babies.

In the girls' rooms, Susie lay with one fair cheek against her favorite woolly lamb. Dorothy's bed was tucked in as neat and tight as a hospital bed, but Diane's was rumpled and looked like a magpie's nest. Rita's lashes lay like black lace against the creamy tan of her face. Laura had crawled into Elaine's bed, and they had fallen asleep with small hands still clasped over the quilt.

As we tiptoed back downstairs, I said, "In my prayers, I give thanks that we never had children of our own, after all. Of our own blood, I mean, because children couldn't be any more my own than these. Somehow I feel that our family was meant to be just this way."

"I do, too."

I looked at him. "You truly don't regret it?"

"If I had it to do over again, I'd still want it this way. You're looking at a happy man who has his quiver full."

"Full of what?"

"Children." He laughed at my puzzled face. "It's a phrase from a psalm:

"As arrows are in the hand of the warrior,
So are children to a man in his youth.
Happy is the man who has his quiver full of them."

There was no mistaking his sincerity and he was not putting on any front. At last I was at peace with myself, inside. I put my hand in his.

"I'm glad you feel like that. I — I used to wonder, sometimes. You've always been so eager to, well, find God. You wanted to know what the divine will was, and you were often so impatient of things that stood in your way."

"I did find God," Carl said. "Not in my theology textbooks, not completely in a mere church building. I found Him this summer. I found Him in the trusting faces of our little children."

In the morning Carl stirred up the usual gallon of hot oatmeal, sprinkled it, as we always do, with raisins instead of sugar, and poured the fourteen glasses of milk. Richard scrubbed oranges for everyone, and Dorothy filled one counter with bread, spread out for the eighteen school sandwiches.

I gave Gregory his bath, and put him into his high chair in his bathrobe. Laura tied on his bib. The children gathered around the table and bowed their heads to sing grace. In their sweet, treble voices they sang:

> *Morning is here,*
> *The board is spread,*
> *Thanks be to God*
> *Who gives us bread.* AMEN.

"Why do we sing thank you for bread, when we're going to eat oatmeal?" Timmy asked. "Why don't we sing, 'Thanks be to God, who gives us oatmeal?' "

While Carl helped the children with their breakfast, I finished the sandwiches and packed them in the lunch boxes, along with a cookie and a raw carrot. When breakfast was over, the children scrambled for coats and sweaters, while Carl and I flanked the back door. Armed with a washcloth, Carl checked for clean faces and ears, while I held a comb and checked hair partings and cowlicks. Each child grabbed his lunch box on the way out.

When the stampede had left to race noisily down the drive to the school-bus stop in front, Dorothy laughed. "Look what we did, Mama! We forgot, and packed a lunch box for me and Richard, too."

"Doesn't matter," I told her. "We'll take them along. You might get hungry over at Ukiah."

I washed the cereal off Gregory's face and dressed him in the same little white Sunday suit that Donny had worn when we took him to see the judge, ten years before. While I was putting on Greg's white socks and shoes, I heard Richard and Dorothy talking in the kitchen, where they were stacking the breakfast dishes in the dishwasher.

"I sure like it better here than any place I ever been," Richard said. "I wouldn't want to live anywhere else."

"Me, neither," Dorothy said. "When I was up at the orphanage last Christmas, I saw that *Life* magazine with all the pictures in it. And I said to myself, *gosh, I wished I lived in that family*. I never dreamed I'd really get to, and now my wish is come true, and my name is going to be Dorothy *Doss* forever and ever."

Our friend Mrs. Pickles was visiting us, and offered to baby-sit with Alex and Timmy while we were at court, and to welcome home the other children when school was out.

"I've stopped trying to question your sanity, Carl," she said. "I'll admit I don't understand what you're doing, but I guess the good Lord does."

We took the short-cut road, nineteen miles over the mountains, to the county seat at Ukiah. On the way over, Greg bounced between the laps of Dorothy and Richard in the back seat, knocking with his small fist on the windows and the rattling ash tray. When Dorothy and Richard started singing, Greg joined them with his wordless da-da-da, sung in perfect pitch.

"I think he's happy he's going to be adopted today," Richard said.

At the Mendocino County Courthouse, we waited on the second floor. Gregory toddled up and down the corridor, rapping experimentally on the marble walls, the doors, the brass doorknobs. At each varying sound he chuckled delightedly, a big grin across his brown face.

Then it was time for our appointment.

Our lawyer joined us, and we filed into the judge's chambers. The lawyer did the introductions, and we shook hands all around. The clerk of the court came in and asked us to raise our right hands and solemnly swear to tell the truth, the whole truth, and nothing but the truth, which we did. We answered the familiar questions and signed the familiar-looking papers, while I thought: *I, Helen, do take thee Richard, Dorothy, and Gregory, to be my lawfully adopted children, for better or for worse . . . in sickness or in health . . . till death do us part. . . .*

Less than half an hour later we were outside again, going down the courthouse steps. Dorothy and Richard were ahead, Gregory between them, his chubby arms held out so they could hold his hands.

Carl asked me softly, "Well, do you have what you wanted out of life, now?"

"Yes," I said. "Do you?"

Carl looked ahead at his three newest children, and on his face was the look of a proud father, a happy man.

"I sure do," he said.

Epilogue

I NEVER EXPECTED to write this book. When I began *The Family Nobody Wanted*, I had already written many stories for magazines. Still, I never thought of writing a story about my family.

But when our family was half-finished, the *Reader's Digest* published an article: "Why You Can't Adopt a Child." I quickly fired back an article about the six delightful children my minister-husband and I already had adopted. I added that we hoped to adopt at least two more. The story, "Our International Family," was published in the *Reader's Digest* in August 1949.

That article intrigued *Life* magazine. They sent their West Coast editor and a renowned child photographer to cover our family. By then we had adopted nine children. For several days, *Life* became part of our family, photographing me, Carl, and the children in many places and poses.

One night, after a well-photographed day at the beach, I tucked my children into their beds.

"What do you do after your kids are asleep?" the editor asked me.

"I usually go to my typewriter," I said. "I'm writing a book."

"About your wonderful family?" the photographer asked.

"Oh, no," I told them. "I've started a novel. About King David, and his many wives."

We kidded around a little, and then the photographer motioned to my typewriter, which sat in the corner. "Let me take your picture there," he said.

When the *Life* article came out on November 12, 1951, the typing picture was cut. But *Life* did say that I was writing a book about my family. Immediately our phone started ringing; publishers were asking to see my book. The new editor-in-chief of Little, Brown and Company even came to Boonville to see me.

"I wasn't serious, and there isn't any book about my family," I explained. "I was just kidding with the *Life* people."

"But you should do it," the Little, Brown editor told me. "Why not just start writing it, and send me each chapter as you finish?"

It was a writer's dream, having editors begging for my first book—even before I wrote it. I hunted for scraps of paper, still tucked in pockets and drawers all over the house, on which I'd recorded anecdotes and children's conversations. During our marriage, Carl was often away. When he came back, I liked to regale him with happenings he had missed. How lucky I was to have all those jottings!

Eventually the book was finished. Soon after sending it to the publisher, I finished another big project—my college degree. In June 1954, I received my B.A. from the University of Redlands, with Carl and our twelve children sitting proudly in the first row.

The day after my graduation, my editor wrote that *The*

Family Nobody Wanted was going to press, and would be out in the fall. He also reported that *McCall's* had bought first serial rights and was condensing my book for publication. It would appear in their September and October issues, and they were sending out a photographer so family photos could be included in the magazine.

That fall my book arrived, with family photos on the cover. I was uneasy with the title, since I certainly wanted each of our children. My editor explained that my title, *All God's Children*, couldn't be used, as another book was out with that title and orders could be confused.

Soon after *The Family Nobody Wanted* was published, *Playhouse 90* did a CBS movie on our family. It was shot live, and no recording was made. Carl and I were played by Lew Ayres and Nanette Fabray, while our children were played mostly by youngsters from the movie *The King and I.* We visited a rehearsal on the set. The movie children kept running among our children to match up. "Where is the real Elaine? I'm the movie Elaine," one would say. And, "Where is the real Teddy?"

On February 19, 1975, our family was again featured on TV. "The Family Nobody Wanted" had an entirely different script as an ABC "Movie of the Week." Shirley Jones played me; we chatted about our children while we were on the set. James Olson, who played Carl, phoned his father in Hebron, Illinois. "I'm playing Carl Doss, a Methodist minister who once preached in Hebron," the actor told his father. "Did you know him?"

"That crazy guy?" his father shouted. "The one who adopted all those kids?"

My readers probably would like to know much more about "all those kids" and their lives. This would take another book, but I won't write it. I always have wanted my children to live out the rest of their lives in private, if they wished.

But I can tell you a few things about my children. Don, when he finished high school, was class valedictorian, receiving a string of honors and offers of college scholarships. He is a self-taught computer wizard, with large corporations vying for his services.

When Richard finished his stint in the navy, he became a genius with machines. He also went into farming in Idaho and raised his family there.

Tim had just finished high school, and Ted was in the middle of college, when the Vietnam War broke out. Both volunteered for the army, and soon they were shipped to the war zone. They slogged through swamps and jungles. I breathed a huge sigh of relief when at last they came back, intact. Each son finished college under the G.I. Bill. Ted learned computers, and the big oil company he worked for sent him to Bangkok, to Jakarta, and back to the states. Tim and his wife have worked in the real estate and housing field.

Diane, like two of her brothers, also went into the computer field. She is funny and outgoing. Dorothy raised her children and also worked in retail; now she does fascinating crafts. Diane has taught Dorothy to surf the Web, and also to email her children and her siblings.

Elaine was a valuable helper for her father in his last years, and now helps her husband. Like her sisters, she is a doting grandmother. For Elaine, a trip to Japan yielded a full-size samurai suit encased in glass, perhaps a relic of one of her ancestors.

After Susie's children were grown, she went back to college and was graduated with honors. She has become an excellent artist, using her photography skills to create her own line of gorgeous greeting cards.

Laura, who trained as a beautician, changed the spelling of her name to Lora. I have popped in for a visit, unannounced, any time of day, and her house always is as beautifully groomed as she is. She spends many hours keeping up with her children and grandchildren, yet still finds time to manage the apartment complex where she and her Ecuadoran husband live.

Rita warms my heart whenever I think of the work she does, caring for elderly and incapacitated ladies. Carl always said, "Rita is the hub of the wheel, and our other children are the spokes. She is connected to everyone, knows what's going on, and is always ready to help."

Alex had a career in the U.S. Air Force. During his last five years, when stationed in Korea, he fell in love with and married a lovely Korean girl. So, his family is completely Asian.

And as for my youngest, Greg, one episode from his life stands out for me. Every year people from all over come to Laguna Beach, California, to attend its Arts Festival. At the festival, a series of living tableaus is produced. Each one is an amazingly accurate recreation of a famous painting. I was so proud of my grown-up Greg in *End of the Trail*. Like the

Indian he was, he sat perfectly still on his horse, and the audience was spellbound.

But there is sad news as well. Carl died after a painful bout with cancer. Still, he lived long enough to know most of his grandchildren. I also lost my two beloved Indian sons. Richard, already a grandfather, died of cancer. Gregory died after a tragic mugging.

In my sunset years, I live with my present husband, Roger Reed. He served in the U.S. Army Signal Corps, and retired as a lieutenant colonel. We share a love of books and classical music. It pleases me that he enjoys get-togethers with my children as much as I do.

I am proud of my accomplishments as a writer. In addition to *The Family Nobody Wanted*, I have written a handbook on adoption, a complete book of Bible stories, and many children's books. All are now out of print.

But the greatest joy of my whole life has been as the mother of my twelve adopted children. I love each one of my children, as well as their spouses, and my grandchildren and great-grandchildren. And I hope my readers will realize how blessed I have been to be part of "the family nobody wanted."

Yuba City, California　　　　　　　HELEN DOSS REED
January 2001